The effi

Cricket: a

Simon White

the *White* words

The effing c-word
The White Words Limited
Registered in England 5422061
www.thewhitewords.com

First edition paperback 2012
Copyright © Simon White 2012

Simon White reserves the moral right to
be identified as the author of this work.

ISBN-13: 978-1479166909
ISBN-10: 1479166901

A catalogue record for this book is available from the
British Library.

Typeset in Minion Pro
by Neil Smith
Design and Illustration by Neil Smith
www.neilsmithillustration.co.uk

For Soph,
for letting me.

The author is a freelance advertising copywriter living in the New Forest village of Damerham with his wife Sophie and girls Izzy and Maddie. He likes to remember once winning a match with 5-12 off 6 overs. He likes to remember that. But he's far more likely to remember losing one by being bludgeoned for 48 off 2.

contents

introduction

The story of cricket is the story of Empire. The story of how men were groomed to rule. It is the story of how the most civilized and civilizing of games came to be the byword for fair play. Of how the colonies fought back, how nations came of age and forged their own identity, how black came to dominate white, how slaves and convicts and the downtrodden took the game of their former masters and made it theirs. It is the story of class division, of 'gentlemen' and 'players'. It is about politics, racism, oppression, injustice, dirty dealings, match fixing and gambling.

Blimey.

Sounds quite good, doesn't it?

It is. It's all good. I heartily recommend as large and varied a cricket library as you are able to acquire. There is no shortage of choice, for cricket is one of the most written about sports, its literature littered with great writers, past and present: players, journalists, novelists, historians, statesmen.

If you want to understand the broad sweep of the game on the world stage, and how it is inextricably intertwined with class, race, politics, history, and the very concept of sportsmanship, there are numerous options open to you.

This, I should warn you, is not really one of them.

We may touch on these things, but this is more about how much fun cricket is to play, and be a part of, even if you're a bit crap. And how the big, televised, cash-hungry international roadshow relates to the activity that causes marital disharmony on a weekly basis across England concerning who it is precisely in this relationship that needs to take their responsibilities a bit more seriously, actually, sunshine.

a note on gender

Most people I know who play cricket are blokes. No, wait, that's not quite true. Not most: all.

I think that's a bit of a shame. These days, apparently, there are a lot more girls learning to play, inspired no doubt by the continuing success of the ODI World Cup, T20 World Cup and Ashes-in-Australia winning England Women.

There's the odd moment in this book where the ladies come in to the story, and it is usually as an opponent of the game – rather than an opponent in a game. I wish it were otherwise, I fervently do, but that is not my experience.

Where I do mention girls playing, it is solely to poke fun at the juvenile failings of the men they shared a field with. (See chapter 9.)

Elsewhere, I would like to stress – in the keen hope that girls might find these musings of interest – every example or definition could equally well refer to girls as boys; every 'he' could easily be a 'she'. The MCC puts this quite neatly in its introduction to the Laws:

"The players, umpires and scorers in a game of cricket may be of either gender and the Laws apply equally to both. The use, throughout the text, of pronouns indicating the male gender is purely for brevity. Except where specifically stated otherwise, every provision of the Laws is to be read as applying to women and girls equally as to men and boys."

All hail to that.

glossary

Cricket is packed full of jargon.

Some of it is silly and a bit puerile, but no less fun for that. Most of it helps us to understand and discuss the finer subtleties of the game and the way it's played.

To help you get to the bottom of it all, in the back of this book you'll find a glossary and jargon-buster.

If you come across anything in the text that sounds like gibberish, it'll probably be in there. If it isn't, then you can be pretty sure that it really is just gibberish.

I've tried to be exhaustive without being dull, and make the glossary as amusing as it is informative.

In fact, I reckon some of the best bits of the book are in there.

But then I would say that, wouldn't I?

Hopefully you'll find it entertaining anyway – whether you're relatively new to cricket, or you know exactly what a chinaman is and how to deal with his wrong'un.

cricket is:

"A game which the English, not being a spiritual people, invented in order to give themselves some conception of eternity."
Lord Mancroft

"Proof that God loves us and wants us to be happy."
Stephen Fry

"A beautiful and highly stylized medieval war substitute, chess made flesh, a mixture of proud chivalry and base greed."
John Fowles

"Organised loafing."
William Temple, Archbishop of Canterbury

"Not illegal, for it is a manly game."
Queen Anne

"Stupid. I don't know why you bother. It hurts you, it irks you, and you're shit at it. I don't know why you bother."
Sophie White

"Full of theorists who can ruin your game in no time."
Ian Botham

prologue

To the uninitiated observer, cricket looks like a slow, gentle game. And sometimes it can be. But it can also be fast and nasty. That's what makes it interesting.

Sitting watching a game from a table outside the pub on a still summer's evening, with buzzing insects, warm sun and cold beer, only the slow gentle bit is evident.

80 yards away, You've just arrived at the crease. Moments ago, your predecessor's off-stump was sent cartwheeling back past the wicket keeper. You pass your team mate on his way back to the pavilion. He shakes his head. It's hard to tell if it's a rueful shake, or just an aid to removing his helmet. "Doing much?" you ask, pausing.

He shrugs. "Dunno. Didn't even see it." Trudging on, he pulls his gloves off irritably.

Pulling yours on, you walk on towards the middle, and decide he probably is rueing. He's showing all the signs of having a good rue.

The opposition clap you in and you can feel their confidence, it's tangible. You take your guard, look around at the field. Don't do anything silly, just play yourself in. The bowler's back at his mark, pawing at the ground like a bull ready to charge. Or is he just marking out his run-up? Whatever.

The umpire drops his arm and the bowler runs in. Well, ambles in, really. He's pushing 50. Can't be all that. Should be fi– Whoa! Holy crap this chap's sharp! And he's swinging it, that started on middle stump and swung away from you sharply, miles past the outside edge of your hastily lowered bat. You were nowhere near that, despite the oooos from the close fielders.

The next one pitches shorter and jags the other way – what?! – thudding into your pads like a bullet hitting a sandbag. The bowler leaps in the air, twisting 180 degrees with remarkable athleticism and pointing accusingly at the umpire, issuing a primal, red-faced scream in which the words "I say, how was that, Umpire?" are not remotely discernable. The umpire shakes his head and the shout stops abruptly, the bowler ambling back to his mark, smiling to himself. That was missing leg stump and he knew it. You can feel your own pulse quicken indignantly in your ears.

The next ball is speared in at your toes, dead straight. You get your feet out of the way and jam the bat down where they just were. By some miracle, the ball finds the middle of the bat, squirts away behind square and races to the boundary. Your team mates in the pavilion cheer, and a bloke having a pint outside the pub claps lazily. Presumably he only saw the result, not the shot.

Last ball of the over. It's on a length, you see it early, you're forward to it, foot to the pitch and, amazingly, you've got time. With soft hands, you bring the bat into line, angled forward, smothering the ball. A perfect forward defensive.

"That's the over," says the umpire.

The bloke outside the pub claps again. Isn't this pleasant, he thinks. Such a lovely thing to watch, village cricket. So gentle and unhurried.

chapter ■■◻

effing cricket

On why cricket is not everyone's favourite thing

Cricket is not a quick game.

It is among the least family-friendly of sports, for the simple reason that it takes most of the day. I imagine around-the-world-yachtsmen have less sympathetic wives, but there's always someone, isn't there?

Superficially, it looks idyllic. Children play with their own little bats and balls around the boundary, toddlers gambol around tartan picnic blankets, pretty Mums in floaty sundresses laugh tinkling laughs and drink ice cold rosé.

Birds twitter in the boughs of majestic oaks, cows graze in the middle distance, rabbits frolic in the dappled sunshine beneath the hedgerows, and bees buzz lazily between wild flowers.

Sometimes, it really is like that.

Quite magical, it is, when it happens.

Other times though, there is mizzle. Mizzle is a particular kind of English weather which favours summer weekends. A cross between mist and drizzle, it's the kind of rain that doesn't so much fall as hang. It gets you wet by attrition, without you really noticing. Not wet enough to stop play, but definitely wet enough to stop picnics, mizzle is an English summer staple.

On this kind of day, "Why don't you come over the field with the kids and watch?" is not something a wise man would suggest.

To be honest, even if the weather was still fantastic, the picnic blanket might begin to lose its appeal after a few weekends in succession.

And I can absolutely see why. If my wife took up a leisure activity which required me to sacrifice a day every weekend to sit around in a field on childcare duty, I'd be as enthusiastic about it as she is. Which is 'not even slightly', in case that's unclear.

There's not really a compromise to be reached here. If you're young and single, obviously your weekends are yours to do with as you wish. Even if you're attached, chances are your other half will be more than happy to amuse herself while you go and get grass stains on your whites. Most girls relish a Saturday afternoon to themselves, whether she's shopping or gardening, getting her hair done or riding a horse, going to the gym or staying in bed with the papers.

But if you have kids, there's a very good chance she might not be quite so easy going about it.

This is because of the immutable law of parenthood: if one of you is having me-time, the other one is having the kids.

And cricket represents a fair proportion out of a weekend. Much worse than football or rugby. Even worse than golf. (Worse still, it goes without saying, if you're one of those foolhardy lunatics who's prepared to admit that he's monstrously selfish enough to harbour hopes of playing cricket AND golf. Shhh. Best not mention it.)

Sometimes it's more than just one day out of a weekend. We play in a midweek league too, though that's not generally a problem, as Wednesday evenings are simply not as precious as Saturday afternoons in anyone's book.

One of the things that causes real problems is 'fixture congestion'. There's always one mad week, usually at the end of May or beginning of June, a few weeks or maybe a month into the season. Before anyone's really got used to the idea of cricket again, it completely takes over.

This congestion is largely caused by knockout competitions. For us the problem tends to be short lived, as we get knocked out fairly quickly, which clears the calendar nicely.

The other factor is the Great British Summer, which as everyone knows can be capricious at best, especially in May, and tends to exacerbate the situation.

Here's an example from a couple of years ago:

Saturday league game at home, then a National Village Cup fixture away on Sunday, which had been rained off from the previous week. Then, similarly postponed from the week before, a midweek Cup game away on Monday evening. Then a Wednesday evening league game at home, then, assuming we won on Monday, a third round Midweek Cup game on Thursday, also at home. Then Saturday league away, then a long standing friendly game at home on Sunday – unless we won the previous Sunday, in which case we'd have to cancel the friendly because we'd be in a regional semi-final that day. Either way, that's seven games in nine days.

Was there ever more cause for marital disharmony than seven games in nine days?

In case there's any doubt let me add that this particular week also happened to be half term, and for good measure my wife's parents were arriving on Wednesday, to stay for the weekend.

Fortunately, (I hesitate to say 'fortunately' about losing, but in this case it definitely was,) we lost both cup fixtures, so the busiest week of the year was six games, of which I played four. Which made me feel I was being perfectly reasonable and observing the spirit of compromise, and made Soph feel I was deliberately being awkward by being out of the house, like, ALL THE TIME, and playing as much cricket as I conceivably could at the least convenient time OF THE WHOLE YEAR and generally making her life as difficult as possible. On purpose, with malice aforethought.

It is this kind of thing that has led cricket to acquire a prefix in our house, which from May to September it is rarely to be found without. It is routinely referred to, sometimes jokily, sometimes not entirely without heat, as "Fucking Cricket."

Often the epithet carries sufficient venom to convey either the deep rooted unfairness of it all, or wearily resigned acceptance, depending on what stage of the summer, and indeed what stage of the week, we are in.

So ubiquitous has the prefix become, that even when the she is censoring herself – usually due to the proximity of children – she leaves a slight pause in the sentence to indicate its presence, as in "what time have you got to be at… cricket tomorrow?" so that I know she's thinking it, even if she can't say it.

For two-fifths of the year, the calendar is liberally riddled with cricket fixtures, highlighted in red (home) or yellow (away) to signify their "unbreakable commitment" status. I do this to try to be helpful, to keep conversations starting "Well, it wasn't on the calendar," to a bare minimum, but in more honest moments I can see that this could easily be interpreted as deeply annoying.

By the end of April she despairs of ever being able to offer friends 'free' weekends that we can see them, as most, if not all, involve the effing c-word somewhere. Sometimes, whisper it, twice.

Dennis Norden knew of this problem: "It's a funny kind of month, October. For the really keen cricket fan, it's when you discover your wife left you in May."

I know it's not just Dennis and me in this one, either. I know I'm not alone because it is a constant topic of conversation on the bench outside the pavilion.

"You playing next Sunday?"

Marky D is rolling a cigarette. Without looking up from his task, he grimaces and sucks in a breath dramatically, like a plumber surveying a leak.

"Don't think so mate."

Mark is not a plumber. He's a tree surgeon, or something like that, and so never has conversations like this with customers. He's clearly wasting a talent. There are a couple of real plumbers who play for us, and they can't pull off the cliché plumber voice at all. Though maybe they've consciously worked hard not to 'do' that voice. Or maybe it's something, like a 'CORGI' badge, they only put on during work hours.

"I'm playing Saturday, see, so Sunday, y'know…"

Of course I know. Mark's kid Frankie is still very little. It needs no further explanation.

But Mark likes Sundays. Saturdays are important, because they're league matches and the league *matters*, but Sundays are fun. Sundays are 'casual' games, friendlies. On a Sunday, Mark is more likely to bat, more likely to bowl, more likely to take catches, more likely to laugh.

The week after Frankie was born, Mark's first game after a month or so of I'm-about-to-pop-so-no-you-are-not-playing-fucking-cricket was on a Sunday. He took five-fer eleven off four overs and hung on to two steepling catches in the deep.

Still concentrating on the construction of his cigarette, Mark is now doing a rather childish and inaccurate impression of his wife in a silly squeaky voice, which includes the phrases "ner ner ner ner" and "fucking cricket".

The rendition provokes titters of recognition. Not of Heidi, who we all know as a lovely, friendly, reasonable person, but of the speech itself, which we all recognise as a familiar and intrinsically unwinnable argument.

"Nahhhh," he finishes, to illustrate that he's not blaming her, but, well, y'know.

Yeah, we know.

"I can do Sunday," James pipes up, adjusting the velcro straps on a pad.

"Yeah? How come?"

"Broke up with the misses."

There's a silence, during which we try and assess whether he's serious. And if he is serious, whether he's upset about it.

"Sorry to hear that mate."

"Yeah, well. It was all getting a bit... y'know."

"Sure. Put you down for Sunday then, shall I?

"Yeah, mate. Every Sunday."

This tends to be as in depth and personal as relationship talk gets at cricket. This is one of the reasons it's so convivial, I think. During six or seven hours in each other's company, the conversation will be in-depth only about cricket itself: the fortunes (or lack of) of the national side; musings on the game generally; our specific situation in this match in particular. Otherwise it will be silly, inane, untaxing, safe. It is generally, as all sport is, a safe haven from the serious business of real life.

Henry and Joel are scoring. Both are young, working, but still living at home, in that brief, blissful period in life where you've got yourself some disposable income but have yet to acquire commitments for it. As a result, they are almost entirely unfamiliar with the 'fucking cricket' phenomenon.

"H, Sunday?"

"Yeah, 'course."

"Joel?"

"Yep."

They'll find out. Couple of years, a decade if they're lucky, their weekends will no longer be theirs to command. They might still get to play cricket, but boy will they know about it.

"Ah," says one.

"What?"

"Paul's out," the other confirms.

James passes Paul on his way out to the middle. They pause for a few words. It's more likely to be commiseration than a 'what's it doing' chat. Neither of them are big on finding out what's happening out there till they actually get out there. Some people like those chats, some don't. These two don't.

Paul trudges the rest of the way in, sighs heavily, and leans his cherished bat carefully against the pavilion wall, muttering under his breath, "Fucking cricket."

"Unlucky mate."

"Nah. Stupid. Should have left it alone."

He sits, still padded up, sighs again, and reaches for his papers and backy. Paul and Mark belong to an age where sportsmen actively advocated smoking; when the England Captain did cheesy to-camera endorsements for tobacco companies, and the proof that you'd arrived in top flight sport was not a sports drink sponsorship deal, but your appearance on a cigarette card.

"You playing Sunday?"

He pauses before answering, like he's not sure.

But we all know he is.

He shakes his head slowly, in the universal, unspoken negative. "Yeah," he says.

chapter 22

great expectations

On how reality gets in the way

I've got an ornamental cherry tree in my front garden. I think that's what it is.

For 50 weeks of the year, it just sits there dormant, almost leafless, looking like it might even be dead.

But it holds the promise of two weeks in spring. Two weeks when people stop and look, and everyone says how pretty it is.

Promise is a fantastic thing, and springtime is when you feel it most.

It's the best time of any season, just before it starts. Plump with potential, ripe with expectations. The long months away from the game have dimmed the reality of your limitations. This could be the year.

This could be the year of five-fers and fifties, the year of punched sixes, magical slower balls and diving catches. Heroic defences, huge totals, dramatic last ball wins.

The year Man-U get thrashed by a non-league side in the cup, the year a Brit wins the Masters, the year we regain the Ashes in a nail biting summer. The year it all comes together.

This could be the year.

The year you finally start to bowl like Anderson, bat like Pietersen and field like Collingwood, just like, deep down, you always suspected you probably could, if everything came together just so. This could be the year.

Just before the first game, this could always be the year.

Until you actually start playing of course, and you realise that, as it happens, perhaps no, maybe this isn't going to be the year after all. It only takes one little omen. One little duck. One little over that goes for 20.

It really is quite beautiful when it blooms, that cherry tree. A thick mass of delicate pink blossom, it looks like a giant's wedding bouquet dropped on the lawn.

Of course, blossom is all it's got.

It's an 'ornamental' tree, so there's no fruit. Not a single cherry from that cherry tree. It's the flora world's equivalent of 'all talk'.

It flowers, and it starts to shed its blossom almost immediately, as if when it came to it, what it was building up to was too much for it to cope with after all. At the end of its two weeks, the ground all around it is covered in a deep carpet of candyfloss confetti.

Then it settles back to sleep, waiting for the slow build up of potential, until it comes alive again.

By that time, the cricket season is well underway.

There's something I should probably make clear from the off: I'm really not very good at cricket. I'd dearly love to be, but I'm just not.

There's no sense hiding from it.

There may be times in this book where I get into my stride and really start to sound like I know what I'm talking about. I hope there are, anyway.

And I do, to a certain extent. I mean, I'm a student of the game. I think deeply about it and its nuances, its history, its present and future, its place in the grand scheme of things. But I am not, by any measure, a great practitioner. This doesn't matter, of course; many of sport's greatest theorists, pundits and writers were never great practitioners. Not that I'm lumping myself in with the 'greats'. I'm just saying.

My mate Eds has a theory about coaches, which I think applies equally to writers and commentators. Truly great, naturally gifted players rarely make good coaches – or pundits. Someone who is a complete natural is often quite unable to explain how he does what he does, or even place his ability in context. He's always been able to do it, his superiority has come easily to him, so he's never examined it, or even thought about it much. Was Alex Ferguson an exceptional footballer? Was Jonathon Agnew an outstanding cricketer? Journeymen make the best coaches and commentators, because they know what it's like to be the best, they've seen it up close; they've shared dressing rooms and fields with it; they've spent their life in pursuit of it; they've almost touched it. (As with all rules, there are exceptions to this one. The one that leaps to mind is Mike Atherton, former England captain and opening bat, now among the very best writers on the game.)

I, of course, can only dream of the giddy heights of the journeyman. I'm not sure I'd even make the journeyman grade in village terms.

Don't get me wrong, I'm not completely awful. I am competent: an alright bat, a pretty decent leggie, an adequate close fielder. A village all-rounder. (This will not be the last time that expression crops up. If you can't wait for a definition, look it up in the glossary at the back.)

Somebody once said that golf and sex are the only things you don't have to be any good at to enjoy. I was never quite sure that was true on either front, but anyway, I would cheerfully add cricket to the list.

I'm a better golfer than I am a cricketer. (I don't know how good I am at sex and this is not that sort of book.) I tend to stay at about a steady 14 handicap even when my golfing frequency is reduced to below once a month. (I'd say my cricket handicap, if such a thing were possible, would be about an 18, with a fair wind. Ok maybe 20 then.) I'm reasonably confident that if I played golf consistently two or three times a week for six months or so, I'd make single figures without any drama. Fortunately my life is unlikely to let that happen, so I'm not going to have to prove it.

I'm not positive about it, and I hesitate to commit this thought to paper in case it makes it truer than it really is, but I don't think the same can be said of cricket. I think I could practice every day for a year, and still remain a competent village all-rounder who's weak off his pads and prone to bowling leg-side wides. I also think, luckily, that I'm probably ok with that.

Yes, I spend a lot of time in the winter nets, (see chapter 13) but that's because it's so much fun, not because it's good for me. I am not labouring under the misapprehension that it'll make me a better cricketer. A few years ago I had some batting lessons. To be honest, I'm not sure what they achieved, other than confirmation of a couple of things from someone who knew what he was talking about that I had pretty solid suspicions about anyway: a) no, I am not a natural technical genius, and b) my bat was far too heavy for me.

What's important to note here is that I derived happiness from these conclusions, because a) well, we were pretty sure about that anyway, and b) did you ever hear a more cast iron excuse – nay, *reason*, dammit – to buy a new bat?

I don't mind being only-ok at cricket, because when I do have a good game, it feels like I've really achieved something.

Back to the golf/sex wisdom, I think perhaps what that expression is trying to say is not that you don't *have* to be good at them to enjoy them, but rather that you'll enjoy them more if you're *not* good at them.

Certainly sex can rarely be more joyful and fun than when performed by enthusiastic teenagers, unencumbered by experience or expectations, careers or mortgages.

And it works for golf too. A bogey achieved by a novice is good work, a par hugely satisfying. A birdie will probably make his week. But for a good golfer, a par is just another birdie putt he didn't make.

It's hard to shake that, but it's understandable. The better you get at a game, the higher your expectations the next time you play. That's natural enough. What you've got to be careful of is that your expectations don't rob you of your enjoyment. If every par is cause for tutting, every bogey for a despairing head wag, and every birdie is dismissed wryly as too little too late, are you really enjoying yourself any more?

But I think that says more about golf than golfers. Golf's problem is that it's a game of almosts. Perfection is impossible – no-one has ever shot 18 for 18 holes, nor is anyone ever going to. The winner is whoever misses least.

You can get really up tight about it, and become a club thrower.

I've been there, and fortunately I got over it. I was lucky that it didn't cost me any clubs, though I have witnessed many of my playing partners snapping them in anger. I remember two from my brother-in-law off the top of my head, one of which was his favourite club, and my cousin's 5-iron was so well hidden that it may still to this day be quietly rusting in the patch of nettles to the left of the third fairway at Old Petersfield where he flung it in disgust. This is not exclusive to amateurs either. Picture this perfect marriage of picture and commentary: a slow zoom in to a £500 driver bobbing forlornly in a lake, while the voiceover deadpans: "John Daly not entirely happy with his drive there..."

It is a uniquely frustrating game, but it can also be remarkably relaxing, if you let it. If you surrender to the vagaries of it, and accept each mistake as an unavoidable inevitability, it can be a great de-stress. Providing it's not how you make your living. Alan Hansen, of all people, a low-single-figure handicapper, said something that has stayed with me: "I do this for fun. I'm not good enough to get annoyed with it."

Cricket is not like that. It's not about beating the course, playing against yourself, or any of golf's other clichés. It has many variables, most of them caused by your opponents.

Each situation is pretty much unique – this bowler, this field, this pitch, this target. You're unlikely to have faced the same combination before or to face it again.

I am, at heart, an optimist. Every time I go out to bat, I fully expect to score heavily, quickly and fluently. I am however a philosophical optimist, so somewhere deep down, I know that it is just as likely that I'll make an ugly swipe at a straight one and be back on the bench outside the pavilion before my cup of tea's got cold.

And that's the strange thing about it: it *feels* like both possibilities are equally likely.

I know they're not. There are only a few times I've ever really scored quickly, and 'fluent' is an adjective I'm sure even my most benevolent team-mates would hesitate to apply to my batting, even when feeling a bit drunk and generous. Whereas I don't think they'd have any problems with 'ugly' and 'swipe'.

I will play the occasional drive that's every bit as good as it looks, but it's the exception rather than the rule, if we're honest.

What I am famous for, batting wise, is running. Not in a good way.

Judging a run is an art. It requires you to know where the gaps in the field are, how well you've hit the ball, how quick you, your batting partner and the fielder in question are, and how good the fielder's 'arm' is – meaning how hard and fast and accurately he can throw.

Some batsmen are excellent judges of a run. Tendulkar, for all his silky ability as a shotmaker, has made many hundreds of his many thousands of runs by inches. He's an exquisite judge of a run. Inzaman al Huq on the other hand, while a world class batsman, was, I can comfortably say, an even worse runner than me.

Even so, I'm pretty bad. At a club presentation evening a few years ago, I won a special award for most run-outs. The award was a four-pack of Red Bull. I still have that four-pack, languishing out of date in the back of a cupboard. Well, you certainly can't drink the vile stuff.

I'm not the most decisive person, to be honest. Am I? I don't know. Maybe I am. Anyway. Probably not, and this shows in my running. I have been guilty many times of the comedy "Yes/No/Sorry" call. I don't even know I'm doing it, until I replay what I've just said in my head afterwards. "Yes!" I call confidently, and we set off, oh wait, no, hang on, that fielder is closer than he looked, "NOOOOO!!!" and we both scramble back to our ends, making it by the smallest of margins. I look over at my partner, perhaps a bit muddy now from a desperate dive back into his crease, and hold up my hand placatingly. "Sorry, mate. My fault." The classic Yes/No/Sorry.

But I bowl okay.

My leg breaks do not turn prodigiously, and are more in the mould of Kumble than Warne. Yes, I am aware of how ridiculously pretentious that sounds – "Yah, I'm more of a 600 than 700 Test wickets sort of chap, see?" – but I just mean that my stock ball has more topspin than sidespin, so often bounce is more of a weapon than turn. (To really appreciate the enormity of pretentiousness in that claim, look up those two former greats on Wikipedia when you've got an idle five minutes. You won't be sorry you did. Unless you're on a deadline. Then you probably will be.)

Occasionally a perfect Warnie 'century' ball one will come out, pitch outside leg stump and rip to off, but more often than not when that happens there'll be enough bounce to take it over the stumps. They have a tendency to waver in length, and to drift down leg.

I have a straight topspinner too, which can work quite well and garner the odd top edge, as it looks very inviting. Though it's just as likely to deliver on its invite, and go sailing over the rope for six.

My wrong'un turns the most, but is prone to being dragged down. Its biggest plus is that it's very difficult to read, so I'm told. When it's right it cramps you for room, and has a good chance of bowling the unwary through the gate. But when the wrong'un is wrong, if you see what I mean, it's a rank long hop, pitched way too short, and likely to get mercilessly thumped through midwicket.

(Incidentally, does all this jargon sound like utter gibberish to you? Ball of the century, bounce, dragged down, drift down leg, leg break, midwicket, rip, stock ball, through the gate, topspinner, wrong'un – to name just a few alphabetically in the last couple of paragraphs. If it does, look them up in the back. The glossary is your friend. All will become clear. If you hadn't even noticed there being any jargon, clearly you are already fluent. As you were.)

I'm probably a better bowler than I am a batsman, but, by dint of the same psychology that makes girls with curls want straight hair and brunettes want to be blonde, I'd rather bat.

Unless I'm taking wickets, of course. In which case bowling is the best thing in the whole wide world and I never want to stop.

Go fetch

We're playing Gary's lot, the Firemen. Gary's played for us for years. A former vice captain, and a crafty left hand bat. He's also Watch Manager over at Redbridge Fire Station in Southampton, and for a good few summers now Green Watch come out to play us in a friendly. It really is very friendly, too, unlike some of the so-called friendlies which can be much more spiky and barbed than league games. We don't tend to invite those ones back. But the firemen are always a great bunch, dead friendly and up for a laugh, both in the game and in the beer garden afterwards.

As well as Gary, they've got a couple of guys who play regular cricket. Tim, another fireman and fine bat who plays for us on Wednesdays, he plays for them sometimes. And Gary's boss who plays Saturday league somewhere in the Forest.

Often they come to us a bit hungover, as sometimes the game is the culmination of a weekend camping in the forest. But they're fit, they can handle it. They're mostly rugby players, rather than cricketers. They have the look of guys who are not going to let a little thing like a hangover stop them running all day.

There have been some memorable incidents with the firemen.

When they were batting last year, one of them really got hold of a cross-batted slog. It was a rank full toss, and he swung like a home run and middled it, but it went straight back and stayed low, rather than up towards cow corner where you'd have thought. It was nearly caught-and-bowled, but he hit it so hard the bowler didn't get near it and a split second later it slammed into the non-striker's chest, dead centre, knocking him backwards.

I don't think he was watching, and it caught him completely by surprise. Must have felt like a bodyblow from Tyson.

It was one of those strange moments which is quite funny, but you're trying desperately to stifle the laughter in case the guy's really hurt. He wasn't, fortunately, just winded, so after a minute or two it was okay to chuckle. But if it had been a foot higher... best not to think about it.

On the subject of getting hurt though, a few years ago we were playing them on a baking sunny midsummer's day. Some chap wandered out of the pub after one too many in the sun with his Sunday lunch, tripped and fell on his face in the road. A car coming past stopped and helped him up, woozy and bleeding quite heavily, and someone went into the pub for help.

Chinese whispers worked their magic, and a few seconds later a different someone came running out onto the cricket pitch, thinking the guy had been run over and looking quite panicked, yelling "Are there any first-aiders here?!"

All 11 firemen, who were fielding, turned as one and ran off the field, bless 'em, leaving the two batsmen and two umpires alone and bemused out in the middle.

Right now though, I'm out in the middle feeling bemused for a different reason.

We're playing a two-innings-T20-reverse-the-order game. It's been another crap summer, so the pitch is slow and it's a fairly low scoring game. We both got around three figures in the first innings, but they only set us 60 to win in the second.

We're going comfortably, scoring freely. We're going to walk it, no need for anything hectic.

Then something weird happens.

Out of nowhere, I hit a six. This is unheard of. I don't hit sixes.

I wasn't thinking about hitting one (I often do that), it just happened.

It must have been just so in my slot that even I couldn't refuse it, and suddenly there I am watching it sail over the fence at midwicket into the nettles by the tumbledown old barn. I can't believe it.

It's so simple. Front foot forward, smooth flow of the bat. Sweetly timed, didn't even feel it.

I can't believe it.

But it must have happened because the bowler's giving me the old 'double teapot', glaring at me with both hands on his hips.

And here I am, leaning nonchalantly on my bat, grinning like an idiot, watching a few fielders and a few of our lot from the pavilion climb over the barbed wire fence and start gingerly parting the nettles where the ball went in.

In the pavilion, Burroughs is enjoying it almost as much as me, yelling between the woops and belly laughs: "Look at him! Leaning on 'is bat like 'e does it all the time!"

Selfconsciously, I stop leaning on my bat. Then I think, no, actually, sod it, I've done enough fetching in my time, it's my turn to lean. I've earned a bit of a lean.

I lean on my bat, resume grinning like an idiot, thinking: I'm gonna do this more often.

I have yet to hit another six.

There's a very real possibility that it may never happen again.

chapter ■ ■ 3

quaint, beautiful, ugly

On the many faces of cricket's foibles

Traditional village cricket is so quintessentially English, it can come across as slightly twee. It can look like such a chocolate box cliché. Like someone has staged it, and arranged for those dozen or so chaps to dress all in white and stand on the village green all day for the benefit of tourists.

Like summer fetes and village fairs, there is an element of self consciousness to it, which only exists in the minds of onlookers – for those involved, it's a mighty serious business. As John Arlott gravely noted, "Villagers do not think village cricket is funny."

Village teams have played cricket pretty much unchanged for hundreds of years. Sure, today's village player may be attired in high tech dry-wicking sports fabrics, but his team probably still includes some traditional flannels.

Bats have improved. (Every ex-player who ever comments on the game is guaranteed to bleat on about this with high indignation, the implicit criticism being that these days any competent toddler could hit sixes with those bats, whereas in MY day, well, it was like batting with a pencil, and a chewed one at that, so basically we were playing a more noble and skilful game than these clueless chancers, who clearly don't know they're born.)

And protection now extends beyond cane leg guards and cotton gloves covered in rubber spikes – arm guards, chest guards, thigh pads, hip protectors and helmets.

But in essence, the game is very much as it always has been.

There's a comfort to it. It has rhythms and patterns that feel solid, unshakable, carved in stone.

There's tea, for a start. The quiet solidity of cricket tea is a strange and wonderful thing. Like the game itself (which really amounts to fully grown adults chasing a ball around a field, when it comes down to it,) tea is taken very seriously by otherwise thoroughly nononsense people.

It's almost ceremonial. I've seen a few cricket teas in my time, ranging from excellent through indifferent to awful. What I don't remember seeing, ever, is a square sandwich. Cricket tea sandwiches are triangular, cut from corner to corner into four. This is not a suggestion, it is an unbreakable law.

Tea itself is universally served from enormous chipped enamel teapots, usually dating from sometime around the war.

Crisps will be served from a bowl, not from a packet.

There may be pork pies. There may be sausage rolls. There may even be sausages on a stick. There will absolutely not be cheese and pineapple on a stick.

There will be cake. There will not be trifle.

League sides rate the facilities at away matches, and this includes the teas. That's how seriously tea is taken.

Damerham's teas, I should stress, are among the very best. They're provided by Joyce and Liz, and you'll be hard pushed to find a better cup-of-tea-and-egg-mayo-sarnie combination at any ground in the land.

Few visiting captains find much to complain about with the teas. The outfield may be a bit lumpy on the football pitch side, but there's nothing wrong with that tea, matey. Indeed, visiting sides rarely leave without a compliment, and frequently (especially for friendly fixtures) they email afterwards solely to express their thanks and appreciation for the tea.

But that's quite enough tea; get your pads on lad, there's a game to be played here. And that too is steeped in behaviour handed down from generation to generation.

From a distance, it looks like the outer fielders are just standing around, not really involved in the game. If you watch closely, however, provided the team are a half decent one, you'll notice they're all keenly attentive at the moment the ball is bowled. The wicketkeeper, slips and any other close fielders are crouched and still as the bowler runs in, but fielders beyond them will all walk slowly towards the batsmen, everyone watching him as he watches the ball.

The purpose of this is simple: it is easier to react when the ball comes your way if you're already on the move, on the balls of your feet, rather than uprooting planted legs.

The effect is a curious and rather lovely one.

The gentle in-out movement is like the field breathing. A single entity, guided by a common purpose, going about its business.

It is powerfully inclusive. Cohesive, even. To move collectively in towards the foe in this manner makes a team feel like a team, united in their efforts. It is an immensely enjoyable sensation, and one of cricket's unique pleasures. You'll be hard pushed to feel more involved in sport while expending less energy.

If a fielder plays regular cricket, you will see him relax almost instantly if the ball goes safely through to the keeper. If the ball is hit away from him, and his team mates on the opposite side of the pitch launch into action, he may move into position behind the stumps to back up, but otherwise, he is off duty until the next delivery.

This switching on and off of concentration is quite necessary, and very much a part of the rhythm of cricket. It means good sides can keep alert and 'on the ball' all day, focussing tightly when they need to, relaxed and enjoying each other's company when they don't.

Cricket has, more than most games, an abundance of rituals and traditions. Things that seem quaint to those looking in, their sense and meaning only clear to those who play.

A particular favourite of mine is the fielding side clapping each new batsman in. It sometimes feels like a moment from a bygone age, an act of chivalry for chivalry's sake. Yet it is so much a part of the fabric of the game at its grass roots, that not to do it is beyond rude. It is actually aggressive.

Most village teams include the odd tosser. The guy who wants to fight, start a row, argue with every umpiring decision. The vast majority of the time, they will be overwhelmed by their own players, told firmly to calm down or shut up. Often their team mates are visibly embarrassed by the hooligan in their midst.

Some sides have more idiots than normal people, and these can be hard work and not much fun to play against. When a 45-year-old sales manager with a Napoleon complex starts to behave like he's Merv Hughes, you can be fairly sure you're in for a long afternoon.

And yet, no matter how unpleasant they are, every amateur side will clap in the opposition batsmen. Every single one. Whether they're a league below you, or seven leagues above you, a bunch of vicars or a bunch or lawyers.

"Batsman in, lads," someone will cry, and the applause will spatter around the field, unacknowledged by the chap with the bat it is welcoming to the game.

It seems a great shame to me that it doesn't happen in the professional game. I'm sure it must have done in the past, and probably not that long ago. They have the crowd to greet the batsman, of course, but it lacks the significance of saluting a challenger before battle. It is a gesture of respect. It has nothing to do with how hard you will try, or how much you want to win. It is a simple recognition of your opponent, valiant or not, and there is something quite wonderful about that.

You're unlikely to see much recognition for the opposition's efforts in the professional game, but good play is usually acknowledged on a village green. If someone strokes a flowing four, he'll most likely receive a hearty if monosyllabic "shot" from any number of his opponents. (Though with diminishing enthusiasm if he starts to make a habit of it.) Often you will hear bowlers – usually the better ones, significantly – praise a batsman for keeping out his yorker, or keeping a brutal rising ball down. And often the applause will ripple out from the pavilion when a ball is well fielded, the batting side appreciating some feat of athleticism that has denied their team runs.

There is something about these little rituals that help lift cricket above the ordinary. It has these inbuilt social conventions that players learn when they first play the game, to the extent that they are performed unconsciously after a while.

It is typical of the game, and surely no accident, that these rituals channel those who play it into behaving like gentlemen, even if, off the field, they are patently not.

The appreciation of the aesthetics of cricket is something else that sets it apart. Lovers of the game will appreciate a good looking shot no matter who hits it. Australians, even with the Ashes at stake, will be warmly applauded by English crowds for classy cricket shots. It's a rare football fan, conversely, who appreciates a goal scored against his side, regardless of how brilliantly skilful it may be.

There's a perfection to cricket when it is done well that transcends the competition between one side and another.

It is simply bigger than the game, that perfection. It makes you wonder if perhaps the game evolved around it, to give the confluence of clinical precision and easy flowing grace that is the sweetly timed cover drive a reason to exist.

You can spot elegance from a long way off, and you can't fake it. You only have to watch someone caress a back foot drive to the fence once, and you instantly know the kind of refined, effortless player he is.

The golf swing has a similar mystique. Everyone's is unique, like a fingerprint. But you can tell with one look if it works or not. Watch a golfer in silhouette two fairways away, and with one swing you can tell if he can play. And probably hazard a reasonable guess at his handicap.

In marshal arts at a high level, there are moments when you can't believe that the two protagonists are not on the same side. A throw looks like it has the full cooperation of the one being thrown. In striking sports like karate or fencing, the combination of attack/parry/defend/attack looks fixed, choreographed.

Cricket is the same. Surely the bowler has agreed to bowl the ball exactly there so the batsman can hit it. There's no way it could look that stylish if the bowler was trying his best to put the ball where the batsman least wanted it, is there?

It looks like an act of collusion.

From Vaughan's cover drive to Tendulkar's wristy flick off the pads, from Lara's cut to Ponting's pull, from Pietersen's 'switch hit' to Dilshan's 'ramp shot' – they all looked for all the world like the bowler was a willing accomplice.

When Stuart Broad was hit for six sixes in an over in the first T20 World Cup, he seemed deliberately to keep putting the ball exactly where Yuvraj Singh had next decided he could most easily smash it out of the ground.

And when Virender Sehwag has his eye in, there isn't a bowler on the planet who can send down anything he can't crash to the boundary with contemptuous ease.

Of course it's not always like that, and what makes the game interesting is that some days the opposite is true. The bowlers are on top, and even the world's best batsmen have no chance.

Jimmy Anderson's scorching outswinger to rip out Brendon McCullum's off stump, Harmison's vicious bouncer into Ponting's grill, Glenn McGrath's relentless accuracy, the swing of Wasim Akram, the naked aggression of Andrew Donald, the raw animal pace of Shoaib Akhtar.

To bowl truly fast is to squeeze the maximum out of toned muscles in a flowing movement of grace and controlled power, and to bat well against pace like that is to react like a fighter pilot, to let training and instinct take over, as it's all happening far too fast for conscious thought (see chapter 13 for more on this).

Like most things done well, when you see both together, it is a joy to watch. Especially if you know from personal experience just how difficult it is.

But of course for every front foot drive there's a cross-batted swipe. (Actually there's probably a good dozen, lets be honest.) They can both get you four, they can both get you out. One's pretty, the other's downright ugly.

On a Wednesday night in June needing a dozen to win off the last over in the Midweek Evening League, does anyone care about style?

Do they draw pictures next to the numbers in the scorebook? They do not. One is not awarded runs for 'presentation'. (But sometimes Test places.)

Ugly runs are just as valuable as pretty ones. Ultimately, as the saying goes, what matters is not how, but how many.

One of cricket's great strengths as a team game, paradoxically, is that it relies on individuals. Team game it may be, but no-one can help you when you're batting. You and you alone must keep that yorker out. Bowling, too, can be lonely, especially if it's all going horribly wrong and you can't figure out why. Three wides in a row and another six balls to come is no fun at all. Ask Steve Harmison.

There are few more unifying experiences for a bunch of people who don't know each other that well than winning a game they all thought they were going to lose.

There are few better – or quicker – ways to make a new friend than to take a catch off his bowling.

And scoring runs or taking wickets is a great feeling not just personally, but also because it benefits both you and the guys you're sharing a changing room with.

You can have a terrible game as a player – your bowling can get carted all over the place and you can be out cheaply – but if your team wins you've still got something to smile about. By the same token, if you lose but played well, you can be quietly pleased with yourself. Emphasis on the quietly though.

Of course, there are always days when everything goes horribly wrong, everyone's bowling gets spanked, you're one of six ducks and you get roundly thrashed. In that instance, all you can really do is moan about it together in the pub afterwards and look forward to next week, when it'll all come together. Bound to.

Is the pope catholic?

We're up at Barnsley Beeches near Cirencester for a friendly, a sort of mini-tour to Paul's old club, where he used to play when he was a kid.

The ground is small-ish, and as picturesque as they come. It's within a country estate, which lets the club use the pitch for nothing, and always has.

It's bordered on all sides by the trees that give the club its name and a three-foot fence – which the ball has to go over, not just hit, to be a six. The fence's other purpose is to keep out the natives: it's completely surrounded by sheep.

The pavilion is a large shed, which is homely, characterful, and appears to have been held together with roof felt, tlc and optimism for many long years. Among the photos crowding the wall we spot a 14-year-old Paul in their 1979 line up.

The toilets are hilarious. Behind the pavilion there's a sort of make-shift urinal made out of a piece of guttering at an angle that just stops so everything runs straight onto the floor. There are no actual toilets. If you need anything more than a wee, there's the woods out the back.

Unchanged for God knows how long, it's a great place to play cricket, especially on a beautiful hot sunny day in September. They win the toss and bat, making 165 for 3 from 40 overs, while we toil in the heat.

We have tea in the shade while Paul, guest-skippering against his formative side, (which includes a guy he used to play with, now in his 44th consecutive playing year) muses that he never got a 50 on this ground, and maybe now, 27 years later, it's time to put that right.

After tea I do a bit of scoring, which I loathe, and make an excuse to wander off at the first available opportunity to find a loo. There really isn't one.

Mark's out. Joel's out. Where am I batting? Six? Really?

Oh shit, really? Oh shit indeed. The more it sinks in that I really can't have one, the more I really need one.

I need to make a decision here, and sharpish.

So I faff indecisively for ten minutes.

I put my pads on, trying to convince myself I don't need to go. You know how sometimes you think you need to, and then something unexpected crops up so you don't go, and the need just quietly dissipates for a few hours? I'm trying for that.

The normal nervous feeling I always get before going in to bat is not helping. I think every muscle in my whole abdomen is clenched.

Henry's out.

Nope, sorry. This isn't going to work. I really do need to go.

Right that's it. The pads are off again and, armed with tissues and a flat stick for burial purposes, I scurry into the woods.

I'm just coming back into earshot when I hear the shout go up in the field. Is that another wicket? Please don't be another wicket.

As I round the side of the pavilion James is trudging back in that I-can't-believe-it way we all have when we get out cheaply or stupidly, bat swinging, head down. That'll be another wicket then. Walk slowly James.

Box, thigh pads, pads, gloves, lid, bat. Fastest pad-up ever.

"Come on Si, what are you playing at?"

I don't tell anyone till after the game.

Boy am I glad I did it though. It's the longest I bat all year, must be two hours if it's a minute. I'd never have made it.

I'd have had to stop the game and make everyone wait. Running wildly off into the woods, leaving a trail of discarded protective clothing in my wake. And they'd all be standing around, fully aware of what I was doing and politely not talking about it. It'd be like one of those Jungian childhood anxiety dreams coming true. The longer I'm out there in the middle, the more relieved I feel that it didn't happen. This imagined nightmare scenario not having happened is actually making me happy.

Though it feels like ages, I only make 25. We're digging in, trying to steady the ship. Me and Paul have a nice little partnership going and he's set, looking on course for that 50.

And then I run him out.

The field's back and I knock it down into leg and shout 'Yes!' immediately. Paul sets off full steam, but as he's running towards me he's already yelling 'Noooooooooooo!' in slow motion, like Willem Dafoe getting gunned down from the chopper to Barber's Adagio in Platoon. I must have connected better than I thought. It's a terrible call. Never a run. He's out by miles. Gunned down in cold blood by his own side.

After that, wickets fall steadily again. We're 9 down and 30 odd short with a few overs left when I hole out to midwicket, trying to get on with it. Bugger. If I hadn't run Paul out we'd probably have won this, and he'd probably have got his 50. Bugger.

The cricketing calamity has made me completely forget about the toilet trauma, and just how unthinkably badly the afternoon might have gone, if I hadn't decided to make like a bear.

all in the mind

On where most sport, good and bad, is really played

Psychology is a big part of all competitive sport.

Golf, particularly, is mostly psychological. Once you are consistently playing bogey golf and get below a handicap of 18, you clearly have a firm grasp of the basics.

You know what you're doing. You've got most of the shots, can probably move the ball both ways in the air, if not always exactly when you want to, have a sound putting stroke, and are capable of an occasionally majestic short game. Every round you'll play several shots that any pro would be happy with.

You know how to make pars and will have days when there are strings of them and you shoot in the 70s. But you have no control over when those days are. Your success or failure has little if anything to do with your technique, and everything to do with what's going on in your head.

Take this 100 yard pitch, here, for instance. It's easy. The lie is good. You know you can do it, you've done it a thousand times. But, if it's over water, or to win a match, or for a fiver, or to break 80, no matter how much you try and tell yourself to relax and just get on with it, you can't. The consequences are there, up in lights in front of you, and you cannot ignore them. You can pretend to ignore them, which is what most of us do, but you can't really. If you make the shot it will be in spite of the consequences, not because of them.

The opposite phenomenon – when it matters most is when

you play best – is often seen in top sportsmen, rarely if ever in amateurs.

Give an 18-handicapper 10 chances to hit a green at 200 yards, he might make it half the time.

Give him one chance. Tell him it's worth £500 if he hits it, but will cost him £1000 if he misses. Most would miss. In fact most, quite sensibly, would walk away.

Ask someone like Sergio Garcia though, and he would probably want to know what a hole-in-one would be worth, before he decided if it was worth really concentrating. Or if you'd go double or quits if he did it with his 9 iron. Or your putter. Left handed.

Perhaps the ability to focus your ability, back yourself utterly, and be spurred on by barriers rather than intimidated by them, is the raw difference between amateurs and professionals in any sport.

This is why most of us can hit straight drives on the driving range, but on a hole with Out Of Bounds down the right: well hello there Mr Slice, where've you been?

By my reckoning – and this I stress is a survey of one – once you've mastered the basic techniques of the game, golf is 90% psychology.

Your success in convincing yourself that it doesn't really matter will determine your success on the course. And the more you fail, the more it matters, and the harder it becomes to convince yourself that it doesn't matter.

Though highly sociable, golf is by nature a solitary game. There is nowhere to hide, no-one to share blame or glory with, and in this respect it's quite different from cricket.

Forgive the golf talk. "A game," according to Hampshire legend Colin Ingleby-McKenzie, "to be played between cricket and death." I wonder what he'd make of the new 18 hole development at the Rose Bowl? I think he's being a bit harsh there anyway. What's wrong with between September and April, Colin?

Anyway, back to the cricket. There are, as noted before, aspects of cricket that are entirely solitary.

A batsman or bowler 'in the zone' is a powerful thing, a wonderful pairing of confidence in his own ability and focussed determination. It is something his team mates can encourage him in, but cannot otherwise influence.

I was lucky enough to be at Lord's with a bunch of the Damerham boys for the fifth morning of the second 2009 Ashes Test when Freddie bowled his brutal swansong five-fer. That, if ever there was one, was a bowler in the zone.

(Here's an odd little aside about how unconnected and just plain weird the MCC, ECB, or whoever's responsible for such things can be with their audience. Days one through four for that Test cost three figures minimum and were sold out before they got to joe public. I and several others were in the Lord's ballot for tickets and we all got nowhere. The Home of Cricket was full of corporate boxes packed with suits on a jolly who couldn't give a flying slip about cricket. Nice one old chaps, way to keep the game alive. But then they put fifth day tickets on sale in advance for £25. Brilliant! A nice scrap from the top table for us plebs. So we went, saw Freddie get on the honours board, and enjoyed the best atmosphere I've experienced at a live sporting event. And guess what they do. No. No. No, forget it, you'll never guess, I'll tell you. They gave us a refund. The game finished ten minutes before lunch, so they refunded half the ticket prices, whether we asked for it or not, for being inconvenienced by a thrilling England win with the retiring talisman the hero of the hour. They seem to have no concept of what cricket fans want, what they think is important, and what they think is worth paying for. Still. Gotta love Lord's. End of aside.)

Great individual performances can often win games, and can even make mediocre teams consistently competitive where they would otherwise not be.

The West Indies provide excellent examples of this on the world stage. Shivnarine Chanderpaul has for a while been a world-class Test batsman in what is otherwise a pretty ordinary side, and before him the batting phenomenon that was Brian Lara bestrode the game, leaving shattered records in his wake, for some years the buoyancy that kept an otherwise sunk Windies afloat.

There are countless village teams with giants similarly ensconced within their ranks of pygmies. Sides where you know, if you get *that* guy out cheaply, you'll probably run through them. But can you get him out? You can not. By the time he's notched up another 80-odd, they're well on their way to a decent total. You know that without him you'd beat them easily (he usually bowls, too, this bloke) and in some odd way it feels vaguely unfair. But the really good player surrounded by rank and file journeymen is very much part of cricket at every level, and in fact a distinct aspect of a game which is played by a team, but so manifestly won or lost by individuals.

Anyone who has followed England for any length of time will be familiar with the classic English batting collapse. They'll be going fine, then someone will get out. Then shortly afterwards someone else will. Then, with crushing inevitability, someone else will. And then it's like the next guy coming out has already resigned himself to the fact that he's going to be out for single figures. Adelaide December 2006 was a perfect example. Look at this middle order scorecard: 2, 2, 10, 0, 4, 8, 1. Dismal, but somehow inevitable. Only the inestimable Paul Collingwood dropped anchor against the relentless tide of McGrath and Warne. In fact, if you can get hold of it, the match is worth rewatching for an England fan, even though we were crushed. Warne is on fire, which is always good to watch: he turned a draw into a win pretty much by force of personality, simply because he had decided it was there to be won. But it was possibly Collingwood's best game in an England shirt. There can't be too many Test batsmen who've got a double century in the first innings and carried their bat in the second and still managed to end up on the losing side. What Colly did, though in this instance it still wasn't enough, was the pro-phenomenon: play his very best when he needed it most.

Of course the collective hysteria of the batting collapse is by no means exclusive to the big boys. I was fortunate enough to miss a game the other year in which we were all out for 20. Which included a top score of 13 (batted, Matt) and no less than six big fat nothings.

So back to those mind games. The real force of psychology on most of us who play the game (including England batsmen) is a negative one. When things start to go wrong, no-one can help.

When that ball comes to you in the field, no-one is going to catch it for you, or stop it going for four, or make the return that runs someone out. Here, as much as anywhere else, is the individual in the team game, for those moments turn matches.

For a bowler, loss of form can mean all sorts of little things. You lose your line and keep bowling wides. Your length goes, and it's either a long-hop or a full-toss. Or worse, a succession of juicy half volleys. ('Juicy' is the only legally acceptable adjective for half volleys.) You keep overstepping and bowling no-balls; you can't get it to swing; your pace drops; it won't turn.

All these things are repairable.

Sometimes there's something technically wrong, and team-mates can tell you what looks different: you're dropping your shoulder, your run's too long, get your left arm up higher, get more sideways.

Usually though, all this well-meaning amateur advise serves only to confuse and muddy the issue.

More often than not, whatever's temporarily deserted you will come back of its own volition with a minimum of fuss, just as inexplicably as when it left.

At the time it's all going wrong though, the poor chap will be inconsolable, perhaps made worse by being taken off after one disastrous over, and not bowled again all match.

There are few more tragic figures than an out of form bowler patrolling the outfield, shaking his head in incomprehension, railing against the unfairness of it all. "I don't understand it," he'll mutter, kicking the ground. Then, moments later, almost to himself, he'll whine plaintively "I'm not doing anything different," and sigh, staring at his feet. No wonder few of us can resist offering all that conflicting advice.

One of those few figures who is indeed more tragic than that though, is the batsman in similar straits.

Without doubt the greatest of all cricket's psychological horrors is a run of ducks.

Every player gets out for a duck sooner or later. Everyone.

Batsmen need to acclimatise, to 'get in', to become 'set'. For some this takes a few balls, for some it takes half a dozen overs. For some of us, it might be said that it never really happens at all.

Very few can arrive at the crease ready to play each ball on its merits. Relatively innocuous deliveries will remove a batsman early on that, had he survived long enough, ten minutes later he would have negotiated with ease.

Facing a quick yorker, a hooping outswinger or a sharp googly first ball up can be enough to remove anyone. This is why bowlers get so annoyed with themselves if they offer poor or easy balls to a batsmen new to the crease – it's the best time to throw all your tricks at him.

Perhaps the most famous duck of all was Bradman's last Test innings. He needed to score just four runs to finish his career with a three figure average. He was bowled through the gate second ball by an Eric Hollies googly, and retired with a test average of 99.94. He probably got over it. History has not forgotten him because of that lapse. (Though it has remembered Eric Hollies, whom it might otherwise have forgotten. Well, perhaps not. He did once take 10-49 in a County innings without assistance – 7 bowled, 3 LBW. He also showed astonishing ineptitude as a batsman, way more remarkable than his ability as a bowler: he accrued 650 more wickets than runs in his career. But it is as Bradman's denier that posterity knows him.)

A flurry of ducks (there are some great collective nouns for ducks: a bunch, a paddling, a raft, a brace, a flush, a safe, or, heaven forbid, a team) is the most insidious thing of all though.

They take on a significance they do not posses, and become massive in the mind. Yes, they happen to better players than you, yes they're often not your fault, yes it will end, and no, there's nothing you can do about it.

It is not a pleasant experience.

Ducks in a row
Saturday league, first away game of the season and we're somewhere up near Winchester. They batted first and were all out for one-seventy-something. I bowled well and feel good about it, got a few to really bounce and leave the bat off the pitch. Took 3-26, all top edges, my usual.

Now we're in a spot of bother. Big Marky H and Henry got twenties, but other than that we're not looking clever, with a couple of ducks and a couple of single figures. Gotta settle in here, plenty of time, just play yourself in boy, nothing silly.

They guy's bowling a good line, not quick. It comes out well and

I stick with the plan, first ball, don't try to hit it, just get behind it, solid, block it. I get forward, bat to the pitch. And miss. I hear the death rattle behind me and see the field leap in celebration. I don't know if the ball did something, moved off the pitch, or if I just totally misjudged it. All I know is that I'm trudging back to the pavilion, any warm fuzzy feelings I might have had about bowling well completely evaporated.

We're near Winchester again, north of it this time at a rural ground inside a country estate. It's a lovely setting, the only building in sight is the tumbledown pavilion with its marvellous scoreboard made from old barrels. It's a village cup draw on an unseasonably sweltering Sunday in May. We are comprehensively outclassed, and had a loooooong hot day in the field while they blasted 330something. We haven't got a whelk's chance in a supernova of chasing that down, so our sole aim for the day is not to be all out.

We've not done too badly. Mark and Joely got runs, Paul's still in. There's only eight overs left and we still have a few wickets left to play with. This is perfect for me. I'm never going to be one of those guys who can come in and start biffing it straight away, but usually I can block all day, and that's all we need to do here: make like we're batting out a draw. I reassure myself of this as I stride out from the shade of a little tree near the pavilion where we're all gathered, sitting or lying on the grass.

Bat tucked purposefully under my arm, I line the velcro up on my gloves and continue my inner monologue. They've got some very quick, very accurate bowlers. I wouldn't mind facing them, to be honest. They're not going to bowl short and nasty at us – if they were going to do that they'd have done it by now – and there are no demons in this road of a pitch. Blocking straight length balls is fairly straightforward on a pitch with reliable bounce. You can cope with it up to 80mph from a bowling machine, as long as it's length-ish. Very short or very full are quite different propositions.

But anyway, those guys came off long ago, and now it's their second team guys and youngsters getting a go, since it became obvious that their victory was not in doubt. The chap bowling now is an offy. Well, he's bowling sort of off-cutters, or that's what it *looked like from under the tree.*

I reach the crease and take two, scratching it carefully in front of the batting crease with the outside spike of my right foot. The keeper's standing up to this guy, so I'll be staying back in my crease, foot behind the line. I'm tall enough and have a longish reach, and I'm ready to get right forward to him, unless he drops it short. I'm focussed, determined. Not to do anything flash, just not to get out.

The first ball pitches outside off on a good length: a good ball. I'm forward to it, bat angled down, arms extended. It turns. Not much, just a little bit. Just enough.

Bowled through the gate. Golden Ducks in consecutive innings. I have completely failed even to hit the ball in those encounters.

In a well meaning but futile (and as it turns out inaccurate) attempt to make me feel better, my team-mates will later point out that it can't get any worse.

But how did I miss that ball? How, plausibly, could I have not made contact with it? How? How is that possible? It's not possible. Is there something wrong with my eyes? Is there a hole in my bat? I check. My eyes appear fine as I look down at my bat in the brilliant sunshine and study the evenly spaced grain of the willow and the red smudges of previous contacts in 20/20 clarity. I am also able to confirm that the bat is, without question, without holes. I sigh, turn, and trudge back towards the shade under the tree, defeated in every conceivable sense.

Three days later I'm on my way out to open with Paul. Paul's one of those people I'd have had no chance of meeting, let alone becoming friends with, if it wasn't for cricket.

He seems abrasive when you first meet him, but he's not at all really. He's a lovely bloke, and a bit of an old hippy. He's an artist; a stone sculptor. Tall and whippet-thin, he doesn't drive, so he cycles everywhere – rides to every away game, though he'll sometimes get a lift back. You can pick his bike up with one finger, and he reckons he does 8,000 miles a year on it. He's one of the fittest people I know, despite the fact that when he's not on his bike or playing cricket, he's either smoking or rolling a fag. Often both at the same time.

He loves his cricket and is a fine bat, strong through the offside with an elegant, flashing cut. As is so often the case in this infuriating game, it's as much a weakness as a strength: his preferred mode of dismissal is caught at cover/point.

It's a Wednesday evening, at home, early in the season, and we won the toss. Often there's some discussion over whether to bat or bowl first on a Saturday or Sunday, but on a Wednesday there's no question, especially early or late in the season. In May and August you start in the gloom and it gets steadily gloomier, so if you get the choice you bat first.

The team we're playing are mostly kids and mostly gobby. Not in a nasty or aggressive way, just in an exuberant mouthy teenager way.

As Paul and I walk out to the square, their skipper gives the customary shout: "Batsmen in, lads!" and they all clap us in, this little ritual signalling to everyone that the game is afoot.

Still clapping, extra-cover says to his mate at point with a completely straight face, "Have I got time for a wank?"

His mate wrinkles his nose at him distastefully. "What?"

"Come on, I wanna rub it in your hair."

"Fuck off you idiot."

"All right, that's enough, c'mon lads, here we go." It's not clear if the skipper heard the exchange or not.

Paul looks at me with raised eyebrows, and I'm amused to realise that my eyebrows are raised too. "That's not the sort of conversation one's used to overhearing on one's way out to bat, is it?"

"Indeed not." Paul strokes at a nonexistent WG Grace beard and leans on his bat with both hands on the top, like it's a Gentleman's cane. "Do you want the first ball?"

"Don't mind."

"I don't either."

"You have it then."

"Nice loud calls, okay?" All business now, he reels half-seriously through his favourite clichés. "Backin' up, Si, yeah? Plenty of time, nothin' silly, have a look first."

"Yeah yeah."

Paul takes centre, knocks in his guard, and settles himself.

"Play," says the umpire.

The first ball is decent, not too fast but on a good length. Paul plays it down into the offside. "YES!!" he bellows, and sets off.

I hesitate, I can see mid-off swooping in for it, there's never a run here. Not now, anyway. "NOOOOOO!" I yell back. Paul shudders to a stop a third of the way down and hurls himself back. His bat hits his crease as the ball hits the keeper's gloves.

We meet in the middle while they're all congratulating each other on what a good start it was.

"Easy fella."

"There's a run there if we're quick."

"You reckon?"

"Backin' up, Si, backin' up."

The next ball is similar but wide of off stump and he lets it go. The third ball is like the first, and Paul plays it down into off, just like before. "YES!!"

This time I set off without looking. I'm not the quickest between the sticks, and I was probably guilty of sitting on my heels then, rather than half way down the track on the balls of my feet ready to take off, not believing he'd go for another sharp single straight away. I'm at full tilt, bat outstretched, ready to run it in along the floor when I get near the crease. I'm still six feet away when the direct hit breaks the stumps. I carry on running past them, not looking back, head down. I slow to a trot as I get near the pavilion but don't catch anyone's eye as I jog straight back through the door into the home changing room I left not two minutes before, having not faced a ball.

The summer is turning out conspicuously and stubbornly to be not as advertised. We were promised a heatwave, warned we'd have difficulty getting hold of suncream and barbeques. We got persistent drizzle.

We're away somewhere near Romsey. We're early, and congregate on the cut strip. It's a weird looking one. Looks like the wet grass has been ironed flat by a heavy roller, rather than cut short. It's been raining most of the week and everything's damp.

For once, most of us agree that we might even want to bowl first *on it, it looks that dodgy to bat on. This is highly unusual.*

Mark is relieved of the decision and we're put in. It's pretty processional. Henry hits a quick 40, but everyone else is rubbish. I don't know how many we've got when I go in but it's not many. Maybe 70 for six or seven, something like that. We're not even half way through the overs yet.

But again, you see, this is great for me. This is my kind of crisis. The task here is not to score fast, it's not to get out.

The bowlers on are not quick, and they're not spinners, but the ball is darting about all over the place off the seam, every ball a grenade. Whatever the opposite of 'flat' is for a pitch, this is it. 'Fizzy,' perhaps.

I pat the first ball back to the bowler. The next is wide outside off and I leave it very deliberately, bat high out of the way. The next is straighter and pushed away to point.

It goes on. With every ball I feel better. There aren't that many demons in this pitch after all, are there? It's simple, I tell myself. Leave the wide ones, block the straight ones.

I have this conversation with the skipper in the middle after a single at the end of an over, and he agrees. But Mark is allergic to the forward defensive, and moments later he hammers a straight ball for four. Moments after that he's back in the hutch, caught chasing a wide one.

Leave the wide ones, block the straight ones. I block one a bit firmer and it runs out towards mid off. Not worth the run. Just carry on as you are. There's still 20 overs left to bat. Block the straight ones, leave the wide ones.

I leave another one well wide of off-stump, bat raised high. The ball must have hit a stone or something. Either that or this straight-up-and-down guy's got a secret Murali offbreak and has just been toying with us up till now. Seriously, it pitches at least eighteen inches outside. Maybe two foot. Dammit, it was nearly a bloody wide. There's no way it could come back in enough to hit the stumps. Except of course that it does. Bowled on a leave. I can't believe it. Judging by his somewhat sheepish celebration, neither can the bowler.

I reach the boundary to a chorus of straight-faced "nice leave"s from my side-splitting comrades who have bravely risen above our dire predicament in the game to find amusement at my indignation. Their mirth is garnished by Henry, who reports from the scorer's hut that that, actually, believe it or not, was a six over duck.

Wednesday night. The first ball I face is dragged down and wide of leg, a classic long hop. I wait for it and then club it away through square. There's a man out there, so it's only a single.

But it's a run.

Walking to the other end I take my lid off, raise my bat and bow to the pavilion where the comedians are cheering.

My cheeks blow out in a huge sigh of relief, and I'm grinning despite myself.

A run.

it's just not golf

On language, fair play and manners

Cricket is full of jargon with which players and fans talk about it. Like most jargon, this is pure gibberish to those not in the know. (Consequently, in the back of this book you'll find a handy glossary.) But unlike most, a lot of cricket jargon has been around so long that it's become part of the language.

To 'play a straight bat' is one of the more obvious, with a clear path from the game to the wider world. It has several meanings. One is to be honest and trustworthy; another is to hold traditional ideas and beliefs, especially about behaviour and etiquette; and a third is to obstinately refuse to submit to questioning or give up information. All of which make perfect sense in the context of a well bred forward defensive, and are as identifiably English, or at least as colonial, as a stiff upper lip. (Although I am reliably informed that the phrase 'stiff upper lip' is American in origin. That is inconvenient of it, but need not concern us here.)

A 'sticky wicket' has come to be a metaphor for any sort of tricky situation that requires extreme care to navigate. Ironically its original meaning has been more or less destroyed by the ubiquitous use of covers in the first class game. Much to its detriment, traditionalists claim, being just one of the many slow creeps the game has made unfairly weighting the contest between bat and ball in the batsman's favour. A sticky wicket, or a 'sticky dog' as it was also known, is a drying pitch after overnight rain that turns prodigiously and bounces unpredictably. The master spinners of yore like Laker and Lock could exploit those conditions and render such a surface practically unplayable. The great English left arm spinner Hedley Verity to this day holds the record for the best first class bowling figures ever, on what must have been a beauty of a sticky wicket: 19.4 overs, 16 maidens, 10 for 10. That was in the summer of 1932, before his tour to Australia that winter, infamous for rather faster bowling than Hedley's, of which more later. Today, village cricketers at clubs without the funds for such niceties as covers still know the sticky wicket well of course, though few can exploit them quite like Verity.

Then there's the duck. Can there be anyone, even someone with no interest in cricket whatsoever, who doesn't know what it means to be out for a duck? The term is thought to have come from the shape of a duck's egg, being a big fat zero. (Interestingly, sports fans, the same source is also thought to apply to 'love', meaning nothing, in tennis, being a contraction and Anglicisation of the French l'oeuf.)

Cricket – not football – gave us 'hat-trick'. (Its etymology is disputed, but only within cricket. See glossary.)

Someone who's lived to a ripe old age will invariably be said to have had 'a good innings', even if they never ventured anywhere near a cricket pitch. This is often said in a compensatory sort of way after a person's demise, intimating that one mustn't grumble, really, 96 is not bad going. Of course, any cricketer who was out for 96 would be far more likely to be livid with himself for being one blow away from a century, rather than sanguinely accepting that he did well to get that far, all things considered.

Arguably, to be stumped – meaning to be confused, flummoxed, without an answer – could come from cricket, though there are other conceivable roots for it, as anyone who has ever tried to dig out a tree stump will attest.

The most obvious idiom that cricket has given us is a more general one. "It's just not cricket" is still widely used today, even though rarely without someone affecting a silly posh accent and comically knitted brows. It is somewhat strange that to the wider world the game is defined by what it is not. For something to be 'not cricket' is for it to be unfair, unsporting, or not in the right spirit.

The Chambers Dictionary of Etymology lists under the meanings of the word 'cricket' 'sense of fair play, good sportsmanship' first recorded in English usage in 1851. The word was first recorded at all, incidentally, in 1598. Intriguingly, in 1809 it was noted that it was also used as a verb, by none other than Lord Byron. You don't tend to hear people yelling goodbye up the stairs to the wife and kids of a Saturday lunchtime, declaring jauntily that they are 'just off for a cricket' too much anymore.

Clearly the game has for a long time been regarded as a gentleman's pursuit were fair play was paramount. But it hardly holds the monopoly on that. Golf could equally have a pretty fair a claim on its reputation for fairness.

In the 1969 Ryder Cup, Jack Nicklaus made one of the great sporting gestures of all time, which brings a lump to my throat whenever I think about it. The all-conquering Nicklaus was playing the inexperienced young Tony Jacklin in the last match. The tournament was level, Nicklaus and Jacklin were all square on the 18th tee. America were holders, so only needed a tie to retain it. They both drove off, and on the way down the final fairway Nicklaus asked how the younger man felt. "Bloody awful," Jacklin replied. They both scrambled onto the green, and Nicklaus sank a four foot putt for par, leaving his opponent a three footer to tie. The pressure on that three footer would have been immense. It could easily have been the defining moment of the young Jacklin's career. Instead, it became a defining moment of a different sort. After collecting his ball from the hole, Nicklaus picked up Jacklin's ball marker, conceding the putt. Shaking hands with his speechless opponent, he told him: "I don't think you were going to miss that, Tony, but I wasn't going to give you the opportunity." His gesture so incensed US skipper Sam Snead, who wanted an outright win, that he didn't speak to Nicklaus for weeks. But it won Nicklaus friends throughout the world. Even among those who were only six months old at the time.

Decades earlier, Augusta National and Masters founder Bobby Jones famously called a penalty on himself in the US Open when the ball moved as he addressed it. Even though he hadn't touched it and the movement was just the ball settling in the long grass, because he was addressing it (lining his club up, ready to hit it), it counted as a shot. Jones knew the rules. No-one else had seen it, but he went and told the match referee that the ball had moved. Congratulated afterwards on his integrity, he replied "You might as well congratulate a man for not robbing a bank."

Golf is one of the few games where players call penalties on themselves. Snooker is another. No-one who saw it could forget Stephen Hendry calling a foul on himself in the final frame of the World Championship against Jimmy White, seemingly handing the title to him at last. (As is happened the nerves were too much, Jimmy missed a sitter and Hendry cleared up to thwart him in his fifth final in a row, but that's beside the point.) Fencing, curiously, is another, from which another word has leaked into mainstream use. Before there were electronic vests to register a hit, each protagonist would be expected to acknowledge their opponent's success. They would do this by declaring "Touché!", the French for touched. If the striker considered that he had not in fact scored a hit, he would respond "Pas de touche," – no touch – indicating that it should not count. Outside fencing, the word "touché" is still generally used in the cut and thrust of argument and debate to acknowledge a point well made.

But golf and cricket are the two mainstream sports where players call penalties on themselves. Yet you do not hear anyone proclaim that something is 'just not golf'. Cricket, in the public imagination at least, retains its reputation for sportsmanship and even-handed fairness. The reality of the modern game at the highest level, is sadly a little different.

The all-seeing eye of television removes a lot of decisions from the players these days. (Back to golf for a second, it's unlikely that a player of Bobby Jones' profile would be the only one who witnessed a ball move in a Major Championship today.) But only at the very highest level, and even then it is not always to be trusted. The foreshortening effect of powerful zoom lenses can mean that low catches look like they've been grassed when they were actually taken cleanly. This not only robs a fielder of a catch, it also makes him look like a cheat for claiming it, which seems desperately unfair. Even technological innovations like snicko (which registers sound at the supposed moment of impact), hawkeye (which projects the probable movement of the ball after it was interrupted), hotspot (an infra-red camera that shows up the heat of impact marks on bats and pads), and the super-slow-motion 100-frames-a-second high definition camera, can sometimes not conclusively decide whether a batsman got a nick or not. (See chapter 7.) But he'll know. Oh yes, the batsman knows.

To me, if he thinks he's out he should walk. He just should. It's the game: you hit it, they catch it, you're out. That's what we're doing here, not what you think you can get away with.

There is a lot of pressure in the modern game on players at the top level – from coaches, boards and sponsors – to transfer that pressure onto the umpires by not walking. And to enthusiastically appeal for decisions they know they shouldn't get. To cheat, basically.

This attitude undermines the very soul of the game. It reduces cricket to the same level as preening prima donnas diving in the penalty box. And who thinks that's a good idea? Find me one person who thinks it has improved football as a spectacle.

I will personally always remember Australian wicketkeeper Adam Gilchrist as the author and endless repeater of the phrase "Awww! Nice area, Shane!!" and variations on that theme, as he kept wicket to the wizardry of Warne.

He was more widely famous as one of the most entertaining and exhilarating batsmen of his or any other era, and Test cricket's most prolific six hitter – he is, and is likely to remain for some time, the only player to have hit 100 Test sixes.

But he is perhaps most famous to fans of the game as a walker. If Gilchrist thought he was out, he walked. On one occasion, he even walked after being given not out in the 2003 World Cup semi final against Sri Lanka. Here it is in his own words:

"He pitched it up and I went for an aggressive sweep, trying to hit it behind square. I got a thick, loud bottom edge. It bounced off my pad and I had no idea where it went. 'Catch it! Catch it!' I heard. I stood and turned to see that Sangakkara had it. I knew I was done. It was so obvious. Then, to see the umpire shaking his head, meaning, 'not out', gave me the strangest feeling. I don't recall what my exact thoughts were, but somewhere in the back of my mind, all that history was swirling around, [all those] batsmen, both in my team and against us, who had stood their ground in 'close' catching incidents were definitely a factor in what happened in the following seconds. I had spent all summer wondering if it was possible to take ownership of these incidents and still be successful. I had wondered what I would do. I was about to find out. The voice in my head was emphatic. Go. Walk. And I did."

Gilchrist's gesture momentarily re-opened the 'walking debate' in the professional game, and again, made him a lot of friends around the world.

It didn't seem to change too many minds though, and with his retirement, I can't think of any other walkers in international cricket.

In the village game though, the phenomenon is very much alive.

It has to be, really. If you don't have access to TV replays and third umpire decisions, you have to rely on the honesty of the batsman.

And amateur umpires (who in the vast majority of cases will be the batsman's team-mates, ex-players, secretaries or treasurers anyway) cannot be expected to be ruthless, and will naturally give the batsman the benefit of the doubt if he maintains he hasn't hit it. And by not walking, of course, that is exactly what he is doing.

No, on village games, whether league or friendly, batsmen will usually go gracefully, in the same way that they will own up if a catch is grassed, or if a ball sneaks over the rope for four.

That, is cricket. It just is.

As we have seen, cricket's meaning of fairness and sportsmanship was already well established by the middle of the nineteenth century. But it was an incident some 80 years later that would cement the phrase 'it's not cricket' firmly in place.

The 1932 Ashes tour to Australia has become known as the Bodyline series, and is squarely in the public domain, known to millions who know nothing else about cricket, purely because of its status as neatly defining the kind of behaviour that is very definitely 'not cricket'.

I'm not going to go into detail here (if it's detail you crave, the book you need is David Frith's excellent *Bodyline Autopsy,* which is every bit as forensic and exhaustive as its title suggests) but basically, the English needed a plan to combat Don Bradman, who was then and remains today the most prolific run-scorer ever to wield a bat.

The plan hatched by England captain Douglas Jardine was to bowl not at the stumps, but at the body, forcing the batsman to defend himself with his bat, thus offering simple catches to the specially placed ring of close fielders on the leg side. Jardine called it 'leg theory'; posterity knows it as Bodyline. The main weapon used to implement this plan, and the name synonymous with it, was Harold Larwood.

It's impossible to know how quick Larwood was, but contemporary accounts certainly place him at the rapid end of fast. Many first class batsmen were bowled by balls they never even saw, and Larwood hospitalised plenty, way before bodyline was even thought of. He was definitely a handful. It's reasonable to assume he was at least as fast as today's fastest – 90 to 95mph – and he may well have been faster.

Half a century before helmets became the norm, and some time before any protection other than rudimentary ruber-spiked gloves and cane pads, the Aussies took blow after blow, the most serious resulting in a cracked scull.

When bowlers bowl fast, batmen will get hit. It's part of the game, and the game is infinitely poorer without that risk, as will be obvious to anyone who has ever played cricket with a tennis ball. But this was different. It was meant. He was aiming at you. One of the many remarkable things about Bodyline – and there really are a lot of them – is that no-one was killed.

In theory, it could not happen now. The ferocity of feeling Bodyline whipped up provoked changes to the Laws of Cricket to ensure it wouldn't be repeated. Shortly after the series, the MCC introduced a new law under the heading "Intimidatory Short Pitched Bowling" issuing umpires with the imperative to intervene if they considered a bowler was deliberately aiming to hit a batsman with intent to cause him harm.

This is today part of Law 42 (Fair and Unfair Play) parts 6-8 'Dangerous and Unfair Bowling', and even, rather sweetly, takes into account the "relative skill of the batsman", in other words, you can bowl fast and short at a good batsman, but you can't at a crap one. The law obliges the umpire to take action if he thinks such bowling is "likely to inflict physical injury on the striker, irrespective of the protective equipment he may be wearing."

There are also guidelines for ODI and Test Match playing conditions which limit the amount of 'bouncers' (a term not recognised in the Laws) in an over: one in ODIs, two in Tests. But there is nothing to limit such deliveries in the Laws themselves, unless the umpire considers them to be dangerous.

It's arguable that these guidelines are more a result of the highly skilled, vicious, bouncer-happy and largely unplayable West Indies attack of the eighties than anything that happened in the thirties. Anyone who remembers that side could be forgiven for thinking that the MCC's attempt to make sure Bodyline didn't happen again had rather profoundly failed. But also, just as importantly, bouncer after bouncer after bouncer made for pretty dull viewing.

It all gets quite murky and complex, seeing as a bouncer that's going over your head can't really be considered dangerous, as by definition it's not going to hit you, but it could certainly be considered 'intimidatory', a term that was dropped from the laws some time ago. (It could also, of course, be considered a wide, but let's try and stick to the point.)

Some years later another rule was introduced which must, though rather belatedly, have been a direct attempt to limit the profitability of 'leg theory'. Law 41 part 5 'Limitation of on side fielders' states that "there shall not be more than two fielders, other than the wicket-keeper, behind the popping crease on the on side", thus making any attempt to repeat Jardine's 'leg trap' cordon of close catchers an automatic no-ball.

Bodyline is a great story, full of drama. The international incident it very nearly caused, the riots it very nearly sparked, the resentment that still lingers.

But the most dramatic thing of all was that the Aussies did not fight back. They had some very fast bowlers themselves, and could easily have retaliated in kind. If they had, cricket might be a different game today. Because they didn't, Bodyline was an English outrage, not a cricketing one. Australian captain Bill Woodfull, son of a Methodist Minister, turned the other cheek. It made the English, and specifically Jardine, into the villains, and inverted the lazy stereotype of the Aussies as violent criminals and the English as cultured gentlemen.

There is a brilliant anecdote which is almost certainly apocryphal, but worth repeating nonetheless. Jardine knocks on the door of the Aussie dressing room one evening looking for an apology because one of the Aussie players had questioned the veracity of his parentage during play that day. From the dressing room door, Woodfull turns to his men and demands wearily "All right. Which one of you bastards called this bastard a bastard?"

I think I like that exchange better in the knowledge that it didn't happen. It seems willed to have happened by those who thought it probably should have. Highly satisfying though it may be to modern minds, Woodfull would, I suspect, have deemed such a profane rebuke to have reduced him to Jardine's level.

The point, I think, is that Bodyline was the height of bad manners, and Woodfull simply refused to stoop. Cricket is a lesson in manners, in many ways, and if nothing else it teaches us that you will be judged on *how* you play the game every bit as much as how *well* you play it. The means are absolutely as important as the end.

Bradman himself was never hit, (well, not properly: he turned his back on Larwood once and was hit on the arse, but that hardly counts,) and still averaged over 50 for the series. Which was poor by his lofty standards but hardly a bowler's triumph. So Bodyline could be said to have failed against the man it was invented to curb. England did win the series though, so perhaps that failure was irrelevant.

But I don't think so. England won, yes. But even now we as a cricketing nation are not proud of it. We're proud of squeaking the glorious 2005 series when they were the better side, and delighted at trouncing them in their own back yard in 2011 when the pendulum had finally swung, and we at last were decisively the better side. Both quite different, and both with plenty to be proud of.

But are we proud of Bodyline?

Who could be proud of manners like that.

Whippersnapper glory

A few years ago we played a couple of friendlies against a side from up Salisbury way. I can't remember where the contact came from. They got my number from some other village side, I think. They just phoned up looking for a game.

They were a new team, who stood out for the fact that they were both incredibly young and incredibly keen. Usually with young sides there's a captain or coach or someone older around to keep them in check and steer the ship, who tends to get lumbered with all the fixtures and subs and admin and stuff. But this lot were steered by a lad of about twenty, their most senior member by three or four years.

They had just got on and put a team together themselves because they wanted to play, and I liked that about them a lot – it's the kind of thing adults are always complaining that 'kids today' never do. Well, they did.

Working out fixtures with them was tricky, because they all had pre-pay phones which never had any credit on them. No-one seemed sure who was responsible for what, and all of them held typically teenage attitudes to organisation. We only played two fixtures against them, in consecutive years, but they both involved a disproportionate amount of voicemail, text, and 'I'll-call-you-back' conversations. Extracting a contribution towards tea from them was a slightly more arduous task than I'm in favour of too, I seem to recall. Though I had the impression it was largely because they were genuinely skint, not trying to pull a fast one. Unless of course giving me that impression was in fact the fast one. If so, they did it well.

They played under several different names, one of them was a Salisbury housing estate, something-or-other Farm, which I think is what they eventually settled on. To us, for obvious reasons, they were always referred to as Whippersnapper Farm.

The first year we played, they won. And pretty well, too. They got us all out when we only needed 20 to win off the last 22 balls. They were mouthy in the field and rarely shut up, but not in a nasty way. They played hard and wanted to win.

The next year they must have been a year older, but they didn't look it. If anything they seemed younger. And keener. And mouthier. But still hard not to like.

It was as ever a horrible wet summer, and our tireless groundsman Derek had worked a small miracle to get us out there at all. The wicket was dead, low and slow – a bowlers' wicket. I lost the toss and they put us in.

We struggled to get it away, and were a miserable 40 odd for 4 at not far off the halfway stage. Henry, blithely unencumbered with the notion that pitches can be hard to score on, doubled the score in ten minutes before he was out, and Clive stuck around till the end and gave us something to bowl at with an unbeaten 50, including two sixes off the last two balls which, as it turned out, would come in quite handy. We made 162.

The Whippersnappers' innings started beautifully for them. We did not bowl badly, just unsuccessfully. Their openers were a decent left/right combination who defended solidly and picked their shots.

By drinks the Whippernappers were 106 without loss, and no one who was there was in any doubt at all of the outcome. They needed 57 to win with 132 balls and 10 wickets remaining. I don't think 1000-1 would have been unreasonable at that stage.

The first ball back after the break Chris held on to a sharp catch at square-leg. Maybe 500-1 then. The following over Joel took a blinder diving forward at slip. Two overs later another one was bowled. Next over Marky D held on to a ballooning skier at cow corner. It was off my bowling so I remember it vividly: it was in the air for several long seconds, and for the first few we all told him loudly what to do. The last second passed in absolute silence until it dropped safely into his bucket hands and the yelling started up again. They'd stopped scoring too. Four wickets in five overs for 11 runs.

They were still favourites. Maybe only 10-1 now though.

But 'the big mo' had swung our way. We were on fire. Bunch of little Collingwoods, we were. Bats were crowded, runs were smothered by diving saves, catches were held. We looked suspiciously like a cricket team that afternoon.

Mark Matthews ran someone out with a direct hit from fine leg, which surprised him as much as it delighted everyone else.

A skewed drive stuck in my fist at silly-mid-on. Henry came back on from the church end and bowled his last two in maidens, for once ending wicketless, but tightening the screw as they ran low on runs, overs and batsmen. Chris replaced him and bowled another one first over.

I was starting to believe.

After 33 overs they were 137-7. 26 needed off 42 balls. They were definitely still favourites.

Can you feel that tension though?

Maiden.

Just two off the next one.

Mix up in the middle – another Whippersnapper run out.

Then Joel clean bowled their number nine two balls later and suddenly they weren't favourites any more.

But then they scored a few runs and maybe they were again.

Finally, just eight runs short with 10 balls remaining, Henry hung on to a skied top-edge running away from the wicket, and it was over.

My nails haven't been that badly chewed since that ridiculous Sunday morning at Edgbaston in 2005. It honestly felt like that same kind of tension, even though this was only a friendly game against a bunch of local kids.

The Whippersnappers should have won easily. They should have walked it, and they knew it. They played their socks off, but if wasn't enough against a 1000-1 shot.

It was a game we should never have won.

And those, beyond any doubt at all, are the best ones to win.

11 good men and true

On cricket people, character, and characters

Cricket, more than most sports, is defined by the nature of the men who play it. It's a sweeping statement and a ridiculous generalisation, but I'm going to make it: cricketers are a decent lot.

The comparison does no-one any good, and it's a silly one to make, but compared to footballers... I'm just going to leave that thought hanging there.

Suffice it to say that the game of cricket is blessed to be populated not just by talented sportsmen, but by men of character. And by men who are characters.

If there's a defining moment in the last decade or so, it must surely be the Flintoff and Lee encounter after the climax of the Edgbaston Test in 2005.

If you are a hardened cricket fan, you will not need telling about it. But if you're anything like me you'll probably enjoy hearing about it again even though you know every nuance backwards. And if you don't know about it, well, you should.

In ancient times, I imagine it was moments and men of this calibre that populated tales told around campfires. Of course, it would have been swords and axes they were wielding in those tales, rather than bats and balls, but the core of the stories would have been the same: bravery, self-sacrifice, grace and humility.

England had lost the first game of the five-Test Ashes series. Australia were indisputably the best side in the world at the time, and if England went 2-0 down at Edgbaston, though mathematically they could still win 3-2, psychologically, there was just no way. Realistically, if they lost this game, the Ashes were gone.

It was an epic four days, in which Flintoff came of age as the talismanic all-rounder he had so long promised to be, excelling in both disciplines. (I just checked online, and you can buy a brand new 3-disc box set of the whole magical 2005 series for £1.27. Now that is a bargain.) But the details don't matter much to this story.

All that matters is that on the fourth morning, Australia were still over 100 short and had just two wickets remaining. A formality, surely. England's finest pace attack for years would do for the Aussie tail in no time.

Except that Warne and Lee didn't look like being done for at all, and began chipping away at the total with some panache. Then Warne, the most capable batsman among the Aussie bowlers, fell to Flintoff and Kasprowicz joined Lee in the middle. The final pair. Just one wicket needed. And still they hung on. And on, and on. It was ludicrously tense, and they tried so hard to get them out.

Flintoff hit Lee again and again. Beneath his whites he must have looked like he'd been sparring with half a dozen heavyweights afterwards, as Freddie slammed the ball into him time after time. He tried yorkers, bouncers, and everything in between. Several times he knocked the bat out of his hands, the rest of the time he was trying to knock his head off. Lee took it all, and stood firm.

Slowly, agonisingly, the target inched down. 30 to win. 20. 10. Then it was within one blow. Five. Three. Three to win it was when finally Kasprowicz gloved Harmison behind and England had won by two runs, the narrowest result in Ashes history.

I was only watching on telly, and I jumped up and down and shouted like an idiot. To have been on that field in that moment, it must have been very difficult to contain the heady mixture of elation and relief, bubbling up like suddenly opened Champagne.

Flintoff though, found time amid the running shouting and hugging, to salute a brave and worthy opponent. At the non-striker's end, Lee sank to his haunches, a beaten man in both senses. Batting at 10, he was 43 not-out and top scorer in Australia's second innings. Freddie walked over, squatted down with him, put one hand on his shoulder, and offered him the other.

Neither Flintoff or Lee will be drawn on precisely what was

said between them. Strangely, I can easily believe that neither can remember exactly. It's almost not important. Freddie has done speaking engagements where he tells the story that what he said was "That's 1-1 you Aussie bastard!" but this is clearly played for laughs, a well rehearsed pre-empt to the much-asked question.

Like the moment Bill Murray catches up with Scarlett Johansson at the end of Lost in Translation; it doesn't matter what he said, what matters is that he went and said it.

Besides, Flintoff's expression says everything that needs saying. Compassion, respect, admiration; not even a hint of smugness, gloating or schadenfreude. Had there been, in the mood he must have been in, Lee would surely have brushed that hand aside. But he didn't, he took it, and one of cricket's most thrilling matches was crowned with one of sport's most noble gestures.

Tales of heroic sporting feats are often given more flavour when sprinkled with humanity. And sometimes humour.

Sometime West Indies captain Chris Gayle is a fine candidate for both. Gayle is an incredibly laid back man, who gives the impression even at the crease that if he relaxes any more he's likely to lose consciousness.

This appears in direct contrast to the enormous power with which he hits the ball. During the World T20 in England, he hit a six clean out of the Oval into the road outside with what appeared to be a nonchalant flick of the wrists. In the 2011 IPL he took 49 balls to race to 107, 94 of them coming in boundaries.

This is a man who relinquished the Test captaincy of his country, observing that his temperament is more suited to the shorter forms of the game so he might not bother with Test cricket at all any more. Fair enough, you might think, perhaps he's right. Then he wanders over to Sri Lanka and lollops to 333, becoming only the fourth man in history to score more than one Test triple century (Bradman, Lara and Sehwag, since you ask), and you wonder if perhaps, just maybe, he ought to carry on.

Here's a Gayle anecdote that conjures up the most glorious

image. He is sat next to a stuffed blazer – MCC, ECB, ICC, it doesn't matter – at some official cricket dinner function. We can guess the nature of the conversation: polite establishment smalltalk, steered by the blazer, in his element, surrounded by silver service.

Most would endure in silence, nodding occasionally, hazarding an opinion when on safe ground. Not Gayle. He listens for a while before abruptly leaning in to the blazer and interrupting, asking him earnestly, "You get much pussy?"

On a similar theme, Gayle, who from these two stories at least appears to be something of a ladies' man, was at a West Indies team photo-call in Australia. The pretty young photographer asked him if he wouldn't mind sitting with his knees together. "I'd love to, but I can't," Gayle responded, with an almighty grin. Poor girl.

WG Grace is perhaps the most famous larger-than-life character in cricket, but dozens of books have been filled with his stories, and his tales have a particular flavour, so I won't recount them here.

CB Fry on the other hand, is a man not celebrated nearly enough. Just a few generations on, his life is almost unimaginable now.

He was an incredible athlete, and equalled the world long jump record whilst still at college. It was said that he prepared for the attempt by lighting a large cigar, which he allowed himself to finish as a reward. His acrobatic prowess was such that, as a party trick, he would leap backwards onto the mantelpiece.

At the world's first international athletics event in 1894 in London, he won both the long jump and the 100 yard sprint. He would almost certainly have won Olympic medals in the 1896 games, had he not been busy touring South Africa playing cricket for England. Which, lets be honest, is far more important.

He gained 12 sporting blues at Oxford, and at one point he was captain of the university's football, athletics and cricket teams. He also played rugby for Oxford, and Barbarians, as well as football for Southampton – including an FA Cup Final – and England.

But really he was just dabbling at these compared to cricket.

He played for Oxford, Sussex, Hampshire and England, and went on to captain his country. He scored over 30,000 first class runs averaging over 50 in an age of low scores. He led the averages for five English seasons, and made 94 first class hundreds, including six in consecutive innings in 1901, a record that still stands.

John Arlott, always reliable for a quote, called him "probably the most variously gifted Englishman of any age."

He also wrote, edited, published and broadcast, ran for parliament, and very nearly became Charles III of Albania. (That's a long story, too long for here, but worth looking up, I assure you.)

And if all that were not enough, he was often cited as the most handsome man in England.

He paid a high price for his extraordinary gifts though. An unhappy marriage and propensity for depression and mental illness (today he would almost certainly be diagnosed as bipolar) robbed him of a happy ending, but cannot rob posterity of a character Cricinfo summed up as one "you would think twice before having the effrontery to put into a novel."

In recent times many international sportsmen seem to be slavish clones of an insipidly bland 'ideal'. Like politicians, they are focussed, committed, and have known nothing but 'this' since the age of 12. They are correspondingly dull, anodyne, and ignorant of the world outside their field (so to speak). Cricket is less guilty of this than some sports, and still boasts individuals aplenty, including one or two that perhaps even CB Fry would recognise as kindred spirits.

The Dutch Australian Dirk Nannes is one such. He may have nothing like the almost ludicrous variety of talent and experiences granted to Fry, but he has at least taken the scenic route in his career.

Rather than shimmy up the ladders of age-group cricket towards international level, Nannes appears to have nipped of and had a life before deciding to give international cricket a crack.

He studied saxophone and Japanese at university, and was on the fringes of Australia's World Cup skiing squad, making a living running a ski tours business.

He was pushing 30, almost fast bowler retirement age, when his 'left-arm thunderbolts' earned him a first class debut in 2006, and positively ancient at 32 when he made his international debut for Netherlands. Just two months later he made his second international debut, this time for Australia. He was part of the Middlesex T20 cup winning side in 2008, and the highest wicket taker in the 2010 T20 World Cup (playing for Australia). Perhaps, in his eyes at least, his greatest achievement was for the Delhi Daredevils in the 2009 IPL, for whom he led the attack and kept the legendary Aussie seamer Glenn McGrath on the bench. "I'll be able to tell my grandchildren that I kept the greatest fast bowler in the history of the game out of the team," he said with a large grin.

This is a man I can relate to: "I never had any aspirations to play international cricket. I just fell into it. I always played back yard cricket with my brother, but I was in the thirds at school and the thirds at my club side." That's not just humility; you get the impression he genuinely can't believe his luck.

This from a guy who Virender Sehwag, a chap with some experience in such things, classes as the fastest bowler he has ever faced.

My admiration for Nannes was sealed when he was called up as a standby replacement for an injured quick in the 2011 World Cup in the subcontinent. He was 16th man, and highly unlikely to play (he didn't).

"It's certainly unexpected. I was just having fun on the farm at the weekend and got the phone call," he said. "I'm rapt to be going over. I'm not really sure what sort of role I'm going to play, but I'm excited about what it may be. I will prepare myself to carry bags well and make good drinks. That's about all I can do."

I consider myself a cricket fan, and yet I have never seen a whole Test match. Not all of one. I've seen whole days, either in person or on the telly, but never all five days of one match. The closest I've come is probably five consecutive highlights shows. You'd have to have no job and/or no family, or be hell-bent on ridding yourself of both, to really watch all of a Test match. Let alone a series – can you imagine taking two months off work to watch every second of the Ashes? People do, you know.

Watching cricket exposes you to no less a variety of people than playing it.

I sat next to a brilliant bloke at an England v Pakistan ODI at the Rose Bowl at the end of the 2010 season. He was exceptionally polite, and the first thing he did after sitting down was offer around his family pack of Starbursts. He later refused a return offer of Haribo because of their high gelatine content. It wasn't possible to tell if he was serious. This was a recurring feature of his personality.

He was of Pakistani heritage, doubtless, but his accent was pure north London. If you closed your eyes and just listened to him speak, you would never have known he was there to support Pakistan.

His appearance was somewhat ambiguous too. He was draped in a bedsheet-sized Pakistan flag, and had a tea-cosy Rasta hat on his head with dreadlocks flowing out around the sides. Though it later transpired that this was simply a rather convincing comedy hat that he'd bought during a Pakistan tour of the West Indies and had become de rigueur cricket wear for him, and he was in fact shaven headed.

Once the game started, his polite, knowledgeable, quietly spoken cricket conversation would periodically be interrupted as he was taken over by another presence. He would suddenly – often mid-sentence – let forth a bellow in a foghorn voice of literally breathtaking volume "BOOOOOOOOOOOWLING SHOIABBBBBBBBB!" And then something else, either in Pakistani, or in broken English with a tarmac-thick Pakistani accent, almost like a hybrid language, before returning abruptly to his natural London and normal volume, in resumption of his sentence about the bright future and non-Englishness of sparkling new talent Eoin Morgan.

It was quite disconcerting. This was at the height of the spot-fixing story in the press, and he was erudite and thoughtful about the allegations, and especially about the tragedy of the prodigiously gifted young Amir's involvement and – "C'MON C'MON C'MON SHAHID, BOOM BOOM SHAHID VELL DONE VELL DONE" – the incredibly shoddy handling of the situation by the Pakistan Cricket Board.

The only time his two personas crossed, when the exuberance and brashness of the loudmouthed fan inhabited the conversation of the well informed supporter, was in his rather brusque answer to an enquiry after his opinion of Ijaz Butt, the head of the PCB who in the wake of these allegations had hit back by accusing England of cheating as well, like a child in a playground. He shook his head in despair and snarled: "Dickhead. Man's a total prick."

As the game drew on Pakistan lost too many wickets and it became clear that they would never chase down the total. At the fall of the eighth wicket, my Pakistani companion rose to his feet, pointed with both hands towards the players on the field and the dressing room beyond and unleashed a lengthy, incomprehensible, but surely venomous and withering diatribe of ear splitting volume. Then he turned back to me, bowed, shook my hand warmly and thanked me quietly and sincerely for my company, and disappeared into the throng, Pakistan flag pulled around his shoulders against the gathering gloom.

People, in all their wondrous variety, are also of course the essential ingredient that makes village cricket the experience it is.

It's hard to imagine a more productive source of splendidly unlikely and rewarding friendships than this eclectic little mixing bowl.

Perhaps it's just because I'm getting old, but I find it quite ridiculously heartening to see a 13 year old kid and a middle-aged bloke conspiring to take a wicket. Under what circumstances other than as catcher and bowler would those two ever be likely to high five?

And the 20 year-old deferring to the 65 year-old out of what can only possibly be respect. Even if it's respect for the lingering shadow of an ability that shone its brightest many years ago. Before he was even born, perhaps.

The youngsters who get to know someone at the end of his playing career will look to everyone else around them for how to behave around him, how to refer to him, how to speak to him. Respect is absorbed by osmosis, rather than earned.

So someone who, met in other circumstances, might be a rather intimidating authority figure, becomes a 'mate' rather than a 'sir'. Professionals – teachers, doctors, lawyers – who would otherwise be given the widest of births or the merest of consideration, become someone to look up to, and not because of their job. The difference between Dr William Jones and Bill who opens the bowling is inestimable to a gobby teenager, no matter how much he might protest otherwise, and the positive effect on both parties is tangible.

The characters who make up our little club are a tremendous cross section.

A lot are self employed, freelance, contractors, small business owners, company directors, or otherwise working for themselves.

A fair few work outside, still more with their hands, others spend their days behind a desk or a computer.

Just in the last few years, we've had barmen, builders, butchers, bankers and barristers. And a fair few things in between: from accountant to fireman, farrier to pilot, tree surgeon to postman, market trader to nurse, soldier to student, plumber to shopkeeper, gardener to security manager, environmental scientist to chef, welder to air traffic controller, estate agent to stone carver, kitchen salesman to chemical engineer. And of course, being in the country, most kinds of farmer.

And the strange thing is, I had to ask quite a few of them what they did for a living when I was thinking about this bit, because in many cases I just don't know. It simply doesn't come up.

These are people I've shared lifts, changing rooms, drinks and meals with. Not to mention the bench outside the pavilion, where we've had free ranging conversations about everything from food allergies to social media while waiting to bat and trying to think of reasons not to have to do the scorebook. Certainly they are people I would consider to be friends rather than acquaintances – and I have no idea what they do for a living. Or they tell me and a think, oh yeah, actually maybe I did know that.

There's something wonderful about this. Especially in this modern age where so many of us are defined by what we do and how much we make doing it. But in this situation, our backgrounds, foregrounds, (or 'class' and 'success', if you like,) age and ability are all irrelevant, swamped by the one common factor: the game.

So yeah. Everything's rosy in our little world, until it comes to the eternally tricky question of who actually gets to play. Selection is, not to put too fine a point on it, a bit of a bastard for a little village team.

To begin with, you need eleven guys. Not twelve, not ten. Eleven. That's the first hurdle. Some weeks there'll be 14 guys wanting to play. Other weeks there'll be eight.

On weeks when there's 14, you have to find ways to tell three guys they can't play in such a way that they're not so angry about it that they'll tell you where to go in no uncertain terms when you ring them all back next week because all of a sudden you've only got eight.

That is the surprisingly delicate responsibility of the captain, vice captain, secretary, chairman, or whichever other mug they can palm off the ultimate thankless task to.

It's a rare period indeed when nobody's nose is put out of joint. Someone's got a wedding, but someone else is back from holiday. Another has his mother-in-law coming for lunch, but yet another's been let off the leash because his kids have got a sleepover and his Mrs is having the girls round. Sometimes it works out just fine.

In a bigger club it's easy. You have a selection committee that picks your best team for the first 11, your second best team for the second 11, and by the time you get down to the kids and granddads in the sixths, everyone's happy.

National selection too, is a doddle in comparison. You pick the best 11 cricketers available to the country. Easy. Of course, deciding who the best 11 guys are is often contentious and always fun to argue about.

A few years ago, Kevin Pietersen was dropped for poor form. Some said England had been carrying him for a while. Nonsense, said others, he'll come good again soon. Whichever side you were on, there was no denying that what he'd been mostly doing was skulking ruefully around the balcony in a tracksuit following another duck. There was much talk of Bradman (dropped after his first test) and every other great international sent back to the provinces to regain form before stepping once more onto the big stage.

Very recently as I write, he has been dropped again in controversial circumstances, this time his form not in doubt. Some say it was way overdue and no national side can afford to carry arrogant prima donnas who think they're bigger than the game. Nonsense, say others, suck it up: he's our best player by miles, with the ability to flip games in moments, and not to play him is ridiculous. Both arguments have merits. On form, he is devastating, able to make the best bowling attacks in the world look like Sunday pie chuckers. But is he more important than team unity?

By the time you read this his fate will probably have been settled one way or another. Oddly I find myself not much caring which way. It would be a shame for such a talent not to play anymore, but more of a shame for such a fool to ruin something good. Dropping exceptional maverick batsmen until they regain their form or their sense of proportion may not be as big a problem for village sides as it is for national selectors, but there are still parallels with club sides. Many include people that the others don't really get on with. I have heard tell of teams falling apart because of it, or for other players to walk away from a club because they can't stand an individual. That can't be allowed to happen with England, surely.

But often in a village side it's not about sociability or form or ability. It's about who's available, it's about enthusiasm and loyalty – who *wants* to play; who wants to play for *us*. Who's going to be there for you on the evening before the match when you're desperately ringing round to find that eleventh man. Or worse, that ninth, tenth *and* eleventh man.

And there is one issue every bit as relevant and contentious for both, and that's making way for fresh talent.

Youth vs Experience. Potential vs Proof. Morgan vs Collingwood. Kid vs Codger.

Here's the dilemma. We've got a few schoolkids keen to play for us on Saturdays, a few older guys in the twilight of their league-cricket-playing days, and a bunch of us middle aged spreads in between.

In order to thrive as a club, we must encourage the youngsters. In a few years, some if not all of them will probably be capable of playing a higher standard of cricket than our little one-team village can offer. But if we get them early, get them loyal, we'll probably have them for life. Like Joel and Henry, our resident

20-somethings, both of whom could easily walk into higher league cricket at bigger clubs, but both are fiercely loyal to our little club. In their formative years there wasn't a problem because the team was permanently short of players, but now if the kids get a game, it means someone else doesn't.

And this raises interesting questions.

What kind of team do we want to be?

Are we an ambitious side, hungry for every success possible? Should we aggressively pursue new and better players at every opportunity in order to field the best 11 we possibly can – even if that means none of 'us' get to play, and none of the guns-for-hire who do play have any attachment or loyalty to the club?

Or are we a bunch of blokes who enjoy each other's company and like playing cricket together, not too bothered if we win or lose?

Clearly the answer is somewhere in between. Realistically, we are a lower-league village cricket team, so to place too much emphasis on fielding the best side possible is faintly ludicrous. On the other hand, amateur sport is always about making the best of limited potential, and winning is more fun than losing. It just is.

Clearly we must encourage the kids or we'll lose them, and if there is no new blood then the club will die. But we're not a colt's side; we can't alienate the adults who've loyally served the club for many years every time some 15-yr-old who can bowl a bit comes along.

It's a tricky one. In the end it must all be about balance.

After all, these are teenagers we're talking about. Any minute now they will very probably a) discover girls, b) decide cricket is for losers and what's actually cool is [*insert craze here*], c) sod off to college, or, most likely of all, d) all of the above.

Of byes and men

It's a 'season opener' in the latter half of April. Damerham v Damerham, we call it. Before the first proper game of the year, we get everyone who fancies it out on the field for a sort of warm up game, just against ourselves.

There are Saturday league players, casual players, the Wednesday guys, kids, whoever wants to play. We'll get 20-30 or so people, pick two roughly equal teams like you used to at school, and blow away the cobwebs, just happy to be out there in whites again for the first time in seven months.

I'm sat on the pavilion porch, scoring. This is unusual, as I hate scoring. Largely because I am worse than useless at it. I can't help watching the game or chatting to people or wandering off to find tea bags or Deep Heat or bat tape, so invariably by the time the umpire calls 'over' I've only got two balls marked down. I have the concentration of a goldfish with ADHD in the scorer's chair, so I tend to steer clear of it if at all possible. But for this kind of game the score doesn't much matter anyway.

As it happens, for this particular incident, the scorer's chair is the perfect place to be.

Dave and Iain are batting. At the crease, Iain has an enthusiasm that would shame most puppies, which gives him a tendency to run for absolutely everything unless firmly yelled at not to. Dave is enjoying himself, going for cheeky reverse sweeps, full-blooded wallops to cow corner, dancing down the pitch – the sorts of things he'd never dare try on a Saturday.

As a pair they are entertaining if not elegant to watch.

Then it happens, and suddenly entertaining doesn't cover it. They run six. Six byes. Yes, that's right, a six without the ball coming particularly close to either bat or boundary. It is genuinely one of the funniest things I have ever seen. If it were Stan and Oli batting, it could not have been better played for laughs.

Had it been caught on film it would be one of those clips that are always funny no matter how many times you see them – like Del Boy falling through the bar, or a young Rowan Atkinson walking into a lamp post. Fortunately for me, I can play it in my head whenever I want, from the scorer's chair POV.

Dave plays and misses. Well, now, that doesn't really cover it. Dave skips down the track and takes a wild yahoo, pirouetting when he's missed it to watch the inevitable stumping. But no, his ballet chops have evidently put off wicket-keeper Chuckles, who misses the ball as comprehensively as Dave did.

Chuckles gives chase down towards third man, struggling to

get a glove off. Finally he gets his right one off and flings it over his head behind him. Gathering the ball, he turns and throws with such accuracy that he must have wished he hadn't bothered taking his glove off, as at least then he'd have the excuse that it's quite difficult to throw with wicket-keeper's gloves on, actually, don't y'know.

The ball heads off somewhere towards cover.

By this time they've run two, and, seeing the throw, they attempt a third.

Dave's brother Richie charges in and collects the ball cleanly on the run. He looks quicker than Dave, and if he just runs the ball in to the non-striker's end he'll run his brother out by a yard. But he doesn't. He attempts an ambitious hurl at the stumps, mid-run. He misses. His wail of anguish mixes with his brother's squeal of delight.

"Yeeeeaaaahhhhs!" Dave yells as he turns back for a forth.

Iain has also seen what's happened, and is also yelling "YES! YES!". As the pair cross their shouts turn to whoops, waving their bats aloft like swords, warriors screaming into battle.

The overthrow rolls off calmly towards a vacant midwicket, while square leg and mid on have a staring competition to see who's going to chase after it. Mid on cracks first and breaks into a run.

Dave's just home having run five as the throw comes in to Richie, but Iain is not done. He turns, bat still raised, still cackling like an escaped maniac, and comes pelting back for the sixth run, ignoring Dave's pleas of "No, stay there!" until he arrives breathlessly next to his batting partner in the non-striker's crease.

There's a tension-laden moment of stillness while the protagonists absorb their options. Like the moment in Pulp Fiction when Bruce Willis finds the machine gun in his kitchen and John Travolta comes out of the loo.

Then the toaster pops, and Dave is off, sprinting back towards the striker's end, weaving, making himself big, trying to get in the way of the throw.

Richie repays the throw he got from Chuckles with one of similar quality, though Chuckles does now have a wicket-keeping-glove-related excuse for not getting the bails off in time, in that he's only got one.

To a soundtrack of yelled expletives and delighted giggling, Dave completes his 132 yard sprint, the ground is made, the six is run, and a legend is born.

May the tale grow ever taller in the telling.

chapter ■■ 7

I say old chap, how was that?

On counting to six and other daunting tasks

Counting to six can be surprisingly difficult. Accomplished mathematicians, people who can perform complex calculations in their heads – the kind of folk who have a comprehensive grasp of differential calculus – will often turn to their fellow umpire and ask, "Do you make that one ball left or two?"

When you're umpiring, counting is often pushed to the back of the mind. There's so much to think about, to consider, so many possibilities, that the elementary question of how many balls have gone is too tricky to keep track of.

There's a similar phenomenon in poker. You've been dealt your two pocket cards, looked at them, assessed them, placed your bet. The bets go round, the flop comes, and you can't remember what your cards are. Two cards, which 30 seconds ago you thought were worth betting on. What are they? Nope. Completely gone.

Umpiring is worse, of course, because everyone else is depending on you and obliged to go by what you say. So if you say 'over' after only four balls, or keep going after the seventh, it's clearly not only you who is affected.

There are three solutions to this problem.

The first, most widely used, and least likely to fail, is stones. What you do is just get six little pebbles of roughly equal size, or lucky silver sixpences that your Gran gave you, or beer bottle tops, or bits of gravel from the car park, or, a personal favourite, the mud encrusted worn-down nubs of discarded old spikes you found on the dressing room windowsill, and put them in one pocket.

After each legal delivery – not wides or no balls – you transfer one stone from this pocket to the other pocket. So if you start the over with six stones in your left pocket, when you have six stones in your right pocket and the left is empty, it's the end of the over. Simple.

The problems start when something happens: runs, confusion, near run-outs, a dropped catch, someone gets hurt. And then you're back playing again, and was that two balls or three gone, ump? Did you move that stone yet? The only answer to this is to make sure you always transfer your stone *immediately after the ball is dead.* Otherwise it's very easy to either count a ball twice, or not count it at all.

Another problem is when you have two of your counters in your left pocket, three in your right, and, after a bit of searching, you find one on the floor. Oh no. Which pocket did it fall out of? Has one of them got a hole in? Hang on. Which pocket did they start in and which one am I transferring to? WHY IS THIS SO HARD?!?

The second method is a clicker, which is basically a little gadget that counts for you. On simple ones you click it and the count moves from zero to one, one to two, etc. On more complex ones there are separate buttons for no balls, wides and legal deliveries. There are also iPhone apps for it now of course, which will not only help you record how many balls have gone, but also wides, byes, the score in general, each bowler's figures, when the drinks breaks are due, the wicket-keeper's inside leg measurement, your blood/sugar levels and your favourite colour. But they are basically just elaborate aides to help record your count. You still have to remember to do it. Besides, fiddling with your phone between deliveries has a pretty good chance of creating the impression that you're not really paying attention.

The third way is unavailable to most of us, and that's to wear a little microphone and an earpiece and be hooked up to not only your mate at square leg, but also the third umpire who's in a room with a bank of TV screens, and the match referee, and the official scorers, and the commentary teams for several TV and radio networks and national press correspondents. And even for those guys, seven ball overs are not uncommon.

Quite apart from counting, the job of an umpire is unrealistically difficult.

As the bowler runs in you must determine whether it's a 'foot fault' no ball, either with the front foot over the popping crease (the one in front of the wicket), or the back foot touching or 'cutting' the return crease (the one at the side).

Actually let's back up a bit. Before this, you must have had a look around as the bowler begins his approach, making sure there are no transgressions in the field: whether the wicket-keeper or any part of him is in front of the stumps; if there are any fielders other than the wicket-keeper encroaching on the wicket; if there are more than two fielders behind square on the leg side, (see chapter 5 for the changes in the Laws induced by Bodyline) or, for limited-overs games with a fielding circle, that the correct number of fielders are inside or outside of it. Any of which would also be cause for you to call No Ball. And the bowler hasn't even let go of it yet.

When he does, things start to get complicated.

Firstly, there's the question of getting people out.

There are ten ways to be out in cricket, and really only one of them is so obvious you don't even need to bother appealing, and that's 'bowled'. Though actually, 'hit wicket' (treading on or hitting your own stumps) is pretty cut and dried too, usually.

Some catches are obviously out and don't need to involve the umpire, but marginal caught-behind decisions from thin little edges are likely to require your adjudication, though if you're lucky the batsman will walk (see chapter 5 again).

Stumpings require the services of the square leg umpire more than the 'standing' or bowler's end umpire, to confirm whether or not any part of the batsman or his equipment is behind the popping crease at the moment the bails are removed. This is also the case with 'run out' decisions half the time, in fact probably more than half the time, as the ball is more likely to be thrown back to the guy with the gloves, all things being equal.

The one missing from this list of 'normal' ways to be out of course is LBW. We'll come to that in a minute.

The other four ways to be out are 'handled the ball', 'hit the ball twice', 'obstruction of the field', and 'timed out'. (See 'obscure ways to be out' in the glossary.) They're so obscure you can safely ignore them in pretty much all amateur cricket, as they simply don't come up. If they happen in the professional game it's rare enough to be news. If a side does appeal for a batsman to be out in one of these ways, you can be reasonably confident that they're joking. Even if they're not, it's a good idea to behave as if they are: shake your head, smile, roll your eyes in a "Sheesh, you guys!" kind of way and wait for the next ball.

Then there are wides and no-balls and all that stuff to think about, but the game gets interesting when they all start to happen at once.

Can a batsman be stumped off a no-ball, for instance? No he can't. But he can be run out on one, which is a pretty subtle distinction. (The difference being that to be stumped the batsman is in the process of attempting to play the ball, whereas to be run out he is in the process of attempting a run.)

Can he be stumped off a wide? Yes he can. (It's happened to me. I think it was probably the most livid I've been on a cricket pitch.)

Which raises an interesting possibility. Imagine this scenario: final ball of a match, the fielding team needs one wicket, the batting team needs one run, and the batsman is stumped off a wide. Who has won? Or is it a tie?

Tricky, isn't it? All those straightforward little rules are suddenly not straightforward at all anymore.

The answer is simply a matter of chronology. A wide cannot be called until it passes the batsman, and as such might not be called until after the stumping has occurred. But once called it is deemed to have been a wide from the moment of delivery, so the extra run is credited before the wicket, and the batting team win.

But you'd want to be pretty sure of that decision before you made it, because you're going to have to explain it several times to quite a lot of pretty animated people.

If you like that kind of Laws conundrum, you might appreciate a rather marvellous book called 'You are the Umpire', a compendium of the cartoon strip serialised in the Observer, written by international umpire John Holder and beautifully illustrated by 'Roy of the Rovers' artist Paul Trevillion.

It includes such testers as "The Helmet of a close fielder is discarded behind the wicket-keeper. The batsman edges a delivery high above the keeper, who stands on and jumps off the helmet to claim the catch. Is he out?" and "In a village match a cow suddenly steps through a damaged hedge on to the pitch. The batsman strikes the ball, which bounces off the cow's rump and is caught. Is he out?"

(Yes in both cases.)

There are lots of more serious (or at least less frivolous) and controversial things that umpires have to deal with, especially in the professional game.

Ball tampering is a good one, and a very thorny issue it is too at the highest levels of the game, carrying much of the stigma of really base, low cheating that issues like, say, not walking when you know you've hit the ball are, inexplicably, entirely without.

But if you play cricket at anything less than first class or international level, you can pretty much ignore it, because the skill to exploit a tampered ball is simply not available to us mere mortals.

In the longer forms of the game, a ball is used for 80 overs before a new one is due. In order to reverse swing the ball needs to roughen up, get scuffed and lose its sheen.

The Laws state that artificially altering the state of the ball is illegal, yet every fielding side will do their best to help it happen, from purposefully throwing the ball in 'on the bounce', so that it bounces on the hard square before reaching the keeper, to bowling 'cross seamers', to 'fielding' the ball with their spikes, to picking at the seam with their fingernails. Or bottle tops, in one famous case.

Other ways to make it swing include sugary saliva, from boiled sweets or mints, to make the shiny side even shinier, and vaseline or suntan oil. All are against the Laws, all are done all the time. What you are allowed to do, is 'maintain' the ball, ie shine it, hence the long streaky red marks on swing bowler's trousers, but without any assistance other than spit and polish.

For umpires to decide that a bowling side has deliberately and unlawfully altered the state of the ball is a pretty bold call. It recently and most famously happened in 2006 during an England v Pakistan Test at the Oval, when infamous Aussie (gr) ump Darrell Hair awarded England the obligatory five penalty runs and offered them a replacement ball because he deemed their opponents to have been ball tampering, and Pakistan refused to take the field after tea on the fourth day.

I have some sympathy for Hair, as though his actions were insensitive and unlikely to win any man-management prizes, he was clearly intimately acquainted with the Laws and followed them to the letter, and still managed to be universally cast as the villain of the piece. Though admittedly the sympathy sort of evaporated after he asked the ICC (his employers) for half a million US$ to resign.

(I have further reason personally to resent the incident, as I was – still am, in fact – in possession of excellent tickets for the fifth day, which me and Dad were going to go to and looked set to be rather good.)

Hair was banned and has since sued his employers back and forth and there have been settlements in and out of court. He has worked as a top flight umpire since, but is no longer on the ICC 'elite' panel. Suffice it to say ball tampering seems to be worse for an umpire's career than a player's.

Many pundits take the view that the contest is so much in the batsman's favour these days, anything the bowlers can do to make it more difficult for them should be allowed, and the Laws should be changed.

Certainly the Laws as they stand are ambiguous and unenforced – perhaps even unenforceable – and their blurry edges seem as much a mystery to the players and officials as they are to the rest of us.

Another area where the laws are fuzzy at best, and a fascinating one generally, is that of 'chucking' or 'throwing' – a bowler bending his arm during delivery.

The umpire must determine, in accordance with Law 24.3, that: "…once the bowler's arm has reached the level of the shoulder in the delivery swing, the elbow joint is not straightened partially or completely from that point until the ball has left the hand…"

Well, that's what the Laws say.

But this in itself is odd. There have been some very extensive tests performed under the auspices of the ICC in the last couple of decades, and their conclusions suggest that under Law 24.3 as it stands, for pretty much every bowler, from me to Shaun Tait and everyone in between, every ball is a no ball.

So let's just have a quick digression into chucking here, and indulge in a brief delve into the case of Muttiah Muralitharan, known to the cricketing world as the big spinning, big grinning 'Murali'.

During the mid nineties, Sri Lankan off-spinning legend Murali was repeatedly no-balled for throwing, initially by crotchety Aussie ump Darrell Hair (yes, the very same chap who would go on to scale new heights of crotchetyness and controversy with the abandoned Test of 2006). Murali was repeatedly attacked by the Aussies for some reason, and often suffered abuse from Australian crowds, both on and off the field. The then Prime Minister John Howard publicly branded him "a chucker". Aussie Test player turned Sri Lanka coach Tom Moody was "disgusted and embarrassed" by the behaviour of his countrymen, and no less an authority than Sir Don Bradman called Hair's decision the worst example of umpiring he had ever seen, and "against everything the game stands for."

Murali's action underwent lab testing in '96, the conclusion of which was that not only did he not straighten his arm during delivery, but the same congenital defect that made him such a prodigious spinner of the ball actually physically prevented him from fully straightening it. The deduction was that his action created the 'optical illusion of throwing', and he was cleared to bowl by the ICC. A few year's later he was no balled for throwing again, again in Australia. After much spluttering outrage, notably from his captain, he was tested again. And cleared again.

The ICC playing conditions were changed in 2000 to allow a straightening of 5° for spinners, 7.5° for medium pacers and 10° for fast bowlers, but this proved unenforceable, and umpires in the field simply couldn't tell – it was proving difficult enough to tell under laboratory test conditions, let alone under Test conditions.

In 2004 a panel of former Test players and biomechanical experts was convened by the ICC to study the results of extensive research into both professional and amateur bowlers.

Also in 2004, now with 500 Test wickets to his name, Murali's recently developed doosra was called into question by Chris (father of Stuart) Broad, an English umpire officiating in Australia. So Murali underwent a third round of testing at the Department of Human Movement and Exercise Science at the University of Western Australia, where three-dimensional kinematic measurements of his bowling arm were taken using motion capture. (Interestingly, at around the same time, a few thousand miles away in a New Zealand film studio, Peter Jackson was also playing with motion capture, breaking new cinematic ground bringing Gollum to life with Andy Serkis prancing about in a full MoCap suit. But that's just a digression from the digression.)

Meanwhile the panel concluded that, in fact, 99% of ALL bowlers in ALL standards of cricket straighten their arms when bowling. Of those tested, only the West Indies batsman Ramneraesh Sarwan, (very much a part time bowler,) appeared to be capable of bowling a legal delivery under the Laws.

In the light of overwhelming scientific findings, the panel recommended that a flat rate of 15° tolerable 'elbow extension' be used to define the difference between bowling and throwing, a recommendation that the ICC accepted.

Murali's doosra was shown to be legal, with an average elbow flex of 12.2° at 53.75 mph, his off-break averaged 12.9° at 59.03 mph.

The controversy that surrounded Murali and his mystifying action brought the subject to life, and without him and his unique skill it's unlikely anyone would have bothered with such tests, or if they had that anyone would have paid much attention to them.

As just about everyone was routinely breaking them as it stood, the research clearly necessitated a change in the rules. It also showed that Murali himself was operating well within the new limits, and no more or less so than anyone else. But this made no difference to the poor guy's detractors, of course, and it's a little bit sad that the legacy of his extraordinary career – 800 Test wickets at under 23 – will always echo to the cry of "No ball!"

Fortunately, the lasting memory of Murali the man is the literally wide-eyed enthusiasm and irrepressible smile of the zealot. It was clear to all who ever saw him play that Murali just adored the game. Apart from the fact that he happened to be exceptional at it, he was just like us, looking forward to every game before the last one had finished. It is to his eternal credit that whether he was being no-balled by umpires, taunted by crowds or politicians, or bamboozling the finest international batsmen of his era, by default his face was wreathed in an ear-to-ear grin. The guy just never stopped smiling.

The rest of his legacy is the ICC playing condition concerning the allowable 15° of tolerable elbow flex for all bowlers in international cricket. Why it's an ICC playing condition and not simply enshrined in the Laws I just don't know, and have been unable to find out.

(The MCC were very helpful in pointing me towards the playing condition, but carefully elected not to answer the direct question of why it isn't part of the Laws.)

It seems an odd omission, and I can only assume that we're meant to interpret Law 24.3 as an appearance, and if the arm doesn't *visibly* straighten then all is well. Which to all intents and purposes of course is perfectly adequate for all of us not on the international stage. But if that is the case, I wonder why they don't just say so?

After all, Murali's is a fairly well publicised controversy, and anyone with a more than passing interest in the Laws will know that the uncompromising 'is not straightened' is simply wrong.

But anyway. From that very specific controversy sparked by the unique action of one very special talent, let us move to a more democratic, but no less thorny issue. The one that effects everyone who has ever played or watched the game. From school playgrounds to village greens to one-man-and-his dog county draws to sold out international venues – everywhere the game is played, batsmen will have seen the finger raised and felt the burning sting of injustice.

By far the most thorny and problematical issue any umpire will have to deal with is Law 36, Leg Before Wicket (LBW), the cricket rule whose main function is to make people who can't grasp football's off-side rule feel even more stupid.

Here it is, reproduced in full from the MCC Official Laws Of Cricket 2000 Code 4th Edition 2010:

LAW 36   LEG BEFORE WICKET

1. Out LBW

The striker is out LBW in the circumstances set out below.

(a) The bowler delivers a ball, not being a No ball

and   (b) the ball, if it is not intercepted full pitch, pitches in line between wicket and wicket or on the off side of the striker's wicket

and   (c) the ball not having previously touched his bat, the striker intercepts the ball, either full pitch or after pitching, with any part of his person

and   (d) the point of impact, even if above the level of the bails,

either   (i) is between wicket and wicket

or   (ii) if the striker has made no genuine attempt to play the ball with his bat, is either between wicket and wicket or outside the line of the off stump.

and   (e) but for the interception, the ball would have hit the wicket.

2. Interception of the ball

(a) In assessing points (c), (d) and (e) in 1 above, only the first interception is to be considered.

(b) In assessing point (e) in 1 above, it is to be assumed

that the path of the ball before interception would have continued after interception, irrespective of whether the ball might have pitched subsequently or not.

3. Off side of wicket

The off side of the striker's wicket shall be determined by the striker's stance at the moment the ball comes into play for that delivery. See Appendix D.

© *Marylebone Cricket Club 2010*

You may need to read that a couple of times. I know I do. I just typed it and I still need to read it again. Even when you know what it means, it still seems complicated. It's that sort of lawyer-speak that makes you think there must be more too it than you thought, and if you think you've understood it then it probably just means you haven't read it properly.

But it's really not that bad. Basically, the thing of it is, if the ball was going to hit the stumps and hits you instead, you're out.

There are two exceptions: 1. if the ball pitches outside your leg stump you can't be out. 2. if it hits you outside the line of your off stump, you can only be out if you're not playing a shot. This is the only thorny bit really: if you leave the ball and it comes back in and hits you outside the line but would have gone on to hit the stumps, you're out. But if you played a shot – tried to hit the ball – you're not.

That's it.

Of course it gets a lot harder when you have to make a split second call on all those decisions with 11 blokes screaming at you.

The real task is to determine two factors. One is definite: did the bat make contact with the ball first. The other can only ever be speculation: would the ball have hit the stumps if the batsman hadn't been in the way.

All you can do for that one is make your best guess.

The only rule here is to make sure that whatever you decide, you give the appearance of being absolutely 100% convinced about it. Any sign of ambiguity will be considered an admission of doubt, and you will be savaged by a rampaging pack of 11 rabid hyenas. Metaphorically, but still.

In serious league cricket, each team will provide an umpire. Usually they are stalwart club members who have finally accepted that the best of their playing days are behind them. There are courses run by the ECB and others, and most Saturday League umpires are knowledgeable and fair.

Some are not. Some give nothing, others raise the finger if the ball strays into the same postcode as the pads. Neither matters too much, I suppose, as long as they are consistent so it evens out across the game. Some are downright biased, but there's no point dwelling on them.

In friendlies, and less serious leagues like the evening games, the umpires will most likely both be members of the batting side who are either out or have yet to bat. This often means that the umpires will change every couple of overs. As I am usually at either the top or near the bottom of the order, I regularly find myself answering the call of the ump. And this is fine by me; certainly if there is a choice between scoring and umping, I'll be off to the middle holding bowlers' hats and sunglasses before you can say "Is 'w' for 'wide' or 'wicket', I never could remember?"

This is not too bad for me because, as should be fairly clear by now, I am a student of the game and reasonably well acquainted with its laws. But for some of the guys I play with, this is not always the case. I remember once coming in from the middle fairly puffed and sweaty, so I must have had a bit of a bat, and being asked almost immediately if I could go back out and ump, as the guys out there needed to come in and get padded up.

One of my team mates, who I'd never seen umpire before, piped up: "It's all right, I'll go. Have a breather for ten minutes, get changed and that first."

I thanked him gratefully, and went to take my pads off. Seconds later, his head appeared around the changing room door. "Right. LBW, yeah? If it pitches outside… what is it again?"

This guy has been playing the game for at least three decades, pushing for four.

"You don't KNOW?!?"

"Never mind. I'll wing it. No-one'll notice."

A few minutes later I emerged from the changing room to see

him start an argument by calling 'wide' to a ball that definitely would have been a wide, had the batsman not very clearly hit it. "I don't care, it's still a wide," I heard floating across the ground as I went in search of a pint, failing to suppress a snuffle of laughter.

I think they may have been in the process of noticing.

Two of my favourite LBW moments involve my regular drinking buddy Clive. Now he *does* know the rules. The bar at the Compasses rolls its eyes and sighs whenever we start another of our conversations about the inconsistencies, idiosyncrasies and reasons for the laws, etiquette and traditions of the game, which we'll probably still be having when we've long since turned into the two crotchety old men we already sound like.

Clive is a lovely bloke, warm and effusive. He's a big guy, but a thorough gent who wouldn't hurt a fly. He bowls solid medium pace that looks like it used to be quick back in the day, with nagging accuracy.

Bowling in a Wednesday league match, he struck the batsman's pad and turned in his followthrough to enquire of the umpire.

The umpire was a youngster, who responded to Clive's blood chilling caveman bellow just inches from his face as if he'd nodded off in double geography and been hit by a hurled blackboard rubber – he jumped out of his skin.

Clive was adamant that it was 'very definitely out', but the impression was that the poor lad was so startled he would have agreed to anything in that moment.

Another time Clive was batting and I was umpiring. It was a friendly, thankfully. Mind you if it was a serious game I guess I wouldn't have been umpiring in the first place.

Clive was facing what could kindly be called a dibbly dobbly offy, and one of the 'arm balls' got through his defences to strike his pad. The bowler and wicket keeper went up, and as he was back in his crease and it hit him bang smack in line with middle stump with nothing like enough energy to go over the top, I could think of no reason not to give him out, so I nodded sagely and raised my finger.

Normally, Clive would never argue with an umpire, but as it was me I guess he felt he had special dispensation.

"I hit it mate."

"Did you?"

Slip piped up. "Yeah he did."

And then gully. "He did ump, yeah."

Clive again "Massive inside edge."

And cover "I thought so too."

The guy from deep square leg had begun trotting over to tell me even he'd seen it from 80 yards away and he wasn't even really paying attention, but I saved him the bother by signalling dead ball and apologising profusely to everyone, especially Clive, who I felt I'd somehow betrayed.

If there is a worse feeling than being given out unfairly, it is being caught in the act of unfairly giving someone out. Who'd be an umpire?

LBW is a complicated rule, make no mistake. In fact, it is in the laudable pursuit of 'making no mistake' that the game has looked to technology for help.

The relentless march of technology has recently made incredible strides to increase the enjoyment and understanding of the armchair cricket viewer.

Hawk-Eye is chief among them.

It was first used for cricket, but is also now used very effectively in tennis and even snooker. (Top triv: it was developed by a chap called Hawkins, from whence it gets its name, not simply as I had assumed the bird of prey famed for its none-too-shabby eyesight.)

It's basically a triangulation system, using data from a minimum of four and up to 30 high speed cameras (the more there are the more accurate the results) to track the path of a ball, and then extrapolate its probable future path after it's been interrupted.

Its job in tennis is simply to determine what happened: was the ball in or out? In cricket, its task is a little more complicated.

Its main and most contentious function (for other less controversial ones like pitchmaps, beehives, and wagon wheels, see the glossary) is following an appeal for LBW, to predict the probable path of the ball after an interception to determine whether or not it is likely to have hit the stumps.

First, Hawk-Eye will be used to determine where the ball pitched, which is effectively the same as its function in tennis, except there is no line on the pitch, only an imaginary one. Did it pitch in line with the stumps, outside leg, or outside off?

Now, this is a matter of fact. Where the ball pitched is an absolute. It may be difficult to determine in real time at 90 mph, and therefore the Hawk-Eye system or other ultra slow motion cameras can be very useful to help with determining it after the fact. But the important word here is 'fact'. We are dealing with history, hindsight, something that has happened: an absolute and definitively knowable truth.

The next part is the tricky part. Determining the likely path of the ball after it's hit the batsman's pad or body is, by definition, a guess. Triangulation using a couple of dozen high definition digital cameras makes it a very well educated guess. The best available guess, no doubt about it. But still a guess.

I don't want to get all unnecessary and existential but it's an important point – what might have happened in any given circumstance other than what actually does happen is categorically unknowable. That is the nature of the universe. The ball could swing wildly away, or unpredictably upwards, or hit the stumps and not remove the bails, or fly into a hundred pieces or be abducted by aliens. All manner of things *could* happen. All Hawk-Eye can help us with is what *probably would* happen.

Whilst all this was purely for our entertainment, to show whether or not Hawk-Eye's predictions agreed with the opinion of the umpire, it was fine. Now of course it is used by the umpires as a tool to *help* them make their decisions, and its function in the game has fundamentally shifted, from observer to participant.

The situation did become a bit ridiculous, when TV viewers at home had a better understanding of the quality of decisions being made than just about everyone else: better than the crowd at the ground, better than the players on the field and certainly better than the umpires. It was inevitable really, and probably right, that this fascinating piece of technology should be appropriated to help the game's authorities at the highest level in the pursuit of clarity.

And this is fine to an extent. The problems arise when its word is taken as gospel, and the fact that it is not fact is overlooked. The more accustomed to it we have become the more readily we seem prepared to lean on it, and accept its verdict as absolute – which it is absolutely not.

It seems important to me to remember that it is only conjecture, and conjecture is by definition "the formation of a judgement or opinion based on incomplete or inconclusive information."

Use it by all means, take its 'advice' under advisement, but we should not leave something this important in the hands of a machine, however clever it is. The umpire's decision, his opinion in matters of Law 36, sport's greatest game of 'what if', always has been – and for my money always should be – final.

The ICC's Umpire Decision Review System (UDRS), after a series of trials including England's tour of the West Indies where it was somewhat farcically employed, made its official debut in November 2009 during the Pakistan tour of New Zealand.

There were many teething problems. Two of the most notable being that most players didn't want it, and most boards exhibited similar enthusiasm. Especially when told that not only did they have to use it, but they had to pay for it too. (Hawk-Eye is a pretty intensive system, and not cheap to run.)

The UDRS system is in two parts. Firstly there is the Umpire Review, in which the onfield umpires may refer decisions for things like run outs, stumpings, hit-wicket, bump balls and boundary decisions to the third umpire or, in the case of clean catches, consult with the third umpire before making the decision themselves.

No problems there.

The second part is the problem for me, as it is specifically designed only to work when players question the decision of the umpires.

Player Reviews are when players challenge a decision made by the on-field umpires concerning whether or not a batsman is out. The review may be called by the dismissed batsman for 'out' decisions or the fielding captain for 'not out' decisions.

There's a whole load of explanatory notes surrounding the definitions of things like reasonable doubt, conclusive or inconclusive evidence and 'a high degree of confidence'. All of which is fine.

What bothers me is that at its heart, the system asks, encourages, nay *demands* that players argue with the umpire.

What happened to the central tenet "The umpire's decision is final"?

Poof; gone.

250 years of acceptance and gentlemanly conduct – one of the defining characteristics of the game, and surely no small part of its reputation for even-handed 'it's not cricket' fairness – gone in a flash.

The system is directly engineered to undermine the authority of the umpires.

It rewards dissent.

The main problem with this is not concerned with the game in question or obtaining the correct decision for any given instance, it's to do with an inevitable shift in the way the game is played in clubs, schools, villages, and urban backstreets with tape-balls.

If kids (and adults, who are we kidding) routinely see their cricketing heroes arguing with umpires, having their decisions reversed and subsequently laughing in their faces and celebrating even harder, there's only one way it's going to affect their behaviour on our village greens. It doesn't matter that the amateur game doesn't have Hawk-Eye and never will. It's about attitude.

Accepting what you perceive to be injustices beyond your control is not only part of the game, it's a life lesson, and doubtless a lot to do with why cricket was seen as a vital facet of the education of the Empire's ruling class. It's part of what makes it what it is. To teach the young that they can profit by arguing with those in power is not only unhelpful, it's worse than that. It's not cricket, that's what it is. Don't get me wrong, I'm all for a bit of rebellion, and there are many situations in which it is right to challenge authority, to refuse to accept injustice, and to make personal sacrifices for the greater good, and examples of these instances are of equal if not greater importance to a rounded and useful education. But a dubious LBW shout is not one of them. It never was and it never will be.

This is not all that's wrong with it. Another problem is that each side gets two 'lives' per innings. They can make as many successful reviews as they like, but if they have two turned down, that's it, no more. So if there is subsequently a truly shocking decision which everyone with eyes can see the umpire has got horribly wrong, even his colleague in front of the banks of monitors upstairs is completely powerless to do anything about it.

This is exacerbated by the fact that, quite understandably, the system is not used by the players as it was intended. Its main purpose is to weed out 'howlers' – patently incorrect decisions. So if someone appears plum LBW but is not given, the bowling side can review it, and if a batsman is given out LBW off an obvious inside edge, he can do likewise. But the players are not interested in what the original intent of the ICC was. That is not their concern. Their concern is that they've got a game to win, and they've been handed a new weapon in the battle to win it. Strategic, tactical and borderline reviews are the rule, not the exception, and the howlers still get through because, almost invariably, both sides will have used up both their reviews fairly quickly on the top order; the batsmen the batting side most want to stay in and the bowling side most want to get out. So the very thing it was intended to curtail persists, and all that happens is we get an abundance of replays that slow the game down, and most marginal reviews are upheld, because the necessary benefit of the doubt for the margin of error rightly goes with the umpire's original decision.

To be clear: I'm all for correct decisions, and all for the employment of technology in a way that brings us closer to truth and justice. I just don't think the UDRS is it.

The generally nauseating Stanford Series (see chapter 10 for the sickening details) threw up (sic – okay I'm stopping) one genuinely visionary innovation.

The matches were officiated by world class umpires, including Kiwi Simon Taufel, at the time ICC Umpire of the year for five years running and widely regarded as the best in the world, and grizzled South African veteran Rudi Koertzen.

But their presence was not felt to be sufficient. (And in this, if this alone, we must concede that Stanford was breaking new ground.)

His pioneering move was to introduce technology into the umpiring mix, but keep it as the sole preserve of the umpires. As is so often the case, the billionaire buffoon did the right thing for the wrong reasons, because rather than the general good of the game for the game's sake, he deemed it to be especially necessary in his case "due to the magnitude of money on offer".

The difference with Stanford's system was a small but important one. Either of the on-field umpires or the third umpire could instigate a review at any time, for any situation where they felt further scrutiny might be useful – there were no player reviews. Of course the series didn't run for long, so the experiment too was short lived. But in that short time there were not unnecessary or frequent delays to query every little point, as had been feared by the ludites. Perfection is impossible, but this was a system that, used sensibly, had a chance of getting closer to it than any other. World class umpires can see as well as anyone when a decision is marginal or just plain wrong. If anyone should be able to tell it's them, surely?

The players were free to concentrate on runs and wickets, and the umpires were left to wrestle with making as many impartial and correct decisions as possible.

Or as Stanford's publicity put it: "The umpires will control and officiate the game and the players will get on with the business of playing." Well knock me down with a feather. There may be a lot wrong with the bloke, but there's nothing wrong with that thought.

What a radical idea.

Bang to rights

We're on tour. It's been a blast. Too much of a blast, if we're honest. The first night involved really rather a lot of drinking and silliness. And Jägerbombs. If you're a fortunate and sensible type you may not be familiar with the concept of the Jägerbomb, so I will explain it. Basically it's a glass about two thirds full of Red Bull, into which a shot glass of Jägermeister is dropped, glass and all.

It is, in other words, the confluence of two of the most disgusting liquid substances known to man. If it was a slug of vomit dropped into a bucket of snot, it would only be marginally more vile and repugnant.

The master of ceremonies for that particular evening was Alan, a man not famous for his reticence. Al is a Londoner of the type often depicted in American movies – brash, loud, cheeky, a bit of a rogue, but basically a decent bloke. He is that guy. He also happens to be a fine off-spinner, of the type who doesn't spin the ball prodigiously, but just enough, and has the knack of persistent, nagging length. He used to be an aggressive bat too, but a few years ago he fell down the stairs and broke his wrist rather nastily and since then has lost power in his all important bottom hand. Fortunately this has, if anything, improved his off-spin. One could draw the conclusion that the fact that this 'tired' tumble down the apples took place upon his return from the annual club presentation evening is of no small moment.

Alan spent the evening tirelessly running between us lot and the bar. Each time he returned with a tray full of the said foul concoction, and demanded "Drink!" Moments later, or so it seemed, he would do the rounds again, this time demanding "Twenty quid!" And he would brook no argument.

"Twenty quid!"

"But we just–"

"Twenty quid!"

"Bu–"

"Twenty quid!"

It is difficult to argue with such insistence, especially if you're trying to enjoy a quiet pint and a conversation. It's easier just to acquiesce. He should work for charity.

And there were no excuses, no missing a round. He was on a mission to rid us of all our cash, sobriety and taste buds at our earliest possible convenience.

At one point, one of us (who it would be unfair to name in case his Mrs picks this book up in the toilet one day,) had become a victim of circumstance and found himself ensconced in the gents, in protracted conversation on the great white telephone. So there he was, hugging the bowl, when there was a light knock on the cubicle door.

"Mate it's Al. You all right?"

"Yeah mate, yeah. Right as rain. Be out in a bit."

"Good man. Twenty quid."

"Wha–"

"Twenty quid!"

Moments later, realising the futility of resistance, a £20 note was duly proffered under the lavatory door.

After that a fair bit happened that is probably best glossed over.

Some time after three in the morning it became clear that two of our number (who again I won't name for marital reasons,) had managed to misplace their room key at the pub we were staying at. They embarked on an extensive and entirely indiscreet knocking-on-doors operation looking for a team-mate's floor to crash on, a campaign which also involved a fair bit of angry shouting and was, understandably, ignored by all of us.

But not so much by the other guests, who, also understandably, duly complained to the management.

In the morning the manageress was looking for Simon, the guy in charge, y'know, the one who booked the rooms. That would be me. She was very sweet. She didn't want to spoil anyone's fun, she understood we were on tour, just messing about, didn't mean any harm, and so on.

"If it was only a couple of complaints, I wouldn't have said anything. But it was all of them." She looked at me puppyishly with her head at an angle, a look that said: come on, I know this is your holiday, but it's also my job. Do me a favour.

What really caused the hilarity over the Bloody Marys after breakfast that morning was that the other large group staying at this place, as well as all the other incidental couples and families, was a party of deaf people.

Yes, we had made the deaf people complain about the noise. We surmised that banging on the walls with a beer bottle could probably cause a fair bit of vibration, as well as noise. So maybe, technically, they were actually complaining about the vibes.

It was all desperately shameful and childish and nothing to be proud of and, as a result, really quite funny. Regardless of what happens on future tours, it will doubtless be regarded as a watermark *moment. Low or high, take your pick.*

It's two days later now, two matches and another night on the piss under our belts. We are nine wickets down chasing a large total with not many overs left. It is a hopeless cause. We have not, I think it is fair to say, given a good account of ourselves in this game. We are tired, hungover, and being soundly spanked.

Of course, as we have seen, a game of cricket is never over till it's over. There's always a chance.

There was a pro T20 game recently where the batting side required 13 to win off the last ball. Game over, you'd have thought. But no – a no-ball was hit for six, as was the free-hit that followed it. Easy.

But this is not that game.

In this one, we're scratching along, seeing out the overs, blocking here, swishing and missing there, the run-rate rising inexorably as the balls tick past.

The fat lady may not yet have sung, but she's warming up in the wings. It's as good as over.

Alan is batting, I am umpiring.

This is never a combination I'm delighted with. I hope I've painted a sufficient picture of Al for you to imagine that he is not the type to go quietly. No one ever thinks they're out LBW, and this applies quadrupley to Al. I have seen him stare down an umpire who dared raise a finger at him, bat clattering at his feet, hands on hips, mouth agape in wordless incredulity that anyone could be so UTTERLY WRONG. He never actually technically argued with the umpire, he would say, but if it was in a Test match I think it's a fair bet he'd have lost his match fee.

Now then. I can honestly say that every single one of the LBW decisions I've ever given looked pretty damn out to me. I may have been wrong, certainly – I'm sure I've made plenty of mistakes – but the important thing is that I thought I was right. I understand the rules, and have applied them to the best of my ability. At the moment I raised that finger, I was convinced the batsman was out or he'd have got the benefit of the doubt.

Right up until now.

It's not premeditated. I'm certainly not thinking 'if there's a marginal LBW shout I'm gonna give it'.

But I do. The ball hits Al's front pad, in line, in front of middle and leg. The bowler goes up, turning to yell at me in appeal. The wicket keeper's not interested at all. Could easily have brushed leg stump, but might just as easily be missing it. Normally I'd say that's not out. Too much doubt.

But I'm overtaken by a wave of compassion for this game, twitching in its death throes, and the feeble pretence at competition that's preventing 22 blokes from heading for the pub.

The finger goes up.

Al starts to protest, then thinks better of it.

"Let's get a pint, shall we?" I say.

"Fair enough mate." He says, turning to shake hands with the bemused keeper, his nearest opponent.

It's the right thing to do. Isn't it? Put the game out of its misery. Like an injured horse.

But the moment I do it I feel bad about it.

If the batsmen want to concede a game, they can leave a straight one, or offer a catch on the boundary. It's up to them to do it, not the umpire – who should make his decisions based only on the facts, not the game situation, and certainly not what he knows about the inebriation or commitment levels of the players.

It was only a friendly, and the gesture may have even made it friendlier. It certainly didn't affect the outcome. But that doesn't make it ok.

The umpire's is simply too big a responsibility to abuse. Even in a game that's already dead.

Long before we get to the pub, in fact before I've shaken everyone's hand and left the field, I've made a pact with myself that I'll never do anything like that again.

I still feel bad about it.

get yer pads on, son

On 'hitting' and 'not getting hit': the equipment junkie's joy of stuff

I love kit. There's something enormously satisfying about specialist equipment, paraphernalia, gear, accoutrements, trappings, stuff.

Plenty of people are po-faced minimalists about it. People who have played cricket every week for thirty years with the same bat and pads and fail to see any reason to go wasting money on any new fangled nonsense. A decade ago they begrudgingly bought a new pair of boots, the spikes on which are now more nubs than spikes. Their thigh pad ties have long since rotted away, but they replaced them with an old neck-tie they were never going to wear again, see? Their whites are not those wussy new breathable tracksuit-type ones, which they "don't hold with." No, these are proper cotton cream slacks, circa 1965. Still going strong, though getting a bit tight around the middle now. And maybe a bit thin in the seat.

And that's fine. I don't have a problem with that attitude at all.

I don't understand it, but, y'know, it's fine. To me it's like saying 'I like beans. I have found a food that suits me. I will eat beans all day everyday forever and never entertain the notion of other food.' But each to their own.

I have always loved kit. In my youth I was heavily into guitars, and that offered a dizzying array of equipment, much more so than cricket could ever compete with.

Sure, you can customize bits and pieces here and there in your cricket bag, but it's never going to compare with re-wiring an old Aria with DiMarzio humbuckers, routing out the body to fit an original FloydRose locking wammy bridge, drilling in a monkey-grip handle, spraying it luminous green and fitting a vintage unfinished left handed (I'm right handed) Strat maple neck. No sir.

And effects. Man, you could spend your life and all your disposable income messing with guitar effects pedals. (U2 have made a very successful career out of it) And amps, of course. Valve, solid state? The answer is still valve, if you're a romantic kit junkie, just as the answer is still vinyl if you're a romantic music junkie.

No, cricket kit is a world away from electronics. And there is somewhat less diversity precisely because technology is less of a factor.

Though sometimes technology plays its part. I recently bought a pair of pads on the strength of a sales demo alone. Even though, rather than being sold it, I had to coax the demo out of the salesman. There's this bright orange stuff called d30 which was apparently on Dragon's Den. Sadly I'm unable to watch Dragon's Den because I'm allergic to smug self-satisfied twats. But still, this is a bright orange substance with a TV career – tell me more Mr cricket shop man…

My cricket shop of choice tends to be cricket-hockey.com. It's a web-based business (you'd never guess from the name, would you?) which operates out of a unit on an industrial estate a few miles south of Salisbury. It's an Aladdin's cave. They've got tons of kit there, and you can just go along and pick it up and get a feel for it. It's important to touch stuff before you buy it, I think. (Never more so than bats, but more on those in a minute.) Or try it on, when it comes to things like pads. Mike and Jamie who run it know me and my addiction well enough by now, and have got good at humouring me.

Jamie rummaged around until he found the splodge of d30 he was looking for. He hadn't done this yet, he confided; the salesman had shown it to him. He took this globule of stuff, which was a luminous orange science fiction gelatinous blob, and put it on the back of his hand. Then he hit it with a mallet.

Extraordinary. Intelligent molecules, the blurb says. (Codswallop of the highest order; what utter piffle. Smart thinking it may be, but we can be fairly confident it's not the molecules themselves that are doing the thinking – if they'd created sentient material, they'd have made it past Dragon's Den onto the actual news.) Marketing bollocks aside though, it is indeed very clever: the substance remains malleable until there's an impact, when it stiffens to absorb it.

It's being used in all sorts of things that benefit from the combination of flexibility and better impact protection. From ski-wear to walking boots, from motorbike gloves to tennis rackets to ipod cases. And cricket pads. My cricket pads, to be exact. I don't mind being taken in by stuff like this: they're light, they look nice, clearly they work, and I'm a sucker for a good story.

There's an old advertising adage that somebody who was feeling wise said once: "If you can demonstrate, demonstrate." Thus the fantastic Araldite glue ads – perhaps the first ever 'ambient media' experiments – where they glued a car to a billboard 20ft up in the air. Or the legend of the Shelby Cobra sales pitch, which was to place a $100 bill on the dashboard, and tell you you could keep it if you could lean forward and grab it while the salesman floored the car and the acceleration shoved you back in your seat.

For my money, the story is worth the sale. Glued a car to a wall? Glued to your seat by a V8? Hit your hand with a mallet? I want THAT one.

There are really only two areas to spend money on cricket kit, and those are protection and bats – ie 'not getting hit' and 'hitting'.

Protection is very necessary, and it's good to have stuff that fits well and feels comfortable.

If you play cricket at all, even once a decade, you want your own box. You want a box because certain types of balls, namely cricket balls, are really very hard indeed. And certain other types of balls, namely the kind you keep in your trousers, are really not. It's best all round (actually the cricket ball won't much care) if the two don't come into contact, and a box is in the business of making sure they don't. You want your own for the same reason that you want your own underwear – no matter how good a friend someone might be, you simply don't ask if you can borrow his pants, especially not immediately after he's just taken them off having spent the last half an hour or so running. You just don't. Get your own. Here, however, is where the metaphor breaks down:

borrowing someone else's disgusting sweaty box is preferable to batting without one. This is not true of underwear.

If you play cricket regularly, you'll probably want your own gloves and pads. This, unlike having your own box, is not about hygiene but about familiarity. They all feel slightly different, and the last thing you want to be thinking when facing your first ball is that these gloves are too tight or this thigh pad's going to fall off or I'm going to trip over these pads in a minute. Even for things like sweatbands and knee braces, it's best to wear them for practice if you intend to wear them to bat, just so you get used to them and they're not going to bug you. Batting's hard enough.

Some people don't bother with thigh pads. They can be a bit restrictive, especially if the only ones in the communal kit bag are the wrong size for you. Mostly, people who don't wear thigh pads are people who haven't been hit on the thigh too often. (Remember dead-legs from the school playground? This is the adult equivalent. You can't believe how much it hurts.) This can be an indicator that they're either one end of the batting spectrum or the other: the kind who are good enough not to get hit by anything much, or the kind whose stumps tend to get hit before their body does.

(The other reason not to bother with thigh pads is that they are incredible collectors of sweat. After even a 20 minute bat, they should really, along with pads and gloves and shoes, be aired somewhere, so they can dry properly, rather than being stuffed in your bag with your jumper on top. If you opt for the latter, be prepared to put them through the washing machine if you or your team-mates are less than keen on the rank stench of stale sweat. I can tell you from personal experience: thigh pads wash fine, gloves do not. They will comprehensively fall apart if you even show them the washing machine. And you'll do well to find a big enough washing machine to get your leg pads in.)

There have been a couple of people I've seen bat without gloves. They tend to be older guys, and what you might call 'blacksmith' types, if not actually by trade then by nature. Whoever they are they'd have to be very confident against the rising ball. Against proper quick bowling it's quite easy to get your fingers broken even with an inch of padding between you and the ball. Without it, I imagine fingers trapped as the filling in a ball/bat sandwich, even big thick blacksmith's fingers, would shatter like a dropped lightbulb. Fortunately I've never witnessed it, and the guys I've seen bat sans gloves have always retained their presumably 100% record of not getting hit.

I did once see someone come out to bat without pads. (Bob Willis once famously went out to bat without a bat.) But he had just absent-mindedly forgotten, and hastily and embarrassedly scurried back to the changing room to put some on. No-one bats without pads.

This is simply because people place a high value on a fully intact pair of shins.

More so, it sometimes seems, than they value a fully intact cranium.

Helmets, or 'lids' as they are invariably called, are a source of much discussion and controversy in village cricket, as they were in professional cricket thirty odd years ago, when they first became popular.

It's odd, but there's a real macho thing at work here: the idea that real men don't need to protect their head, or that even if you do get hit you'll be fine.

This has been perpetuated by the likes of West Indies legend Sir Vivian Richards, who retired around the time helmets became ubiquitous in the professional game, and has declared repeatedly and dismissively since that even were he still playing he would never wear one, relying instead on his 'God-given talents' to protect himself. (I have the utmost respect for Sir Viv, and accept that he means what he says and has the record to back it up, but there's still macho posturing in that attitude – if he was so sure he wouldn't get hit, why countenance any protection at all? Why the pads, why the gloves, why the box? Surely that's the logical conclusion, isn't it?)

I guess the same applied to motorcycle crash helmets. It became compulsory to wear crash helmets on a bike in the UK in the mid seventies, but I certainly remember bikers still complaining about it a decade or so after that, which was about the time I first met any bikers, and probably, not coincidentally, about the time I first came across the phrase 'nanny state'.

Recently, push-bike helmets have quietly become more and more widespread too. When I was a kid they didn't exist, but kids today – and many adults – always wear them. I don't let my kids on a bike without one. And when you think about it, why would you? Why risk a potentially life threatening head injury, especially to people (ie all children) fundamentally unskilled at something so inherently dangerous. It's slightly different for adults, as more competent cyclists are clearly less likely to fall off, and therefore less likely to be injured. Although it only takes one car driver not looking where he's going – the argument is ultimately the same as it is for motorbike helmets, when you think about it.

And this is also the case with cricket lids.

There's no doubt that the better the batsman, the less likely he is to get hit. Sir Viv and his disdain we've covered, and that is perhaps fair, as he was doubtless among the game's more naturally gifted batsmen. Bradman was never hit on the head, even during Bodyline, which was specifically designed to have the world's quickest bowler try and hit him on the head.

David Gower, after being hit on the head – evidently not badly – delighted the crowd by calling not for a helmet, but for a sunhat. But in the end even Mr Laid Back himself acquiesced, and batted out the bitter end of his career from behind a grill.

Brian Close is perhaps also worth a mention here. He was surely one of the hardest men ever to play cricket, and made a habit of standing up to intimidatory short fast bowling, preferring to let it hit him than to flinch. The fearless Yorkshireman, whose autobiography was called *I Don't Bruise Easily*, sometimes appeared to be deliberately chesting the ball away, like a footballer, and even to enjoy being hit. "How can a ball hurt you?" he is reputed to have remarked, with a stubborn lack of logic, "It's only on you for a split second." He was also regularly hit in the field, often at his customary position at short-leg. In a County game against Gloucestershire, he famously had a batsman caught at slip after the ball ricocheted off his forehead from short-leg – as it hit him he shouted "Catch it!", again creating the impression that he had deliberately headed it like a footballer. When he was asked what would have happened had the ball hit him a little lower, he replied, "He'd a bin caught in t'gully."

Helmets are without doubt a bit awkward, and take a bit of getting used to. Modern ones are more or less like horse riding hats, but with a metal grill in front of the face. This restricts the vision a bit, but really not that much, and after a while if you've got one that fits properly, you can pretty much forget it's there – just as a camera can focus through a chain-link fence so that it becomes invisible, with practice batsmen can do the same through the grill of a helmet. Much like thigh pads, with repeated use, they become familiar enough to ignore.

(Also much like thigh pads, they can get mighty sweaty. Often the forehead pad can be removed and wrung out like a sponge, or between balls you'll see players who've been at the crease for a while push the grill back, squeezing the pad onto their forehead so a little waterfall of sweat cascades down through the grill. Nice.)

Many adults can't or won't get on with them. If you've grown up playing cricket and never worn a helmet, it is a difficult thing to just start doing. Under 18s are required to wear them in league cricket, and most adults will refuse to bowl to a kid without one even in casual games. Kids grow up with them now, and are so used to them that batting without one would be as unfamiliar as batting without pads – yes, they're a bit cumbersome, but you need them: just get on with it. Surely as the next generation comes through and the older one begins to stop playing, it's only a matter of time before they're as universal on the village green as they are in the professional game.

Though there are kids who stop wearing them as soon as they have the option. Both Henry and Matt at Damerham discarded their lids the moment they turned 18, saying they found the restricted vision just too much of a compromise.

Fair enough, and you have to bear in mind that the need is less severe in the village game, as really quick short bowling is that much more rare.

It is not the rising ball that gets the amateur though – it's our old favourite, the bad ball. Just as the rank long hop will often get you out, it seems to be the favourite to knock you out too. A few years ago we had two nasty ball-meets-face incidents in one season. Fortunately, I was lucky enough that both games were among the few I missed that year – I'm not a big fan of blood and pain generally speaking, even less so when it belongs to my friends.

Alan first, a good bat, took a cross-batted swipe at a long hop, aiming to smear it in the general direction of cow corner, and got a top edge into the face. It hit him above the eye and he needed a dozen stitches, and left a good deal of blood on the crease. Then James a few weeks later: another good bat, another long hop, another swish, another top edge, another bloody crease. His hit him in the mouth.

Both have undoubtedly had their confidence knocked, as well as their faces. They've both tried wearing helmets, and both declared they can't bat in them so are persisting, perhaps slightly more gingerly than before, without.

Though they could be said to be lucky. One chap, not ten miles from Damerham, playing in a village game in the same year, was paralysed by a ball to the temple.

I've never been hit on the head while batting, but consider this to be more by luck than judgement. Accepting that exceptional batsmen are less likely to get hit, surely the reverse is also true: the lower down the competence scale you go, the greater your need for a lid. I've felt the wind from beamers, short balls and top edges passing millimetres from my face, and that is enough to convince me that life is definitely going to be safer lived behind bars. It's not really like I have stunning good looks to protect, but I'm quite fond of my face, thanks. I'm also strongly averse to pain, just generally. Just seems sensible to me. I was on-and-off with helmets before the guys were hit, but I'm now a firm believer. For those less than keen on unnecessary dentistry and serious head injuries, they are a winner. Also, they keep your ears warm on cold days, and stop your nose getting burnt on sunny ones. What's not to like?

Robin Smith, the original great Hampshire and England South African (long before KP assumed the role), argued there was plenty not to like, and that helmets with grills on them robbed batting against fast bowlers of something vital. "I just loved the excitement and adrenalin of not wearing one, and knowing if you made a mistake you could get seriously hurt." Asked to choose a personal highlight from his career, instead of a century or one of the creamy backward cuts for six for which he was justly famous, he chose a 14-ball battle before tea in Antigua with Ian Bishop and Courtney Walsh, during which he scored no runs and had his jaw broken. "It's the only one of my innings I ever wanted to keep on video. It was unbelievably exhilarating."

Barking mad, perhaps. But even so, there is definitely a laudable nobility in embracing the consequences of one's mistakes.

Of course, even wearing a helmet with a grill doesn't necessarily mean your face is safe from harm. In one of the most thrilling and hostile opening spells of his career at Lord's in 2005, a Steve Harmison bouncer somehow managed to cut Ricky Ponting over the cheekbone, presumably hitting the grill so hard it forced it back into his face.

It may surprise many to learn that it is not a memory Harmy relishes. In fact, he has identified the moment as the biggest regret of his career. "I didn't realise I'd hit him that hard, and by the time I did realise, I was almost back to my mark. But I wish I'd made sure he was all right. I've got so much respect for him. He's the best batsman I've ever bowled against. I bowled against Lara, Tendulkar, Kallis when he was on fire in 2004-5, but for front foot and back foot, steel, stubbornness, Ponting for me is streets ahead of everyone else. So yeah. That's one of those things I'd rather forget."

Harmy is not alone as a vicious fast bowler not keen on the injuries his skills can inflict. A (very) young Brett Lee once left a colts game in tears and had to be persuaded not to give up on cricket entirely, having made a bloody mess of a schoolboy opponent's face.

So that's two great fast bowlers of recent times in the 'pro-lid' camp, at least.

But pundits of both the amateur and professional scene bemoan the fact that helmets have changed the game, made batsmen more fearless and more likely to get on the front foot to pace.

This is most definitely the case, but I'm not convinced it's necessarily a bad thing.

It is part of the new type of cricket, aggressive, impatient, boundary-hungry. Yes, better protection may well have a lot to do with it, and the combination of that and T20 is almost certainly responsible for the faster, harder pace of so much modern cricket, both in world arenas and on village greens. Certainly, without helmets cricket today would be a quite different spectacle – it can hardly be a coincidence that they came to prominence during the reign of the game's great revolutionary Kerry Packer. (See chapter 10 for a brief summary of the Packer factor.) Without them, there may not be T20 at all, and there surely wouldn't be Test run-rates of around 4 an over.

Many people have cited the rise of the helmet as yet another tip in the bat's favour in the battle between bat and ball. Maybe so, but if it's a toss-up between higher run-rates and batsmen getting hit in the face, I know which I'd rather see.

The kind of people who complain about helmets changing the game will almost certainly have an opinion on 'bats these days' or 'modern bats' as they also like to call them, in the kind of tone most people reserve for drug crazed violent youths.

Cricket bats have a unique appeal.

They're made of wood, for a start. The defining factor in how good a bat is going to be is the quality of the bit of wood you start with.

Because they are literally organic things, there is something special about each and every one. They are unique, no two bats are the same.

Invariably they are made of willow, though they don't have to be; the Laws demand only that the bat blade 'be made solely from wood', and doesn't specify willow, much less *salix alba caerulea*, the species of white willow native to Europe and western and central Asia used almost exclusively for cricket bats.

Cheap bats are of course mass produced, shaped, stuck together and finished by machines. Even so, no two will be identical, because there are no identical trees.

But when you go up the price scale a bit, to the good bats, made of the very finest cuts of the very best willow, shaped entirely by hand, by craftsmen who choose the right kind of block for the specific type of bat they have in mind, they can be quite magical things.

Bats have what is called a 'pick up'. Which quite simply means what it feels like when you pick it up.

You hold the bat like you would waiting to face the bowling. So it's almost vertical, toe on the ground, behind or between your feet. And then you pick it up, backwards, so now it's horizontal, ready to flow forwards and meet an imaginary ball.

Regardless of its weight, a well balanced bat has a lightness about it at 'pick up'. The very best feel like they're alive, eager. Like a horse straining at the bit when it hears the hunter's horn; or the sudden tension you can feel in a lead when a dog sees a rabbit. It can't really be, I suppose, but that's what it feels like.

You can have two bats that look identical, same make, same design, same shape, same weight, and when you pick them up one feels lifeless and inert, the other feels like it's crackling with vibrant energy, animate and purposeful, a living thing.

Now then. Which would you want?

Not much of a contest, that.

Which is where the very cunning practice often observed in cricket shops of not putting prices on bats comes in, and having an open invitation for customers to pick them up, get a feel for them, try them out.

Going through 20 or 30 bats that you like the look of, you will usually – not always, as with anything there are occasionally bargains to be had – narrow your search down to the most expensive pieces of wood in the shop.

"How much is this one mate?" You ask tentatively, as matey studies the stickers on the bat and then retreats to look it up on his computer.

"£240 mate," he deadpans. Jesus. You only went because your whites have got a hole in the knee. But now you're in love.

An hour later you'll have either decided that your whites will last a bit longer after all, and talked yourself into this exceptional lump of timber full of the promise of classy runs, or left with a new pair of whites and a nagging feeling that you'll never pick anything up that feels quite that good ever again.

You don't find this with golf clubs. Compared to golf, cricket is a cheap game to be a kit-head. £240 is nothing in golf. You can do that on a driver without breaking a sweat. Then there are the other

13 clubs to worry about.

But you never need worry that the golf club you've got your eye on will be snapped up by someone else, and – like the girl you were too chicken to ask out – will live out its life with the wrong person. There'll always be another golf club behind that one on the shelf, and it will be identical.

They're made of metal. It's all about technology, about R&D and design, about science. It's about launch trajectories, COI (Coefficient Of Restitution: bounciness), stiffness and weight distribution. They don't have souls like cricket bats. One Taylor Made R7 425cc Titanium stiff shaft driver is pretty much the same as the next one. In fact, if it's not you should take it back and complain. Golf club manufacture, like golf itself, is all about repetition.

There are some exceptions, and they're always putters. A few years ago now I bought a second hand Scotty Cameron Pro Platinum mid-slant, hand milled in mild steel. It's beautiful, and has the exquisite feel and balance of a Swiss watch. It is a better putter than I will ever be, and has removed any lingering doubt there might have been in my mind that me missing putts was ever anything to do with the putter. I think it has (for now at least; never say never) removed my need for new putters. Since I've had it, I've never felt the slightest urge to replace it. I love my Scotty.

But generally, apart from my Scotty, you can't fall in love with a golf club. You can like it, you can get on with it, you can appreciate it, but that's as far as it goes. It is not, by definition, one of a kind.

This applies in all walks of life. It's the difference between a drum machine and a drummer, a standard letter and a hand written note.

Bats are different. That's the thing: they really are all different.

People will play with a falling-apart, raggedy old bat held together with string and tape, not because they can't afford a new one, or haven't got round to it, or are not bothered enough to change it (often the case in golf) but because they LOVE it.

"We go back a long way, me and this bat," they'll say, stroking it. "Still plenty of runs in it yet." People are afraid to get bats reconditioned, repaired, or even regripped, because it might change the way it feels.

Eventually, inevitably, the poor old thing will break or crack or split, and off it'll go to that enormous kit bag in the sky. Maybe there'll be a respectful run-less period of mourning, maybe they'll jump straight into bed with the next trendy new 'younger model' that takes their eye. We're all different, we all deal with loss differently. But there will always be another. We're only human, after all.

There are restrictions on a bat's dimensions: they can be no more than 38 inches long and no more than four and a quarter inches at their widest point. But there is no restriction on the depth of the blade, ie the size of the middle or the 'meat', and no restriction on weight. As a result, there are some simply enormous bats around with monstrous middles, far too heavy to play any actual cricket shots with.

There's a chap we play against, Steve, who is one of the more cricket-obsessed guys you're ever likely to meet.

Once, when we were playing them one Wednesday evening, he looked a bit out of breath at the crease, and one of his team mates, umpiring at square leg, was shaking his head and tutting at him. Fielding nearby, I wandered over. "Steve all right?" I asked. "Not really," his mate replied. "He had a stroke at the weekend. His Mrs'll kill him for playing tonight. If this doesn't." In the pub after the game I asked Steve if this was true. He shrugged. "Only a little one."

He's always selling bats and balls and all kinds of stuff, and usually has at least one new bat to show us. He's got a couple that get carried around in a big flight case, like an oversized aluminium photographer's case with foam bits cut to size inside for the bats to nestle in. They're huge. Must be 4lb if they're an ounce. If he swings and connects, it's six, no question. But it must rule out the cut, or any other shot that requires any element of wrist. It's like wielding a sledge hammer – devastating if you hit what you're aiming at, but hardly the most delicate of tools.

Most bats these days are between 2lb 6oz and 3lb. If you want anything outside that range, you get into custom-made territory.

The 'standard' in bat weight has risen steadily in recent times. A generation ago 2lb 6oz was the top end, now it's the bottom. Bradman, widely regarded as the greatest player ever to wield a piece of willow, had a 2lb 2oz bat.

Brian Lara's, a batting behemoth of more recent times, was 2lb 4oz.

These days, a 12 year old's bat will be heavier than that.

It's easy to see why good batsmen prefer lighter bats. It allows you to adjust much later in a shot, and means wristy shots require less raw muscle – neither Bradman nor Lara were big men.

Equally it is often argued that lesser players should go for lighter blades too, as you're less committed than with a big meaty bat, and can get yourself out of trouble easier, whether pulling out of a shot, or adjusting late in either defence or attack – the tack hammer, as opposed to the sledge hammer.

The other school of thought of course is the bigger the bat, the further it goes. There is as much finesse in this argument as in the mighty sixes (and thick outside-edges) it produces.

A good general rule-of-thumb is that an enormous meaty bat will be wielded by a slogger, rather than a craftsman. Not that there's anything wrong with that.

But not always. That would be too easy, wouldn't it?

For a start, enormously be-middled bats these days are not always as weighty as they appear. One of the recent innovations is to dry out the wood a lot more. This reduces weight, so you can have a bigger middle on a lighter bat, at the expense of durability so they don't last as long. Some have as much as 90% of the natural moisture removed. They're often pressed a lot less these days too, again meaning greater 'ping' but leaving them more susceptible to damage.

And sometimes appearances are not deceptive at all. There are many great players who use (or used) very heavy bats. Clive Lloyd, Graeme Hick, Graham Gooch.

Sachin Tendulkar's bats are around 3lb 4oz. 'The Little Master' (he's 5'5") demonstrably has no trouble whatsoever with wristy shots, cuts, pulls or flicks off his pads. His thunderous, bottom-heavy bats with three grips on the handles are exactly what you'd expect to find in the bag of a middle-order hitter on a Saturday afternoon, rather than one of the game's most naturally gifted strokemakers over 30,000 international runs and 100 international 100s to his name.

Although there's no shortage of pundits who argue he'd have more of both if he switched to a lighter bat. But then pundits are not paid to agree with people.

The conclusion then, which should come as no surprise at all for something so personal and individual, must be that after (ahem) weighing up all the options, it comes down to a matter of taste.

And this is excellent news, because it calls for plenty of experimentation. Before you know what you like, you've got to try them all, right? There are bats which feel wonderful when you middle them, awful when you don't. Those you know are too heavy for you to use comfortably, and others that feel they might require more of an artist than you're able to offer.

(I've got a GM Catalyst Original Limited Edition, as used by Vaughan in his heyday. At 2lb 7oz, it's a lovely, poised bat, and cost me over £200 some years ago. But sometimes it feels like perhaps it's a bit too good for me. Like using the best silver. Recently I talked myself into a Gray Nicolls Xiphos, which is four ounces heavier, but has an outrageous middle, and seems a bit more, I don't know, working class, maybe? Sorry Grays – and all the public schoolboy pros who endorse you – don't take that the wrong way. I LOVE it, if that makes up for it.)

To extend the falling-in-love metaphor, (perhaps to breaking point,) you can of course go through life quite convinced that you've got a 'type', and yet end up blissfully happy with the opposite of what you always imagined.

Very often, with apologies to J K Rowling, it seems it is not the wizard that chooses the wand, but the other way around.

Battlefield conversion
We're at a friendly away game on a Sunday, half a dozen of us sitting around the scorers on chairs or lying on the grass, chatting about nothing much.

I've just come back from the middle. I wasn't out there for long. I can't have been really annoyed, or I wouldn't have come and sat with everyone straight away. But I still have all my gear on, just sat there, so I don't imagine I was overly delighted.

I'm in a sort of daydream, reliving the dismissal, only vaguely listening, not contributing to the conversation. There's a lull in it, and I fill it with a sigh. I pull my gloves off slowly, then ease my helmet off and drop the gloves inside it.

"Si?" asks Sam. *He draws the sound out, in the way people do when they're about to ask a question they've been thinking about for a while:* 'Siiiiiiiiiiii???'

I'm back from my reverie. "Yes mate."

"Do you think you're always gonna wear a helmet?"

Sam is about 14. He's an excellent little cricketer, keen as can be. He plays Wednesdays and Sundays for us, Saturdays somewhere else, Thursday somewhere else, trains on Mondays, and he's looking out for games on Tuesdays and Fridays. He's sprawled on the grass, watching the game, with his back to all of us.

He's asking me because most of the older guys don't wear them, whereas most of the younger guys do.

"Yeah, I think so mate."

"I definitely am. Even when I don't have to anymore."

"Yeah? Why's that then."

"I dunno. I mean… why wouldn't you?"

Sam has grown up with lids, through colts cricket with proper coaches, required to wear one from the moment real cricket balls got involved. He keeps wicket too, and when he stands up to the wicket his Mum can often be heard yelling at him from the pavilion to put his helmet on.

"I got hit on the head the other day. Went straight up, keeper caught it and appealed. Wasn't out though." *He can talk, can Sam. He speaks quickly, without apparent breaths.*

Joel, not a big talker, is scoring. "I was at the other end when both Alan and James got hit the other year."

Sam sits up and turns round. "Were you? What was it like?"

Joel shrugs. "Not very nice. Bloody."

There follows a series of stories from our own experiences, what we've read about, and what we've seen on telly.

That bloke down near us who got paralysed. Some geezer up north who was killed. Gatting being hit in the face so hard by Malcolm Marshall that part of his nose got embedded in the ball, and Marshall threw it away in disgust. They had to stop to clear the blood off the pitch and get a new ball. Then some moron at a press conference afterwards asked the immortal question: "So where exactly did the ball hit you, Mike?"

"Remember Harmison hitting Ponting through the grill and cutting his cheekbone, first day of the Ashes at Lord's?" We all do.

"Who was that New Zealander who Anderson got through the grill the other year, lost a tooth? Remember that? You could see his tooth flying out in slow motion; they found it on the pitch later!" Some of us remember it, but no one can remember his name. (It was Daniel Flynn.) And Anderson himself turning his back on a bouncer from Fidel Edwards, getting hit on the back of the head, broke his helmet.

Throughout all this, Simon Chalk, who's padded up, next in to bat, is silent.

Simon's a proper Casual, plays once or twice a year. His son Henry is 11, off in the nets with a few other kids. He's the keen one.

After the anecdotes dry up there's a pause, and we all watch the game for a bit.

Simon clears his throat. "Anyone got a helmet I can borrow?"
We all laugh.

"Here mate, have mine. I didn't even have it on long enough to get it sweaty."

chapter 9

where d'you want me, skip?

On captaincy and all it entails

Entire books have been written on cricket captaincy. Some mind-meltingly turgid, some excellent. Well, one, anyway: Ashes-winning England captain turned shrink and erstwhile MCC President Mike Brearley's wonderful *The Art of Captaincy* is widely regarded as the definitive work on the subject, and is as applicable to life as it is to cricket in places, as you might expect from so eloquent and shrewd a man.

The cricket captain is perhaps more pivotal to the success or otherwise of his side than in any other game. The football captain at the top level, for example, is largely an honour post, awarded to stalwart players for services rendered, and carries little or no tactical responsibility, which everyone these days accepts lies squarely at the manager's door.

In cricket though, a fielding captain affects a game with every bowling change, every field placing, every laugh, frown, celebration, every banterly cajole and every muttered obscenity.

Whether he likes it or not, his players look to him to set the mood, and determine the manner and vigour with which they attack, defend, or wander aimlessly towards a limp draw.

His decisions turn games, especially Test matches, and it is this element of cricket that can lend it a chess-like quality, and can make the duel of the best in the world over five days so fiercely captivating.

Brearley himself is often cited as a batsman who got into the national side largely because of his ability as a captain, rather than his talent with the bat. It is that important.

Conversely, truly gifted players often stop performing when burdened with captaincy. Ian Botham – the most able of Brearley's charges – lost the first and drew the second of the Ashes encounters in 1981 before Brearley was recalled to lead the side for the Headingly Test. (Yes, recalled to lead the side; he wasn't in it for the first two games. The late great Bob Woolmer made way for him.) That glorious game is available and highly recommended on DVD, and I won't linger on the details here, but can it be a coincidence that Beefy, unburdened by captaincy, played the game of his life and made himself a household name that day? He argues vociferously that it was indeed a coincidence, and he would have made a great captain given the right circumstances. To which Brearley would smile, agree with him, take him off and not bowl him again until he was angry enough to kill someone.

Recently we've had a modern equivalent, the first Englishman to come along for whom the moniker "The new Botham" was not actually laughable, the mighty Fred. Given the captaincy, Flintoff bowled himself into the ground in vain at Lord's against India, (a helpfully stark illustration of why captains at the top level are overwhelmingly batsmen) and in Australia suffered the first Ashes whitewash for the best part of a century.

Like Botham, Freddie argued that the timing was wrong and he was unlucky. And like Botham, he may have been right, but we'd all rather he'd just got over it and concentrated on the task in hand. A difficult job though captaincy may be, National Hero is harder, and precious few have the CV for it.

Shane Warne is now firmly saddled with the label 'The Greatest Captain Australia Never Had'. A mass of contradictions, Warne is a brilliant tactician. He is (or would have been) the exception to the rule that front line bowlers don't make outstanding captains. His mind games as a bowler, and his personal ability to turn matches on their head with his once-in-a-generation skill, have equipped him with a burning hunger as a skipper. His efforts at Hampshire made them play exciting cricket, out of the blue. Nothing changed except the captain, but they were a different side under him, steely and indignant. Similarly, given the reins of the Rajasthan Royals, the least expensive of the underdogs at the inaugural IPL in 2008, he led a side he hadn't met six weeks earlier to skin-of-the-teeth victories time and again against sides that were vastly superior on paper. Proving thrillingly (to paraphrase Brian Clough, one of football's master tacticians,) that sport is not played on paper.

Not that Australia suffered for its lack of Warne's captaincy. During the time when he might have been captain they were effectively invincible and would probably have beaten everyone even with David Beckham at the tactical helm. (Though imagine: would Warne have put England in at Edgbaston 2005 with his best new-ball bowler out? Come to that, would Beckham? Poor old Ricky.) But purely because Warne has the kind of 'colourful' character that gets him into endless streams of low grade trouble, cricket missed out. Which is a shame. He said of himself, rather profoundly, that it was his ability to compartmentalise that was the key to his successes on the field, and his failures off it. The same criticism might be levelled at Cricket Australia.

A mate of mine used to play poker. That doesn't really cover it – I mean, I play poker, I love poker. I'm not very good at it, but I love it. Up to £20 buy-ins and I'm fine, over that, and I become the incredible human jelly and my brain runs away, throwing chips behind it left right and centre to distract its pursuers. I love the game, the infiniteness of its possibilities appeals to me hugely, but I am powerless in the face of them.

My old mate Tom, on the other hand, was not. He was a proper poker player. Years ago, when I was living in a west London flat, Tom came round late one night after a good night in a Kensington card room. He had a wad of £50 notes over an inch thick. Me and him and Soph stood in the middle of our lounge and he threw them all up in the air, so they rained down on us like they do in all the best clichés. It was a brilliant feeling, being rained on by thousands of pounds, even though none of it was mine. In 2002 Tom won the London leg of the European Poker Championship and bought himself a flat.

One drunken night in Tom's bought-and-paid-for new pad, I fell to asking him what he'd learned that made him a better player these days; in other words, now you *really* know how to play it, what is poker actually *about*. I know it's not about the money. Just like professional golf, if you're a serious player the money is just a way of keeping score, and if you're not, it scares you off so the serious players can get on with it without the jelly men getting in the way. And everyone knows it's not about the cards. You've got to have a hand occasionally of course, but only so other times you can pretend you've got one and get away with it, that is the majesty and the mystery of it. So what is it really about?

"Well, it's not about what you've got. And it's not about what they've got."

"No," I agree slurrily. Yes, you can slur that word, if you're drunk enough.

"Sometimes, it's about what you think they've got, and what they think you've got."

"Mmm." Safe there. No matter how drunk you are you can't slur 'mmm'.

"But mostly it's about what you think *they* think you've got. And what you think they think you think *they*'ve got. And then sometimes, it's about what *they* think *you* think they think *you've* got."

I'm sure you can see how he developed that theme.

Cricket is similarly complicated, and, at any point in a game, it is along these lines that a captain may find himself thinking.

What does a cricket captain actually do?

Like many complicated things – even poker – it is in essence very simple. In most games of cricket, from Test matches to T20 to County cricket to village leagues, the captain's aim is clearly understood by everyone.

He is trying to win.

His job is to use the players, pitch and conditions at his disposal in the most effective way possible, within the laws and spirit of the game and whatever other constraints the format may place upon him (limited overs, time, fielding restrictions, etc). How he goes about this might be straightforward, quiet, brash, safe, experimental, innovative or devilishly cunning, but his only priority is to make sure he and his side do their very best to win. Or at least not to lose, in forms of the game where draws are possible.

What is at stake in league and County cricket is points, determining a side's standing in the league. In the case of internationals of course it's pride, world cups, little four inch urns, MBEs all round, lucrative sponsorship deals, that sort of thing.

So it may be demanding, tactically and technically, but it's not difficult to see what is actually required.

It is my contention, and I will argue it here, that it is way more complex and difficult to captain a casual side than a serious one.

In a friendly, a captain has far more to consider than mere trifles like batting points and national pride. There are a host of subtleties which can alter many aspects of a game, much of which will go unnoticed to all but the most in-tune observer. It's a complicated, nuanced affair, requiring unexpectedly sophisticated understanding and empathy.

Friendlies are often played by people who don't play regular cricket. Or haven't played for ages, or never really played, or used to but don't so much any more. Plenty of people look forward very fondly to the one or two games they play a year.

There's a responsibility for the casual captain to make sure everyone who turns up gets a game. Ideally, this should mean everyone bats and everyone bowls, but that is not always feasible.

There is nothing more guaranteed to put off the occasional cricketer than standing around in a field all day not doing anything except being forcibly reminded why he doesn't much like cricket.

He hasn't played for years but his lad's getting into it; he's been talking about doing some exercise for a while; it's about time he got to know some people locally to have a beer with; he watches enough of it on the telly why not give it a go – there are plenty of reasons the 'occasional' player might get tempted out to play.

And probably only one why you'll never see him again. Captaining a casual game is as much about social organisation as anything else, but the one thing you must try your hardest to ensure is that the guy you've never seen before doesn't have a thoroughly shit time. That, quite simply, is more of a priority than winning.

Also, of course, he *might* have an eighty-mile-an-hour outswinger, which you'll never find out if you don't give him a bowl. The chances of it are pretty slim, but he could have.

Just in order to set up a thin little analogy, let me share with you briefly the best thing about working in advertising. It's a point in the process, just a little moment really, but it comes again and again. The client's given the agency a brief, the agency's planners have sexed it up and re-written it and briefed the creatives. The creatives have gone away and thought up some exciting new ways to sell the client's stuff that the client never thought of before and now you're all back in front of the client, just about to show them what they're paying you for. That moment, right then, is so powerful, so pregnant with possibilities, that I'm sure it's what keeps most of the people who work in advertising from finding something more useful to do with their lives. Right then, at that moment, it could be awesome. It could be career-defining. It could be market-changing. It could be the best thing ever. It *might* be genuinely brilliant. Everyone in the room is willing it to be. Whether it actually is or not is largely irrelevant – the moment is sweet, whether the work turns out to be or not.

Equally, every time you go and see a band, the support act could turn out to be your new favourite band in the whole world ever. After all, the band you came to see must like them. Until that opening chord, how are you to know?

By the same token, whenever someone comes along to play for us that no-one knows, there's always that moment before they do anything when I like to imagine the least likely of scenarios.

There he is, wheezing in to bowl, and you can tell from the run up that he's no more of an athlete than the rest of us. He's repeatedly assured anyone listening that he hasn't played since school, and even then he wasn't any good.

But. But, right – bear with me – what if his idea of 'any good' is wildly different from ours? What if he didn't play for his school because he happened to go to school with most of the national youth squad? Or because he was a gifted chess player or something and was shielded from the distraction of sport by the cardies-with-elbow-patches brigade? What if this ungainly trundle actually culminates in a ferocious inswinging yorker that rips leg stump out like an exocet?

Invariably it's a slow wide half tracker. But in the moment before he bowls it, it *might* be an exocet.

It might be.

So friendly cricket is full of people who don't play it that often, but fancy the odd game. This is part of its charm. Sometimes they haven't played since they were kids, sometimes they still *are* kids.

Friendlies are a great way for kids to experience the adult game. 'Colts' cricket is a wonderful thing, to be strenuously encouraged, and obviously the best way for youngsters to learn. But ask a 15 year old if he'd rather take the wicket of another 15 year old he'll never see again or one of his Dad's mates, and I doubt you'll get many opting for the anonymous acne machine.

But kids bring complications. We have a few youngsters who play for us. 12, 13, 14, 15. Great kids, keen as. They all have better throwing arms than those of us the wrong side of 40, and they all bowl well. A few are already good bats, the others will be in a few years when they've grown a bit.

But if you stick a 12-year-old in to bat, people won't bowl fast at them. And understandably so; who wants to be the hulking great be-beer-bellied bully who has to explain to junior's distraught mother how his little wrist got broken? That sort of thing can really put a crimp on your weekend. Not to mention your image of yourself as a basically decent bloke.

This creates both problems and opportunities for the casual captain. The problems are largely concerned with encouraging the lad, making sure he enjoys it and is not intimidated (you want him to come back, of course; in five years time he'll probably be your star player) whilst not patronising him to the point that he'd rather face a beamer from Shoaib Akhtar than have you step in on his behalf ever again.

The opportunities are more interesting than the problems. If your opponents have a fast bowler who's just hitting his straps nicely, there are few better ways to disrupt his rhythm than a nervous looking youngster. In all likelihood, your opposite number will take his star bowler off and bowl someone slower while the youngster's in, leaving your big hitter at the other end to milk the strike. Genius.

Of course this is terribly underhand, and hardly conforms to the spirit of the game. No self respecting cricketer would ever admit to such low behaviour, so it must always be couched in terms of 'giving the lad a proper go'. The really slam dunk tactic here of course, if you'll forgive the mixed sporting metaphor, is to find yourself a youngster with not only batting but acting talent, so he can behave like a rabbit long enough for the quicks to be taken off and then start carting it all round the park like a particularly diminutive Ponting.

For this reason alone, kids are definitely best kept for friendlies. But this kind of thing actually happens more often than you'd have thought in league matches. It shouldn't, but it does. There's a wedding. Four or five of the regular side are going. You get a few peripherals in, perhaps one of the older players who these days is more happy umpiring than playing, and a couple of youngsters. They're keen, often as good if not better than the adults, kitted out in all the latest gear and dying to do well. But they're kids. There are few properly fast bowlers happy to bowl at a 12-year-old exactly as they would at a 25-year-old. It's psychologically impossible.

Normally, if a nipper comes to the wicket, the quicks will slow down or the spinners will come on, even in a league game. This is cricket, after all, and village cricket at least retains the well-buffed sheen of fair play, and long may that be the case.

But 'fair' is of course a relative concept. If they need 50 to win off 10 overs when the kid comes out at number 11, you can be pretty sure he'll get some friendly bowling, at least to begin with. But if he stays in and they need a-run-a-ball off the last two or three, the game has changed. Is it 'fair' then, to put a youngster in? Frankly no, to either the kid or the opposition.

Unless he's any good. In competitive cricket, from the highest standard to the lowliest league, when it comes down to the wire it's about winning, not about everyone getting a go. If you send a nipper out to bat in a competitive game, he'd better know what he's doing. No one is going to bowl him bouncers, but don't rule out the full pace yorker. And oddly enough, if the kid in question *is* any good, he won't want the quicks to bowl slow at him. How's he going to get good – or indeed know how good he is – if no-one will bowl at him properly?

Sachin Tendulkar made his Test debut against Pakistan in 1989 when he was sixteen facing one of the finest fast bowling partnerships in history. Can you imagine Imran Khan telling Wasim Akram and Waqar Younis to go easy on him? "Listen lads, just bung him a few first up, eh, let him have a bit of a go. None of that 90mph reverse swing nonsense, eh? Don't want to put the lad off. That's it, yeah, just come off two paces, see how he does." I think not.

One of our "Champagne Moments" from recent years was when Dave Burroughs was bowling in the Saturday league. He'd just got a wicket and was feeling buoyant when a little kid came to the crease. Impossible to tell how old he was under his lid, but he looked about twelve. Dave's a canny bowler, rather than a proper quick, so he wouldn't need to throttle back. But he brought the field in, thinking the lad might be nervous enough to chip the ball in the air early on. His first ball was beautifully, fluidly driven straight back over his head for a one-bounce four. No-one who saw it could possibly have refrained from smiling, least of all Dave. Certainly not the fledgling Sachin he was bowling to.

Kids also create extra pressure as bowlers. Partly because they're short, which makes it harder to judge the length and tends to make them skiddy, but mostly because grown men don't much like being got out by little kids.

But do you know who they like being got out by even less?

Girls. Oh, yes. Girls, girls, girls. If you want to thoroughly discombobulate a side, get yourself a girl who can bowl.

Life – even cricket, I'm afraid – is full of idiots.

Idiots who think there's nothing more hilarious in the world than their mate getting out to a girl.

And even if you're a level-headed, even-handed, modern sort of chap who believes in equality and applauds feminism and fair pay and meritocracy and equal rights and EVERYthing, no-one likes being laughed at by his mates. Even if they are idiots.

This gives female bowlers in casual cricket a spectacular advantage.

Great bowlers are preceded by their reputations. Batsmen would quake before Holding, Marshall, Garner and the other great pacemen of the West Indies in their pomp. Facing that attack, no-one could honestly claim to be playing the ball rather than the men.

There have always been bowlers who inspire fear in batsmen. The two great spinners of recent times, Warne and Murali, had the hardest part of their job done in any game before their captains tossed them the ball, anticipation always building to when the master would take centre stage – what a gift it is, before you've bowled a ball, to already have the batsman at such a psychological disadvantage.

A girl playing village cricket has a similar affect. She doesn't even have to be that good. All she has to be is a girl.

We played a side once who had a girl bowling off-breaks. She was not quick, didn't get much turn or bounce, and was not particularly accurate. In short, she was a thoroughly unremarkable village off-spinner, of the type you meet as a second change bowler all the time.

But she took plenty of wickets, and her economy was excellent.

Why? Her economy was excellent because half the guys thought 'well I'm not getting out to her' so were extra careful against her, not risking playing what by rights ought to have been boundary balls. She got wickets because the other half thought 'it's a girl, it's going for six,' and either holed out or swished and missed.

Such absence of sense in the presence of girls is not exclusive to amateur cricket. (No game, at any level, and indeed no walk of life, can claim the monopoly on that one.) When Mike Atherton was caught out by Emily Drumm in a charity match in New Zealand in 1997, the papers predictably wet themselves in excitement. "England Captain Dismissed By Woman!"

Full of idiots, you see.

One of a captain's main responsibilities is deciding who gets to do what when. Who fields where, who bowls and when, and, most contentious of all, the batting order.

In a professional or good-standard amateur team, deciding who does what when is easy. You can ask any batsman who plays to a decent standard where he bats in the order, and he'll be able to tell you. I'm an opener. I'm a number three. I'm a middle order hitter. The point is, you'll have half a dozen batsmen, who just bat. They can probably bowl a bit too, but they know that at their level, there are specialist bowlers who are way better than they are. Your four or five bowlers are probably pretty decent bats too, but their job is to bowl, and they'll only get to bat if the 'proper' batsmen fail.

If you're lucky you might have an all-rounder in your middle order – an all-rounder being a player who bats and bowls well enough to get into a cricket side on the merits of either.

There are four types: a batting all-rounder is an excellent bat who bowls a bit (Paul Collingwood, Ravi Bopara), a bowling all-rounder is a specialist bowler who can bat (Andrew Flintoff, Stuart Broad).

A genuine all-rounder excels at both. (Ian Botham, Imran Khan, Gary Sobers.) These are very, very rare.

Notice that the examples of batting and bowling all-rounders are recent England players. The genuine examples are all legends and all retired and only one is English. I'm not sure there is a genuine all-rounder currently playing top-flight cricket. With the possible exception of Jacques Kallis, but I think even he might admit that he is past his prime as a bowler, and is now a world class bat and a pretty decent, rather than genuinely excellent, bowler.

That's how rare they are.

There are plenty who's batting and bowling skills are about on a par with each other, but neither are quite good enough to ensure that if they didn't do both, they'd get in on just one of them. They are balanced all-rounders, but they're not Class-A. England ODI stalwarts Luke Wright and Dimitri Mascarenhas are fine examples.

There are a few who might yet make the grade: Stuart Broad again, Graeme Swann, Adil Rashid perhaps. All bowling all-rounders whose batting just might kick-on sufficiently to make them the genuine article before retirement.

The fourth type of all-rounder, however, is far from rare.

He is, in fact, rather ubiquitous across this green and pleasant land.

The village all-rounder is a cricketer who bats and bowls okay, but excels at neither. Which, lets be honest, is most of us.

One of the great things about cricket (this won't be the only time I mention it) is that it's a team game that is entirely dependent on individual performances. This is both a strength and a weakness, depending on how you look at it. You can play and enjoy the game without being brilliant at it, and still make a valuable contribution with wickets runs and catches, and be part of a whole. Or you can stand around kicking the turf railing that it wasn't your ton or your five-fer and wondering why you bother. It's all about attitude, really.

At village league level, teams are often dependent on three or four guys. Sometimes only one. We've played teams we would thrash every time but for one guy. It's an odd conundrum that in league cricket, there are likely to be several players in any side – half a dozen in some – who don't get to do much. Not all village sides are like that, but there are plenty where the same five names appear in the score book at the top of the batting order and the bowling columns week after week. Must be pretty dull for those other half a dozen guys.

In Damerham Saturday League games, the top order is relatively set, but our poor old captain Mark has the regular headache of who bats where in the bottom half of the order. Should it be that the guys who didn't bowl bat higher up? Even if some of the bowlers are better bats? Should we mix it up every game? Draw straws? Base it on averages? Attendance? It's a thorny one.

In casual games, everyone wants a go. That is the point and the beauty of them.

There will usually be some players who don't want to bowl, some who are happy to bat 11 if they get a good bowl. There'll be others happy to forgo bowling if they can bat at three. Most will want to do both. Because secretly they harbour the suspicion that they're probably a talented all-rounder, just waiting to flower.

The reality is you'll probably have a couple of players who are genuinely good enough to open both the batting and the bowling, and nine who genuinely aren't.

What to do?

One solution I've hit upon is a new format, specifically engineered to ensure that everyone gets a game, but not to preclude strong individual performances.

It's essentially a two-innings T20 game, which I snappily call T20x2R. The name makes sense (the 'R' will become clear) but has the disadvantage of sounding like a Max Power Peugeot with a full body kit and fluorescent neon lilac under-lighting. Let's say I'm still working on the name.

The format has the same number of potential balls as a normal weekend match, but instead of one innings of 40 overs a side, it's made up of two innings of 20 overs a side, like a miniature Test match. Tea is still half way through the game, by which time both sides have each batted and bowled.

But wait! Here comes the cunning part. Baldrick would love this part: In the second innings, the batting order is reversed. (Hence the 'R'. See?) This is non-negotiable and obviously must be agreed with the opposing captain before you start. (We had one game where, despite extremely careful explanations before the game, it was clear I had failed to get through to the opposing captain when he led his men off the field once we'd passed their first innings total.)

What this format does is make pretty certain – as certain as it's possible to be – that everyone gets a bat. What it doesn't do is mean the captain can stop thinking about his batting order. Quite the contrary. He just has to think about it differently.

Traditional batting orders obviously have the best bats in the top half. If you do that in this format, you're likely to regret it come your second innings, when you sit in the pavilion silently willing all your, shall we say, 'less dynamic' players to be out so your batsmen can get in and start scoring.

Logically, those most likely to bat in both innings in this format are the middle order, 5, 6 and 7. (Curiously – well, you may find it curious if, like mine, your grasp of fundamental arithmetic is below feeble – 6 will be 6 in both innings. 5 in the first innings will be 7 in the second, 4 will be 8, etc. A batsman's positions in the batting orders for both innings will always add up to 12. Neat, huh?)

One thing to do then, is load your middle order with your better batsmen. Another is to stagger them throughout the order.

Bowling wise, tactically, much the same applies. As the opposition's best batsmen are likely to appear later in the game than usual, it's probably wise to hold off on your best bowlers for a bit too.

You can agree anything you like about overs per bowler with the other captain, but a limit that works well in the first innings is three per bowler, so you must use at least seven to make up your 20. This usually means that at least a couple of people who wouldn't normally get a bowl will get one. If everyone wants to have a bowl, two overs each is not a bad idea. In the second innings we usually go for four per bowler, like T20, so the second innings can be a little more competitive.

If you want to get really involved with the format and its strategies, you can say that the first innings can last as few as 10 and as many as 30 overs, and the captain can declare at whatever point in between he chooses. So if you smash 100 off 10 overs, you can declare, put the opposition in, and have a 30 over second innings to build on your total. Your opposite number can then, if he wishes, use say 25 overs to rack up 200 in the first innings, putting the pressure back on you to make a good score with your 30, which he'll then have 15 left to chase your combined total with. Or you could keep the innings rigid at 20 overs, but introduce a 'follow on' rule; 80 feels about right. You can make it as complicated and tactical – or not – as you like.

With a bit of luck, it should result in a balanced, competitive game, that every player has a part to play in.

The best thing about the format is that your tail is also your top order. So an occasional cricketer who would be highly unlikely to open an innings under normal circumstances might have the opportunity to do so, and bowlers who are normally sent in at the death and told to instantly start knocking five kinds of hell out of every ball they face – a tactic almost certain to get anyone who isn't Virender Sehwag out 9 times out of 10 – get a chance to settle down and try to build an innings.

On a good day, this is more likely to mean that everyone enjoys themselves. And that, my Captain, is what it's all about.

The eleventh wicket

One the oddest games I ever played in, let alone captained, was our annual friendly against our neighbouring village, Rockbourne.

Like most of us, the kind of Sunday side Rockbourne can put out depends on all sorts of things. They can be very strong one week, with a couple of guys who play high standard competitive cricket, and the next week they'll be mostly kids and granddads. You never know what you're getting.

The game in question, we both had a pretty good mixture of decent players and kids.

I really struggled to get a side out, and had roped in no less than five youngsters. And then it turned out that someone I thought said he couldn't play thought he'd said he could – so now we had 12. Brilliant.

This is typical of trying to organise a casual side. It's not unlike herding cats.

Anyway, there were a couple of guys sitting around scoring and umpiring who probably weren't going to get a bat, but might get a bowl. Rockbourne skipper Ian was relaxed about it and didn't care, as long as we rotated in the field so there were only 11 at a time.

It was a 35 over game. I lost the toss and we were invited to bat. A decision which, for the first hour at least, made Ian seem like a towering tactical genius.

Speaking of which, I had a plan. In order to make sure the youngsters didn't just end up fielding (or worse perhaps, end up not even fielding) I had devised a cunning two-tier batting order. We would have a kid and an adult batting together: when a lad was out, another replaced him, when an oldie was out, another would replace him. See? Simple. Those who hadn't had a bat for a while were nearer the top of the list. Fair and egalitarian, too. Clearly never going to work.

Just how comprehensively it didn't work is best expressed in numbers. The batting card read: 2, 5, 0, 1, 9, 1, 0, 7, 0, 1

In our defence, they did open the bowling with Ed, who does that on Saturdays for Lymington, a Southern Premier League side. He is not a slow bowler. He passed the bat(s) again and again, and if he'd bowled on the stumps would have had a hatful of wickets. But he didn't, and was too quick to nick, so ended wicketless. Ed's a very pleasant chap who clearly loves the game, competitive or not, and not bowling straight may have been his way of being considerate to the kids. I'm not sure even now if he meant to keep missing the sticks that day or not.

Anyway, at the other end everyone was busy throwing their wickets away. Maybe in relief, I don't know.

Before long we comically collapsed to 56 all out, more than half of which was extras.

Or it would have been all out.

I was batting at 10, and before the last wicket fell, I asked Ian, as it was looking so pathetic, if he minded all 12 of us having a bat. Of course, he said, no problem. Well, 56 for 10, you would, wouldn't you?

11 and 12 in the batting order were Henry and Clive. Which is odd enough in itself, as they are two of the better bats at our disposal on a Sunday. But they'd both enjoyed plenty of time in the middle of late – Henry had got a century the day before in the league game, and Clive lacked an average so far in the year, having yet to be dismissed – so had both volunteered to bat late or not at all.

Both could be described as in good form, without fear of contradiction. This was a democratic final pair.

Forty minutes later, Ian must have been beginning to rue his magnanimous decision to let us bat 12.

The numbers 89 and 42no were added to that batting card, Henry comfortably chalking up 200 runs in a weekend, Clive remaining unbeaten. A partnership of 157. Comfortably a Damerham last wicket record, even if it was for the eleventh rather than tenth.

What had begun as an embarrassingly low total ended up as an embarrassingly high one, and it was a very bizarre apology I was making to Ian over tea. "I'm really sorry, we seem to have got too many runs by mistake."

Rockbourne's collapse was almost as precipitous as ours, with Dave and young Sam both getting four-fer practically nothing.

One of their chaps batted again to make it up to 12, but they lacked the democratically random methods I had unwittingly employed, so they only had kids left at the end and it was never going to happen. All out for 105.

Another game we really shouldn't have won, but this one we didn't quite feel so good about. Except for Clive and Henry, of course. It's still their favourite subject.

chapter ■ 1 0

the media and the money

On the forces that are shaping our game whether we like it or not

In common with most advertising people, I find most advertising pretty distasteful.

It's embarrassing, really.

Like, say, if you work in tv, the way Deal Or No Deal must be embarrassing, even if you have nothing to do with it: it's telly, it's shit, ergo what you do must also be shit. Or if you're a journalist, the way Piers Morgan must be embarrassing.

Sports advertising – or anything a company does creatively to promote itself – can be entertaining, funny, sometimes even moving. Done well, it can be both inspiring and involving; a fan, bringing the game closer to the fans.

When it's bad it can be so terrible as to illicit a reflex out-loud groan, in the same way that awful puns can, or cause you to swear involuntarily at the telly, like Daily Mail columnists on Question Time can.

But when it's good, it can actually enhance your enjoyment of sport. It's part of the game, and even more than that, part of the cool gang.

Here's an example. September 1997. Ian Wright is poised to overtake Cliff Bastin's club record of 178 goals for Arsenal.

The club's kit sponsor, Nike, is among the most innovative and creative advertisers in the world. (Their agency, Wieden & Kennedy, have been doing fabulous work for them for many years. But clients must buy daring work, and the vast majority opt to be boring, so credit must go to Nike too.) Their strapline, 'Just do it', is a wonderful call to arms that resonates deep in the soul of sport itself.

In celebrating his goal, Wright pulled off his shirt over his head in time-honoured fashion. But this time it revealed a t-shirt beneath, printed on which was the Nike swoosh and the legend "179. Just done it."

Now, I'm indifferent about Wright, and Arsenal, and often football, come to that, but that is a simply inspired way to mark such a moment, and it's hard to feel anything but warmth towards a sponsor who is that under the skin, so to speak, of its subject.

(In fact, Wright messed it up, and got so over excited that he did it one goal too early, when he drew level with the record on 178, rather than when he beat it. But nobody cared. Particularly not when he scored again 10 minutes later.)

But when advertising in sport is bad, it is truly awful.

And when I say truly awful, Shane Warne, I am looking at you.

Yes, Warne's ads for hair loss treatment are cringeworthily terrible. It's hard to say if it's the insights into his personal rationale for re-growing his hair, or the to-camera awkwardness, or the horrific forced mateyness with Graham Gooch (who tends to get overlooked for his association just because Warney is so catastrophically bad, but frankly should be every bit as ashamed of himself). I can't quite put my finger on what it is exactly that makes them so terrible, but there's no doubt that they are among the most dismal ads ever created, and serve not only to put you off your dinner, but also to put you off two once very fine cricketers.

In a triumph for creativity as well as truth, the Advertising Standards Authority ruled that the ads – which basically imply they can reverse baldness – were 'misleading', which is industry slang for 'lying', so they were pulled.

The papers had fun with that, of course: "Warne ads have too much spin", "Hair loss claims dismissed", "Ad branded a wrong'un" etc etc. Ah, God bless the papers.

Warne exonerated himself to some extent when he went on to cause much embarrassment to Nicorette, the nicotine replacement therapy people, when he was caught on camera having a sneaky fag whilst he was supposed of have given up with the aid of the magic gum, an exercise for which he was being handsomely paid. He has an uncanny knack, even when he is screwing up, of endearing himself to the public by being such a cheeky schoolboy.

Kevin Pietersen, who it sometimes seems would give his right arm to be able to endear himself to the public, has done some press ads for Citizen watches, written by people who evidently don't follow cricket. They look like this: big picture of KP, big picture of a watch, headline: 'Unstoppable.' This is a well worn formula for celebrity endorsements, the clear implication being that the headline claim applies to both the product and its emissary. In this case, it is so far off the mark, it should be called a wide. Unstoppable? No, he's not. *It* may be, but *he's* definitely not. He's stopped all the time. He gets out to stupid shots – that's the main reason people get so irritated with him, because he's so prodigiously talented and yet insists on throwing his wicket away in ever more inventively stupid ways. Why use your advertising to draw attention to your spokesman's biggest fault? Can nobody involved see that? (More likely nobody involved thinks it's worth losing their job for saying it.) They're not going to get pulled up for it because it's a blatant fib about the player, not about the product. But that doesn't make it any less baffling. There are plenty of positive analogies and parallels that could be drawn between a swanky watch and England's finest South African, but 'unstoppable' isn't one of them.

Freddie's association with Sure deodorant made more sense. The 'tactical' ads running in the sports pages the morning after his Ashes five-fer at Lord's in 2009 worked quite well. A fresh-as-a-daisy Flintoff holding the ball aloft, the headline a simple list of his five Aussie victims, finished off with the assertion: 'No sweat.' All very neatly tied up. Of course, it's clearly a figure of speech rather than an actual product claim, as anyone who believes Flintoff didn't sweat in the course of taking those five wickets, regardless of what he may have sprayed on his armpits, is clearly unfamiliar with Fred and his methods, and certainly didn't bear witness to them that morning, but I suppose you've got to give people some sort of leeway.

There are plenty more, from Botham's breakfasts (three Shredded Wheat – the precursor to a thousand lager ads) and dinners (Beefy and Lamb; quite sweet, really) to the current England camp's collective efforts for Boss (camp is right), and Pedigree (a tad awkward and contrived). But I don't want to bleat on too much about ads; they are the least important of the media money thrown at cricket these days.

Logos. Logos is where it's at. In a lot of sports sponsorship, there's no room or time for a message or a story, all you get is a logo.

Formula One is the ultimate logo pin board, with the tiniest areas of carbon fibre bodyshell fetching astronomical prices.

The reason it commands the big money is that it is seen by so many people. F1 is globally popular, so a little sticker placed on a car in Woking will be seen by millions of people all over the world, week after week.

It used to define what a team looked like. The black and gold of the JPS Lotus was effortlessly cool, probably because it was so uncluttered.

(There's no doubt that it worked, too. As a teenage smoker, only JPS would do, and my love affair with Lotus continues unabated. And I didn't even follow F1.)

The long overdue ban on big tobacco (who, slowly choked of other advertising outlets, until recently hurled their not-inconsiderable budgets at F1) means that primary sponsors are less primary than they were. Today, you will be one of several dozen logos competing for space on a body that gets smaller every year, and as a consequence most cars look pretty much the same.

On a cricket shirt though, you stand alone. A solitary mark on a blank white canvas.

Vodafone spent well over ten times more putting their logo on an F1 car than they did putting it on England cricket shirts. Doubtless they know what they're doing; their association with England came to an end early in 2010. I guess that tells you everything you need to know about which they regarded as better value.

Sponsors on shirts are quite interesting. How big should that logo be? Why are they small and restrained on Test shirts, but allowed to dominate one day kits? Someone somewhere regulates this stuff obviously (the ICC or the ECB or someone; probably both), but I wonder what their reasoning is. Is it simply a tacit understanding that the short forms of the game are newer, brasher, and inherently more commercial, and the long form must be seen to be more deferential to tradition? How do they balance that with the injection of cash? I imagine there are committees for it, on which old men who don't really understand the question hurrumph into their beards.

Here's a subtle one: which sleeve should the sponsor's logo go on? The answer is it depends on his dominant hand. If you bat right handed, it will go on your left sleeve. So that when you're batting, the logo is facing the cameras.

Because cameras are what it's all about here – if you're actually at a game, you won't get close enough to identify the logos on players shirts.

In football now, the reason you don't see players stripping off their shirts as part of goal celebrations so much anymore, is because of pressure from the sponsors. Unlike Ian Wright's moment detailed above, usually there is no message on the striker's chest (unless you count the obligatory tattoos in Chinese or Arabic) and in the moments after a player scores the sponsor gets what he's paying for: a close up.

There it is, he's scored, he's running around the pitch looking ecstatic, the very embodiment of sporting achievement, and he's got YOUR NAME plastered across his chest – and then he takes it off and throws it away. No no no, this won't do at all.

An indication of how shirt sponsors are thinking came from Liverpool's new backers, Standard Chartered Bank, an organisation with no UK branches at all. There is a company clearly not chasing the scouse pound, but interested instead in the many millions of fans Liverpool Football Club has around the world.

There was a very interesting development in rugby recently. I don't profess to even understand much less follow rugby, but a lot of my friends do, so I'll often watch it just for the beer and the company. In a 2010 Six Nations game, to mark some sort of anniversary, England wore a replica of a classic strip: a simple skin-tight white affair with just the red rose over the heart, no logos. I thought (no-one else in the room did) that this was fascinating. That must have been an interesting meeting, the RFU telling O2 and Nike that yes, we still want your money, but no, you can't have your logos. But as the game wore on it became clear how that meeting had actually gone. The sponsors had not gone away empty handed after all. They'd negotiated a bicep each. Their 'stealth logos', as I decided they should be called, were white on white; white gloss transfers on white cotton, so they only showed up when the shirts got muddy. The money shot came close to full time, a thoroughly be-muddied Jonny Wilkinson lining up a penalty kick, absolutely still in close up, his face a study of concentration, the O2 logo burning brightly through the muck, whispering 'See What You Can Do' from one camera angle; the Nike swoosh, unblemished white on a background of mud, calmly urging 'Just Do It' from another. Bingo.

There are other indications that the sponsors are increasingly calling the shots in sport, too. Not only a monopoly on food and drink sold at games – the 'Official Drink', the 'Official Snack', etc – but actively banning rivals, presumably on the logic that if the camera picks out someone drinking Coke, why should Pepsi be footing the bill?

That particular example would be hard to object to, as both are enormous and neither is in need of sympathy or protection from bullying. It's when the little guys get thumped by the big guys that the whole thing becomes unseemly.

2006 seems to have been a good year for brand bullying. Dutch fans had to watch a football World Cup game in Stuttgart in their underwear when they were refused entry in their specially made orange lederhosen emblazoned with Bavaria beer logos. Official FIFA sponsors Budweiser with the graceless muscle flexing and sense of humour failure there. A few weeks later, in another staggeringly insecure bit of territorial posturing, a middle aged woman had her Alpro yogurts and milkshakes confiscated from her packed lunch at Wimbledon, at the behest of tournament sponsors Kraft.

It all sounds vaguely Orwellian, doesn't it? And also contrary to the very spirit of sport, with all its David and Goliath possibilities. For me, and I'm sure I'm not alone in this opinion, such ill-judged bluster has a violently counterproductive effect. Just as in sport itself, the biggest-kid-in-the-playground strutting tactics immediately makes me side with the underdog.

Ten years earlier, there was a terrific anti 'Official Drink' ad from subversive innovators Tango (and agency HHCL) during the European football championships in London. Mostly cross-track tube posters, if I recall, (literally underground advertising) it featured a small dog in a back garden with a burst cheap orange football in its enthusiastic jaws. It's rare for an ad to be plaintive, existential and rebellious all in one line, but this managed it: 'Tango – officially a drink during Euro 96'

I'm often given to wondering what companies get from sponsorship. Why they bother. Is it really beneficial to business for NatWest to sponsor the ODI series? I mean, I can see there's vast capacity for schmoozing there, obviously, lots of big clients treated to a day out and dinner and an endless free bar so that everyone ends the day even more in bed with each other than they were before.

But is that it? Surely they're not hoping for people (real people, I mean; paying punters, not corporate clients and partners) to change their bank account on the basis that they'd rather be with a bank that likes cricket, are they?

It seems unlikely they'd be that naïve. I've done a little bit of work for financial clients, and one of the little nuggets of 'fact' that get thrown at you during briefing sessions in agencies has stayed with me for years. It stuck in my head, I think, because it speaks of basic human laziness. It tells you a great deal about the kind of inconvenience we're prepared to ignore and put up with as just one of life's little irritants, and the kind of thing we will put ourselves through enormous hassle, heartache and expense to avoid. The nugget is this: you are statistically more likely to change your spouse than your bank.

For some companies it's purely about image. The airline Emirates seem to have decided to go for Arsenal and officials. Arsenal is straightforward enough: big London club, worldwide fan base, etc etc, but the officials one is interesting.

By sponsoring both football referees and cricket umpires at the highest level, they're saying something quite out of the ordinary about their brand. Referees and umpires are the voice of authority, often in the face of dissent and even aggression from players and fans (routinely in football, increasingly in cricket). Due to ever improving tv coverage, they're also increasingly in the spotlight for making errors that are apparent to everyone sat at home, and no-one sat in the ground, and so more than ever are the focus of a fair bit of often unfair frustration over controversial or 'bad' decisions. (See chapter 7 for more on umpires and umpiring.)

I think it's pretty bold. Simply by aligning themselves with the much maligned arbiters of top level sport, they are saying "Look, we're doing our best to get this right. We know how important it is to you, and we care about it too. We admit we get it wrong sometimes but our intentions are always honourable." No company, especially not an airline, could actually come out and *say* that. To admit their fallibility in so many words would be professional suicide. But via sponsorship they have conveyed a humility and humanity that no amount of champagne-trolley-dollies-and-legroom advertising could ever convey.

Others are perhaps less subtle. What's in it for npower, for example? An otherwise faceless power company, their relationship with cricket is now pretty entrenched. Most high profile, of course, is their sponsorship of every home Test match that England play. They also run a thing called Urban Cricket with the ECB and some big names like KP, an initiative focussed on getting city kids playing the game. And they sponsor the Village Cup (of which more later). All very worthy and laudable, no mistake.

But why? This is an energy company, operating on the tiniest of margins in an industry that, since privatisation, has become completely commoditised, with nothing to choose between competitors offering essentially identical services at essentially identical prices. They're not doing it out of the goodness of their heart, that much is certain; there must be solid financial reasons, an appreciable return on investment, or they simply wouldn't bother.

I, as it happens, am living testament as to why they bother.

If you've been to a Test match in England in the last decade or so, you will have come across the npower girls. These are pretty, shapely, nubile young women, predominantly blonde, presumably students, who wander around stadia in microscopic dresses in the npower corporate colours: red with flashes of green and white. To be honest they're difficult to miss.

As you file into a ground in the morning they smile sweetly and hand out free stuff. Lanyards to keep your match ticket in, those daft 4 and 6 cards to wave about whenever there's a boundary, that sort of thing. They're chatty and friendly.

At lunch, and particularly at tea, they patrol the walkways with clipboards, looking for mildly inebriated blokes in a good mood, which by that time are not in short supply, especially if both weather and cricket have been good.

In queues for ludicrously overpriced food and beer, they strike up conversations with middle aged men who remember a time (a distant and dimly remembered time, but a time nevertheless,) when pretty young girls used to come up to them and strike up conversations without a commercial imperative.

Even though they know they're being played, these poor fools allow themselves to be drawn into a conversation about who they get their gas and electricity from, and whether or not they'd be interested in the possibility of saving money by switching supplier.

And so it was, one beautiful afternoon between the media centre and the Nursery ground at Lord's, that I found myself signing a clipboard to the effect that yes, on reflection, I would indeed like to switch my energy supplier to npower. Apparently I did anyway. My memory of the event is a little hazy, but I got the confirmation through in the post so I guess I must have done.

Everyone, it seems, succumbs to the sponsor's buck sooner or later. Even at lowly Damerham CC, we now sport a logo across the front of our shirts.

Henry's boss, presumably in response to a certain amount of prompting from his employee, offered to pay for a permanent net cage for the club. As you will have understood, having read this far, we are not a big club, and certainly not a rich one. The idea of having a net up on the field had been floating about for decades before I even moved here. There was even a concrete strip which had been laid for the purpose some years ago. It has been so comprehensively not used, that it not only sprouted weeds, but had a park bench screwed down onto it. A lasting commitment to disuse, if ever there was one.

The problem, as ever, was money. Whichever way you cut it, a permanent weather proof net is expensive. The lion's share of a grand. Who's going to pay for that?

You can't 'fundraise' for that sort of thing. If a few dozen blokes humiliate themselves or otherwise put themselves out in some way to raise money, it needs to be for needy kids or something, not a thousand quid's worth of steel poles and netting. So we just continued to not have one for years and years.

GogoDigital offered to buy us a net, outright, no fuss. All he wanted in return was his logo on our shirts. If he sells a few DVD players as a result of people seeing it, he'll probably make his money back in no time. Who knows, we – and he – might even make the local papers if we have a decent run.

Everyone's a winner.

It's a microcosm, obviously, but that's exactly how sponsorship works at any level. The sponsor gets exposure: the more exposure he gets, the more it costs him. Every club, large or small, will have its sponsors, large or small.

There's an exception to every rule, and this one is Spanish football giants Barcelona.

Founded in 1899, FC Barcelona is one of only three clubs never to have been relegated from the top echelon of Spanish football, La Liga. They are one of the biggest and most successful football clubs in the world in terms of records and trophies, and second only to Real Madrid (arch rivals in every respect) financially. Extremely unusually for a football club, its 170,000 members own and operate it. Its motto "Més que un club" (More than a club) extends to its attitude to commercial sponsorship. For 107 years it never had a sponsor, its unadorned shirts shouting its principles louder than any logo ever could. The non-commercial stance made it iconic, gaining it followers around the world, and the club evidently revels in its status as every right-thinking football fan's second-favourite team.

When in 2006 a logo did appear for the first time on those famous maroon and blue stripes, there was much speculation. There must have been a lot of offers from some very big names for some very big money, as the first corporation to take Barcelona's sponsorship cherry would be guaranteed more exposure than any other.

The deal they struck was, I think, unique. As well as enormous integrity, it showed a complete understanding of the worth of the club as a global brand, and a willingness to exploit its image to the hilt, providing the circumstances were right.

The first logo on their shirt was that of Unicef, the worldwide children's charity, and their sponsorship deal involved a flow of money in the opposite direction from everyone else's: Barcelona paid Unicef for the privilege. Everyone's a winner.

There is one form of advertising that's been going on in cricket for hundreds of years. Ever since there was cricket, I suspect. So much so that it's become part of the game's vocabulary: the maker's name. To show the maker's name to the bowler is to play with a straight bat: correctly, solidly. (See glossary, and chapter 5 for more on cricket's language.) These days sticker designs are often flamboyant and extensive, covering much of the bat's surface, but the top part of the blade, over the splice below the handle, has always been and still is the preserve of the maker's name.

The two really big names in English cricket bats, Gray Nicholls and Gunn & Moore, have had batsmen pointedly showing their names to bowlers for centuries. (In fact, GM had a line on a point-of-sale poster [sorry: a poster in a shop] I saw many years ago which, if I were them, I would adopt as a strapline and slap on absolutely every bit of communication from stationery upwards: 'Making bats for centuries.' Isn't that lovely? Honestly, some people just don't know when they've got it good.)

In professional cricket, the batsman with a naked blade is announcing his lack of a bat sponsor. It's like an invitation to all the bat makers out there, a calling card reading simply 'gun for hire'. Naturally, most good batsmen get snapped up pretty quickly by the big names with the big money. If your business is selling bats, you want your bats in the hands of all the best batsman, so when the fans go bat shopping the first name they think of is yours.

This is basically how kit sponsorship works. We all know that, say, Ricky Ponting, is one of the best batsmen in the world. We see him using Kookaburra bats (and of course everything else: pads, gloves, shoes, etc). Intellectually, even the less bright of us are fully aware that Ricky Ponting would be a phenomenal batsman even if he was wielding the scuffiest old plank of wood from the bottom of the communal kit bag. But we can't shake the sneaking suspicion that if we had a Kookaburra like his, perhaps a little bit of magic might rub off. After all, if it's good enough for Ricky...

There are rumours that contracted batsmen might find a bat they prefer, from small name firms or local independent craftsmen, and then get these stickered up with their bat sponsor's name so that everyone is happy. If this is true – and I have no evidence whatsoever that it is, only hearsay – it would seem terribly underhand to me, and should surely be illegal.

The other end of the spectrum are the bat manufacturers who only seem able to secure the services of bowlers, who are by definition not batsmen. Like the New Zealand firm Aero, who make excellent and innovative pads and protective clothing, but are not famous for their actual bats. They have a good few (and indeed a few good) bowlers on their books, among them the formidably rapid Shane Bond and Lasith Malinger. But the only international player I remember seeing in head-to-toe Aero is Chris Martin, the New Zealand fast bowler who holds the dubious distinction of being the worst international batsman in the world, with an average in all forms of the game hovering around two. Surely that can't be helping their cause, can it? If ever a chap could expect to be lacking a bat sponsor, it would be he. Or maybe they're way ahead of me, and the message is 'If you're this bad, sod the bat, you need the best protection on the market.' I take it back. That's genius.

One of the biggest growth areas for advertising in cricket these days is the back of the bat. It seems an odd place to stick an arbitrary logo, until you think about what a batsman does when he acknowledges applause – he raises his bat. The fashion these days, doubtless driven by such sponsors, is to raise the bat backwards, so the back of it is facing the crowd as the batsman salutes them, displaying to the cameras how NatWest, Barclays Finance or whoever have helped him to his century.

Mostly these are just random institutions, with no link – what the industry calls a 'fit' – with a player at all. The exception seems to be KP; he and Red Bull are clearly made for each other. Most, for no apparent reason, appear to be financial institutions. At the other end of the 'fit' spectrum, it was highly amusing to listen to the indignation of Geoff Boycott as he wondered aloud on TMS what Yorkshire Bank were doing sponsoring fully-paid-up Geordie hero Paul Collingwood, unwittingly giving them way more publicity than they paid for and doubtless breaking all manner of BBC operating rules in the process, bless him. I like to imagine a planner in an agency somewhere (yes, they have people whose job it is to plan) arguing for it like this: "Look, this is the right move *because it's so wrong* – it's a brilliant use of the money because it's going to incense Geoffrey bleeding Boycott so much that all his co-presenters and all the king's men will be simply unable to stop him banging on about it for ten minutes. You just can't buy that kind of publicity." Probably not. Probably no-one really thought about it at all. The truth is more likely to be that someone high up in Yorkshire Bank is a cricket fan, and more specifically a Paul Collingwood fan.

Another odd phenomenon that seems to be gaining pace is the anti-logo. Again, presumably it's because there's an official supplier getting tetchy. Bits of kit – usually protective stuff, but sometimes bats too – will have their trademarks blotted out by bits of tape. It always seems to be bits of tape, and oddly, the favoured kind is the humble elastoplast. It's the damnedest thing. International cricketers, representing their countries, scrutinised by millions of people on telly, going out to bat with haphazardly applied bits of plaster stuck over the names on their pads and helmets. It's all very bizarre, like there wasn't time to remove them properly, or find a nice uniform white label, or even a sticker the same colour as whatever it's going on. It always looks completely unplanned and spontaneous, like it was done at the last possible minute, as if they were just walking out to bat and some brand Nazi at the pavilion door says "Hang on, you can't go out there with that written on there. Come here, I've got an old plaster somewhere, only been used once on me verruca. There. that'll be fine."

When professional sportsmen talk about 'the media' they overwhelmingly mean newspaper sports journalists.

We all like to read the expert's opinion and we all have our favourite experts, but the power they wield over players is sometimes a little too much.

There are countless thousands of examples. Here are just two – both instances of the press having a heavy-handed say in who gets to be England cricket captain.

A few years ago, England opening bat Andrew Strauss looked likely to have come to the end of his Test career.

It was the final Test at Napier, New Zealand, with the series tied 1-1. Strauss was suffering an extended run of poor form and was under enormous pressure to deliver, or lose his place.

The pressure did not appear to come from himself, or from his captain, manager or selectors. It came from the mainstream written media, who had collectively decided that Strauss had had enough chances.

No matter how much they might disagree, no set-up in professional sport can long withstand the collective clamouring for blood from the press box: it was tacitly understood that Strauss was in the red, and either he put some runs in the bank, or his credit was no longer good.

After a first innings duck, the pressure from the media reached a rolling boil. Like a crowd of kids forming a circle around a brawling pair in the playground, you could almost hear them chanting: "Drop, drop, drop, drop…"

Truly great players tend to respond to this kind of do-or-die pressure positively, and I'm all in favour of that – it can only add to the drama. I'm just not sure the press box is where the pressure ought to be coming from.

Strauss scored an imperious 177 in the second innings, steering England to a series victory, and has hardly looked back since.

He could easily have nicked one early, or fallen victim to a terrible LBW decision, and if he had England would have been denied a fine captain by their own media.

And it's not difficult to make the case that England's most successful captain ever was effectively hounded out by the press.

Michael Vaughan was a gifted leader and an excellent communicator. As well as being the possessor of one of the most elegant cover drives ever to grace the game, he spoke well, and was always an interesting interviewee.

But as his career progressed, he became more and more cautious with the press, and with good reason. Hanging on his every word, they sought meaning where there was none, pursued dead ends, and stood yapping endlessly up unoccupied trees. Sometimes their relentless probing yielded results. For instance, after he himself had overcome pressure for runs with a Test ton at his native Headingly, he gave a frank interview which touched on the World Cup 'Freddalo' incident. His disappointment with Flintoff's behaviour was reported as a 'Fred Let Us Down' type splash headline that drove a little extra wedge between the captain and his star player. It would be hard to convince anyone that this angle was chosen with the best of intentions. Was it intended to help further the cause of English cricket, or to help sell newspapers?

Towards the end of his tenure, Vaughan became guarded and bland. In the time-worn clichés the game has in abundance, he spoke of bowling in the right areas, taking out the positives from the situation, and the lads expressing themselves on the field. And who could blame him? If he talked meaningless rubbish, instead of being bright and open and engaging, they would have nothing to come after him with.

If that's what they wanted, that's what Michael Vaughan would give them. Yes, no doubt the most bizarre effect of media pressure on him was that Vaughan began referring to himself in the third person.

At his tearful and heartfelt resignation, he said he had to go because he was just desperate to be himself again. What an appalling way to treat our nation's most important cricketer! Vaughan was perhaps too decent a man to lay the blame for the untenability of his job entirely at the press box door, but it was clear to most observers that it was newsprint, not cricket, that he'd had enough of.

Happily, now that he has jumped ship, the bland Vaughan is gone and the interesting Vaughan is back with us on TMS, where he is a most welcome addition, proving to be as up for a scrap with the truculent Boycott as he was with the strutting Aussies.

Test Match Special is the flat, calm millpond between the two frothing whirlpools of controversy, the press box and the telly. 50 years on, it is as endearing and entertaining as ever.

The lovable cast of characters argue and prattle and opine about all manner of ephemera, cricket related or not, and provide excellent companionship for the five day duration of every Test match England play.

And often indeed when they don't play; in fact, many of the most enjoyable periods of TMS coverage are during rain breaks, when the contributors sit around a microphone and swap anecdotes, or discuss the merits or otherwise of players, grounds, formats, situations and cakes. The experience is one of eavesdropping on a conversation between fascinating strangers on a train or at a restaurant, but one that you feel strangely included in. Certainly the programme rarely fails to fulfil its ancient broadcasting brief, as noted in its excellent biography '50 Not Out', of always providing, over and above ball-by-ball commentary, 'good company'. Apparently, many of its most avid fans have no interest in cricket whatsoever, and tune in solely for the chat. These listeners must pray constantly for rain.

Its most famous moment, and justly so, remains the immortal 'legover incident' from 1991, easily findable online, in which 'Aggers' (Jonathan Agnew) and 'Jonners' (Brian Johnston) corpse spectacularly, collapsing into helpless puddles of upper-class-schoolboy laughter at a childish innuendo. The laughter is incredibly infectious, and I challenge anyone to listen to the entire two minutes of it without at least cracking a smile, and recommend it as medicine to anyone in the midst of a sense of humour failure. What's really funny is that they don't stop, their professionalism drives them forwards, and it's in trying and failing to carry on regardless that their utter helplessness is most hilarious.

It is odd that many journalists I find annoying and snarky in print, I find perfect companions on radio, as if the medium itself is a mellowing, softening influence, and somehow magically makes them more agreeable.

Another recent and welcome addition to the ever shifting voice cast, at least for games involving Australia, is Matthew Hayden, the powerful, bullying, swaggering Aussie opener who garnered grudging respect but never affection in his playing days, who turns out to be an eloquent, thoughtful, softly spoken gentleman in the commentary box, full of grace and insight.

TMS is a constant winter companion when England are touring abroad, and it is a strange thrill to be snuggled in bed at three in the morning with a hot water bottle on your feet and Aggers in your earphones, describing the suffocating dry heat and parched bare earth of Sri Lanka or somewhere equally exotic. You can feel the heat in their voices, and almost see the sweat dripping off bowlers labouring under a pitiless sun, as you weigh up the pros and cons of getting your feet cold for long enough to go downstairs and make another cup of tea. The pictures, as the old saying goes, are better on radio.

Mind you, it's hardly surprising that the TMS team always comes across as having so much fun, seeing as their 'job' is to follow summer around the world and yarn about it. There are many jobs I would love to do had I but the talent and the good fortune, and professional cricketer is certainly not least among them, but TMS summariser would I think be somewhere near the top of the list.

The media power that is really shaping the game of course, is not radio, newspapers, manufacturers, sponsors or advertisers. It's television.

Television is where all the money comes from, and the game is forever bending to feed its insatiable needs.

Sponsors and advertisers may be intrinsically tied up with it, because ultimately they are the forces that steer television, but it is the tv companies that call the shots with cricket's governing bodies.

The government's decision not to safeguard England's home Tests – at the very least the Ashes – on free-to-air telly (like Wimbledon, The Grand National, The FA Cup, The World Cup, The Olympics, etc) is shameless, and inexplicable.

The ECB's subsequent decision to take the money from Sky and have no live England cricket on UK free-to-air television at all was, to say the least, controversial.

Their argument is: the extra money will find its way into the grass-roots of the game, funding youth and local cricket.

My argument is: what's the point of funding kids' cricket if kids never get to *see* cricket? In an age of media saturation, where you can't move for football on every kind of telly, free and subscription, kids are going to struggle to get fired up about a game they never get to watch. Alistair Cook is never going to be any kid's hero if he doesn't know who Alistair Cook is. It is short term, narrow, blinkered thinking, and if we're really lucky it will only suffocate the game for one generation.

If you are already enough of a fan and prepared to pay for it, Sky's live cricket coverage is fine. Their unfathomable insistence that no-one be allowed near the commentary box unless they're an ex-international – preferably an ex captain – can be a little tiresome, as some of them are, shall we say, not microphone naturals. But enough, such as the incomparable zeal of David 'Bumble' Lloyd, are good enough to compensate. Personally, I'd happily listen to Michael Holding's lazy Jamaican treacle-over-gravel drawl saying anything at all, but when he wraps those vowels around such sub-continental tongue twisters as Tillekeratne Dilshan or Mahela Jayewardene, they suddenly sound more like poetry than names.

What's really annoying about Sky though, is their complete incomprehension of the concept of 'highlights'. The only concession they make is a two hour cut-down of a day's Test cricket. Other than that, if you don't watch it live, you're stuffed. All you can do is record it and fast-forward through it, in a sort of do-it-yourself highlights package, if you happen to find yourself with less than six hours spare of an evening. And while we're at it, Mr Murdoch, how about an end-of-Test or end-of-series recap, with some best bits and some expert analysis from all those ex international captains you've got loafing around? Hmm? That too much to ask for £35 a month is it matey?

It's deeply irritating, especially as now they have the exclusive rights, they hardly have the excuse, as terrestrial or other free-to-air channels would, of not having room in the schedule. There are four dedicated Sky Sports channels, mostly showing riveting contests along the lines of International Hedgehog Racing at 4am, so I'm sure they could find room somewhere for a half hour what-happened-today round up or an hour's look-back-at-the-series if they really tried. Unlike live coverage, in these days of Sky+ and the like, it doesn't matter when it's on.

But anyway.

Telly is the real power in cricket, as has been the case for a long time. It began in earnest with Australian mogul Kerry Packer, back in the late seventies.

The 'Packer Revolution' is a story that has been very well documented by far more knowledgeable observers than me, (I particularly recommend the section covering him in the Wisden Anthology 'Cricket's Age of Revolution' 1978-2006) but here's a very quick précis.

It was essentially an argument over TV rights. Packer was a flash, brash, media tycoon, who clearly rubbed Cricket Australia up the wrong way. If they had been reasonable with him from the start, it would probably never have happened. That might perhaps have meant that cricket died a slow, quiet, dignified death, literally while no-one was watching. We'll never know.

Basically, he was cricket-mad, and wanted the rights, and they wouldn't sell them to him. So he thought, sod you then, if you won't let me play your game, I'll buy the players instead of the rights, and put on my own games. My bat, my ball, my telly. The authorities held all the cards, so Packer changed the game, and suddenly the cards they held were worthless. Whatever you think of arrogant Aussie moguls, chutzpah like that deserves respect, however grudging. This guy meant business.

International cricketers at the time where poorly paid, and Packer offered them big money to come and play for him in what he called World Series Cricket. Dozens went, from Australia, England and West Indies, then the dominant forces in the world game. Traditional international cricket was robbed overnight of the cream of world talent, and it blithely tried to carry on as if nothing was happening.

There is more to the story, but in short, Packer won, the authorities backed down and he got his TV rights. But in the process the game had been launched forcibly and awkwardly from the eighteenth into the twentieth century, and there was no going back. Batting helmets, garish clothing covered in logos, white balls, one day games under floodlights, big money sponsorship, superstar millionaire players, multi-camera, gimmick-heavy, over-excitable TV coverage – all of this is thanks to Packer.

At the time, the establishment was deeply fearful and suspicious of him. But on his death in 2005, he was universally lauded by that same establishment as a far-sighted visionary who gave cricket the kick up the backside it needed to make it the global audience money spinner it is today.

Which, if you were feeling charitable, you could use as an argument for why Texan billionaire Sir Allen Stanford wasn't immediately shooed away the moment he started sniffing around Lord's like a horny dog, a few short years after Packer's death.

He was welcomed, one could argue, if one were so inclined, because the ECB felt the hand of history on its shoulder when approached by an obnoxious cricket-mad entrepreneur with no obvious class, but piles and piles of obvious cash.

His cash was so obvious, in fact, that his private helicopter flew $20m of it into Lord's in a large glass box full of used notes, while ECB bigwigs David Collier and Giles Clarke fell over themselves in the rush to fawn at his feet, and knights-of-the-realm cricket legends Ian Botham and Viv Richards lent their approval to his presence.

Yes, even before it all started to go horribly wrong, the whole thing was a desperate embarrassment for all concerned.

That Stanford summer culminated in a much publicised '20 20 for 20' clash between England and the Windies at a purpose built stadium in Antigua – the winning side receiving twenty million dollars. $20,000,000. For one game of T20.

Lunacy. But hard to ignore. Even as we tutted and shook our heads at how venal and crass and generally wrong and bad for the game it all was, I was organising a beer-and-crisps-and-sidebets evening round at mine.

The eleven of us spilling beer and dropping crisp crumbs in my lounge wouldn't have made a bad side. It was remarked upon more than once that we couldn't really have made a worse fist of it than England, losing as they did by 10 wickets. Jack won most of the sidebets, I seem to remember (score after five overs, wickets after 10, etc), though he didn't do quite as well out of it as the 11 West Indian cricketers – most of whom didn't bat or bowl – who became instant dollar millionaires that night.

Stanford spent the evening wandering around his own stadium being filmed by his own camera crew and shaking hands with everyone who couldn't get away fast enough. He then strolled into camp England like he owned the place, which of course he did, and entreated the England WAGs to sit on his lap and bounce on his knee; an episode that looked uncomfortably like the school bully flirting with the cool crowd, and brought to mind Biff from Back to the Future forcing himself on Marty's Mum.

Fortunately, the following spring we were all spared further squirming when Sir Allen was arrested by the FBI, wanted for $8 billion worth of "massive ongoing fraud". No wonder he was happy to hose around $20 million of an evening.

The ECB hastily distanced itself from him, giving back money, cutting all ties and sweeping the whole unhappy affair under the carpet.

Which is where it belongs really. The only people to look back on it fondly are those 11 cricketers, some of whom came from very poor backgrounds indeed, who won the lottery than night in Antigua. And perhaps Jack, who probably won about £30.

(There was one innovation which, amid all the excitement over money and wives and rather cool looking black bats, quietly made its debut. It was a tv umpire review system with the onus placed squarely on the tv umpire, rather than the players; a vastly more sensible procedure than the ICC's 'decision review system' which is currently interfering with Test matches and encouraging kids around the globe to argue with umpires. More of that in chapter 7.)

What Stanford did though, was put T20 firmly in the spotlight, and demonstrate the big tv audience potential of top flight cricketers playing the game's most basic form.

The IPL (Indian Premier League) has taken that to its logical conclusion – a big loud mixture of celebrity, cash, advertising and telly rights that sweeps all before it.

T20 is nothing new. People have been playing it in summer evenings after work for generations. If you want a midweek game of cricket, obviously you need a short one, a game you can start at six o'clock and be all over before nine.

What's new is that no-one ever took it seriously before. If you played cricket for a living, you did so during the day, and you took all day about it.

The IPL is a circus of sponsorship, a feeding frenzy of advertising and association. It arrived pretty much fully formed in 2008, masterminded by commissioner Lalit Modi. An auction was held for the world's best short-format players, and the eight franchised teams snapped them up for up to a million dollars each. The teams represent Indian regions or cities, and each comes attached with a talismanic captain and at least one Bollywood star and one unimaginably rich business mogul. Space for logos on the team shirts is fast becoming more tightly contested than F1 cars. As well as its own dedicated YouTube channel, telly rights are going for hundreds of millions in dozens of countries.

Modi and Packer would have got along just fine.

Before he departed from his brainchild amid a storm of money-related scandal (or simple accountancy oversights, depending on who you believe), Modi was described, seemingly without irony, by serious cricket people, as a 'Moses of the game', as a 'modern Charlemagne, with a little touch of Frederick the Great', and as 'a successor to Gandhi in Gucci loafers'. His stated ambition was for the IPL to be bigger than both English Premier League football and the National Football League in the US. With a cricket-obsessed audience of 1.2 billion in India alone, let alone the rest of the world, it would seem unwise to bet against him. The IPL, with or without Modi (it looks set to be without him, as he's been ostracised by the BCCI), looks here to stay.

It can be exciting. In the very first IPL game in 2008, New Zealand biffer Brendan McCullum smashed 158 not out off just 73 balls, including 13 sixes. It was a hell of a calling card. Modi must have been peeing his pants.

100,000 seater stadiums are routinely packed out, music and dancers and fireworks are constant accompaniments, close games are common, and some of the cricket on display really is astonishing, as you would expect from the world's most aggressive players in such a charged environment.

It is, however, a game completely devoid of subtlety and finesse, and this is reflected in the tv coverage.

Delhi Land and Finance, according to Wikipedia, is the world's largest real estate firm. Not living in India, I had never heard of them. But as soon as they handed over however-many millions to be the tournament's title sponsor, as a cricket fan curious about the IPL, I was guaranteed to.

What they negotiated as part of their deal was that commentators would be forced to embarrass themselves every time a six was hit by referring to it not as a six, but as a "DLF maximum". Considering how many sixes there are in T20 at the very highest level, that's a lot of embarrassment.

I thought that was pretty tacky, but they were just getting warmed up.

Citigroup, the US financial services company, have the poor commentators contractually obliged to drivel on about a "Citi moment of success" every time a wicket falls or fortunes in a game change.

Karbonn Mobile (an Indian mobile phone hardware firm) have sponsored something called a Karbonn Kamaal Katch. This is supposed to be awarded to the best catch in a game, which means the commentators tell us excitedly that every catch could be a Karbonn Kamaal Katch. I had to look this up: kamaal is a Hindi word which translates as 'amazing' or 'magically wonderful'.

I imagine if a ball that would have gone for six is caught on the boundary in a game-changing moment, some poor commentator is likely to explode as he tries to fulfil all of his sponsors' contractual name-checks.

Whilst wiping the rabid foam of raw capitalism from his chin, the poor chap would probably have to call for a Maxx Mobile Strategic Time Out to calm down. There's a slice of real gall – a calculated pause built into the game's shortest format, the purpose of which is thinly dressed up as tactical, but is clearly just an excuse for an extra long ad break, as if one per over was simply not sufficient.

Maybe it's a cultural difference, and in India these things are seen as tasteful and measured. Certainly to western palates they are little short of vomit inducing. The 'Citi moment of success', I think, takes the prize as the most wincingly clumsy, but all of them are pretty loathsome. I have a suspicion it's not cultural though, and the Indian fans just manage to ignore it better than me.

And better than the commentators, it seems. Apparently, on condition of anonymity, some of the former cricketers the IPL employs as commentators told Cricinfo that they didn't want to be seen as 'shameless salesmen', and a deal has been reached whereby only every third six, on average, will have to be called a DLF Maximum. Well, that's them in the clear then. Good job they neatly sidestepped that 'shameless' banana skin. Close call.

How will cricket look when the IPL dust settles? Will the international game lose the cream of its players again, as with Packer? Will the ECB shuffle the County and England seasons to allow players to play IPL without a clash of loyalties? Will the ICC have any clout left at all? Will the YouTube generation stay awake long enough to watch a Test Match? Will balls, bats, stumps and pitches change beyond recognition to make the game yet more exciting and immediate? Will the dust ever settle? Who knows.

There is much talk about T20 being the death of Test cricket, and if that were to happen it would truly be a tragedy.

Certainly it is to some extent in the hands of the players. If the very best players in the world elect to ignore Test cricket, it will cease to be relevant. But that seems unlikely, and the world's best seem to be largely in agreement that it remains the most challenging stage on which to prove real, lasting class.

I have a feeling that the long format of the game will survive because of the richness of the experience it offers spectators, as well as players. No other game can gather a steady crescendo of individual and team efforts to a final morning when all three results – win lose or draw – are equally likely. And for me at least, there are no sporting spectacles more thrilling than a tightly contested Test draw.

Besides, new things are always being heralded as the death of established things. Cinema was going to destroy radio, television was going to wipe out cinema, and the internet was going to sweep them all before it. All continue to thrive. As will cricket, in its many forms, let us hope.

But what sort of place will it thrive in?

Lord's, the home of cricket, is the figurative standard bearer for the game's traditional values, and the literal one for the 'spirit of cricket' as a thing to be revered and cherished.

Though T20 and one-day games are both played there, the kind of cricket it stands for is Test and County cricket. First Class cricket. Men in whites against lush green. The real thing, unchanged, as it's been for centuries.

But Lord's itself is changing*.

The walls are coming down, for a start. The austere 12ft walls around the Nursery Ground end at Wellington Road are to be removed, opening Lord's to the public gaze. Whether or not this is intended as a symbolic gesture, it is one.

Luxury flats will be built, as well as restaurants, shops, a library, more parking, and all manner of other facilities. Including a vast complex *under* the Nursery ground.

A century ago, railway tunnels were built under the nursery ground in exchange for some extra land. Now disused, they will be extended to form a new academy said to house ten pitches that will simulate conditions overseas using different types of synthetic grass. The underground complex will also house a clinic, gym, spa and squash courts.

Stands will be torn down and replaced. Capacity will rise to 40,000.

There was a 10 year plan for redevelopment, but members don't want to watch cricket in a building site for a decade, so the plan now is to get money in quickly to speed up the process.

Advertisements will be placed across the world's press, from the FT to the South China Morning Post. From Wall Street to

---

*At the time of publication, development plans are on hold again, a victim of recession and boardroom disagreements. But it's only a matter of time.

Mumbai, investors will be contemplating putting hundreds of millions into the home of cricket.

One thing the MCC has been very firm about, is that the name is not up for grabs. We will never have to watch the Ashes contested at an Arsenal style Emirate's Stadium. Or Littlewood's Lord's. Or the Hula Hoop Home of Cricket. Whatever else may be different, and however much the ground or the game may change, Lord's will remain, in name at least, Lord's.

Some things, it seems, are sacred after all.

Hallowed turf

In 1970, the president of the MCC had lunch with the editor of The Cricketer *magazine at Lord's. The two discussed ways to promote the National Cricket Association, and together they hatched a plan to start something they would call the National Village Cricket Championship, but everyone else would call the Village Cup.*

They decided it should be a competition between 'proper' cricketing villages. A village, for their purposes, was defined as a rural settlement of not more than 2,500 inhabitants surrounded by open countryside. That figure has today been doubled, which is fair enough, but the organisers are still insistent that to compete, clubs must represent a village. Towns are expressly disqualified.

The organisation of that first competition was quite something. This was nearly 30 years before Google, don't forget, so they looked up potential villages on the map, bless 'em, and wrote to them, sending letters to either the pub or the garage.

Amazingly – and rather reassuringly – they had over 1,000 responses, and nearly 800 teams eventually took part in the first competition two years later, pretty much double the numbers these days.

Damerham was one of those 800 teams. According to Graham, our Secretary then and now, who has an encyclopaedic knowledge of the club's fortunes down the years, we were soundly thrashed in the first and only game, and 'decided to give it a miss' the following year.

These days, however, we have decided to miss it no more. Today the competition is of course run on the internet, and is organised by The Cricketer.

The prize though, is the same today as it was when it started. It is the essence of the idea, the reason, surely, that it was a success, and why it's still going: the final of the Village Cup is played at Lord's.

Whether you have been there or not, if you watch, play or otherwise love the game, Lord's, the home of cricket, holds a special place in your heart.

I love Lord's. It is genuinely one of my favourite places in the world. I know it is ridiculous, a fossil from an England that no longer is, and the ECB/MCC mentality that still hamstrings the progress of cricket in the modern world infuriates me as much as the next inhabitant of the twenty-first century, but I still love it.

For all that is so patently wrong with such an elitist icon to a damp eyed Guardian reader like me, there is something so magnificent about it and its blend of sport and history that I can't help but forgive it. The MCC pavilion is one of the few symbols of Empire that remains exactly as it was, as if it's in some unlikely Dr Who plot, locked in a stasis field, impervious to the passage of time.

In its very ridiculousness lies its appeal. It's the only major sporting venue left in the country where you can take your own bottle of wine. How civilized is that? Watching cricket at Lord's feels bigger, more important, less trivial. More crickety. It is a thick and heady pleasure that even the watered down fizzy beer and endless corporate tattery cannot spoil.

To play at Lord's! There can't be many who've ever felt a ball come off the middle of a bat, or watched stumps splayed and bails fly, who have not daydreamed about doing it at Lord's.

Striding, padded up, through the Long Room, perhaps doffing a cap to the assembled members and wellwishers with a nervous smile, before turning to trot down those steps to the impossibly green, impossibly flat (apart from the slope, of course; did you know the Grand Stand is 8'8" above the Tavern Stand? Yes of course you did,) lush splendidness that is the Lord's outfield.

A daydream such as this lurks in the depths of every middle-aged cricketer's mind, sufficiently well buried as to never be unveiled in public, of course, and therefore safe from ridicule. Except that, really, the only reason to enter the Village Cup is the possibility of playing at Lord's, so in fact all those playing in it reveal precisely that boyhood fantasy to any who care to look. But then, anyone who knows enough about it to be able to point this out to you is probably in the same position, so we're all safe.

The lure of the Village Cup then is that, before it starts, you are nine wins away from a Lord's final. Nine. That's all.

It soon becomes clear, however, that getting to play at Lord's is still almost astronomically unlikely for the average village cricketer.

The standard of cricket in the Village Cup gets very high very quickly as you progress. Winning one game could be likened to getting the first question right on Who Wants to be a Millionaire. *Or getting one lottery number.*

The joy of knockout cup games, for a little village cricket club like ours, is the opportunity to play teams who really should thrash you every time. Teams who run, say, five or six sides. They've got nets and covers and sightscreens and hard bouncy pitches and umpteen colts teams and coaches and slip cradles and a large pool of talent to draw from. Including girlfriends who don't stop at coming to watch: they've been on scoring courses and do the books in a dozen different coloured pens so you can tell who faced which bowlers and all that sort of thing. We might meet their fifths in the league maybe. But in the cup it'll be mostly the first team. There's a lot riding on it – Lord's! – and they are not going to field a weak side. Good players. 16 year olds with trials for Hampshire. 23 year olds with trials for MCC. That sort of thing. It's an experience we would never be afforded otherwise.

We have nothing to lose. They, correspondingly, have everything to lose. "You lost to WHO?" being the essence of cup glory. They're not going to lose, of course, but they don't know that yet.

The giant-killing possibility – a team of mechanics and electricians from Devon beating Chelsea on a puddle of a pitch the size of the Stamford Bridge press box – might even make them a bit nervous, which can only help our cause.

Let's look at the positives here. What else might help our cause? Well, our wicket is by nature low and slow, which they won't be used to. Most of our bowling is similarly low and slow, which they also won't be used to.

The worse case scenario for us is an away game when it's bright and sunny and dry, there's pace and bounce in the pitch, and the ball races on just like classy, orthodox batsmen prefer it to. Who's that going to help?

The best case scenario then, our best chance of giving good sides a good run for their money, is a home game in indifferent weather. Ideally it will have rained a bit in the week, and perhaps the night before. Not too much, but enough to give us a sticky dog (see glossary) of a wicket where the ball mooches reluctantly onto the bat with all the urgency of a stroppy teenager with revision to do. The worse the conditions, the better.

A few years ago we won our first round game, and were then drawn against Tichborne Park, a side half a dozen divisions above us in the Hampshire league. The weather had been dodgy all week, and overnight it tipped down. By nine on Sunday morning, the sun was out and fluffy white clouds were scudding across in a stiff breeze. The wicket looked good, and in five hours it'd be perfectly blow dried.

We dared hope. It was ideal!

Then the wind dropped, it started to rain again, the sun retreated behind a solid bank of grey, it rained some more, then a bit more, and the wicket was reduced to a muddy skid pan.

So close. So close to having a fighting chance.

Though they'd had a wasted hour's journey to us, Tichborne were quite happy. According to the Village Cup rules, a match postponed for rain is held at the other side's ground the following week. They knew the significance of this as they sat by the fire in The Compasses that filthy Sunday afternoon and filled up on Summer Lightning.

The following week got slowly better, and the Sunday was, I think I'm right in saying, the hottest day of the year. Their ground was, as expected, enormous, with a hard bouncy track like a road. Also as expected, they gave us a right good walloping. They won the toss and batted first in unbroken sunshine, strolling to 338-6 in 40 overs, comfortably the highest score against a Damerham side anyone could remember.

I took a wicket that day, my usual type: a skied top-edge. Caught at cover, I think. I nearly got two, but I also nearly got killed. The batsman strode rather than danced down the pitch, and walloped the ball hard and flat. It was a lovely solid shot, the shot of a good batsman no longer prepared to pussyfoot around with average bowling. He didn't quite middle it though so it stayed low, and as it passed me at head height I stuck out my hand to it instinctively, one of those you don't get a say in, and only realise you've done it after the fact. One in ten might have stuck. This time though, it ricocheted off the pad of my thumb into my forehead, leaving a perfectly seam-shaped cut above my eye as a rather pleasing battle scar. Pleasing because it didn't hurt much but bled quite a lot, and gave me the opportunity to say 'No, no, I'm fine' like I was soldiering bravely on, and because it was very clearly a cricket injury and made an excellent 'Ooow, how did you do that?' story for several weeks afterwards. And it stopped a certain four.

The sole ambition at tea was not to be all out.

If they had wanted to, or felt at any point that their total was under threat, they could have kept on with their opening bowlers – one of whom was properly rapid – and doubtless changed up a gear or two to ensure that we didn't make it to 40 overs. Fortunately they were happy to play cricket, and we were 132-8 at the close. Thrashed, but not embarrassed.

We may never know how close we could have run them on a soggy Damerham pitch. Which is probably just as well, as I secretly suspect the answer would have been 'not very close at all', but it was a fun game of "what if" that wet afternoon in the pub.

In fact we generally agreed that being so comprehensively outclassed was actually quite a fun experience. Not one you'd want every week, certainly, but oddly enough it gave us a strange sort of confidence back in our own league.

More recently we had a less positive experience with far more grand hosts. After byes through the first two rounds we were drawn away against the world famous Hambledon.

Talk about hallowed turf. Hambledon is cricket royalty, and I was really rather excited about it. Established sometime in the mid seventeen hundreds, it soon became the foremost club in the country. It attracted noblemen and gentry, largely because of the opportunities for gambling it afforded, as well as early professional players. In the club's heyday, Hambledon sides regularly defeated All England XIs.

Here's Benny Green, from his comprehensive "A History of Cricket":

> "A great miracle was once wrought on this grass, under the patronage of these benign hills. The most complex, the most beautiful, the most profound of all ball games was born here, was nursed and nurtured until it was strong enough to stride out into the great world beyond. Under the skies of Hambledon, to the accompaniment of bird-song and the humming of bees, the plick-plock of the bat against the ball first echoed on the English air. Hambledon is the acknowledged birthplace of cricket, for which reason it will retain for ever a privileged niche in the pavilion of English history."

Though its genuine origins are sparsely documented, the game, or some version of it, was probably at least a few centuries old by the time of Hambledon's golden age, around the 1770's. What it really added, was structure.

The Club was the custodian of the Laws (until 1787, when the responsibility passed to the MCC) and introduced, among other things, the limit of four and a quarter inches as the width of the bat, and, rather fundamentally, the third stump.

It was also here that the game's language was coined, or at least first written down. The 'off' and 'on' sides, 'over', 'wide', 'no ball', 'LBW' and so on. Ever since that time, the game has inspired people to write about it. Benny Green again: "There is a curious symbiotic relationship between cricket and the writing of good English. Not only does cricket, more than any other game, inspire the urge to literary expression; it is almost as though the game itself would not exist at all until written about."

I can't imagine what he means.

Anyway. We arrived at Hambledon's new ground (the original is no longer deemed good enough or big enough for higher league cricket) in dribs and drabs, a bit hungover, a bit tired.

On the outfield, 15 be-six-packed athletes were performing the kind of slick fielding drills you see before internationals. They took every catch, hit a single stump as often as not, and throw after throw came in from the boundary hard and flat. Not intimidating at all.

Al was captain, won the toss and decided to bat. Despite five ducks, we made it to the humiliation-free zone of three figures, due largely to a Paul and H partnership. (The competition's lowest score batting first was Marston St Lawrence, who were all out for six against Abthorpe in 1978. There are four other totals in single figures.)

Disappointingly, a few – not all – of the Hambledon boys felt the need to behave like they were Australia playing England in the 90s. There was a lot of sledging, much of it personal or just plain rude. Their captain was the worst culprit. Why a side seven leagues above us felt the need to behave like spiteful children, as if the manifest superiority of their cricket would not be sufficient, was quite baffling. Clearly it is what they're used to in the Southern Premier League. I do not envy them; it must be an unpleasant way to spend your Saturdays.

They knocked the runs off in 13 overs. The high point of the day came in the first over, when Captain Chippy, having smashed the first ball for four, smashed the third straight to Paul at extra cover. Paul wordlessly favoured him with an enormous toothy grin as he trudged off, presumably in an even worse mood than before, which lifted ours considerably.

Their behaviour was all the more disappointing, perhaps, because of the weight of history their name carries. As a cricket team, they were pretty good. As custodians of the spiritual home of a game world famous for its reputation for decency, fairness and gentlemanly conduct, they left rather a lot to be desired.

The welcome was quite a contrast a mile up the road at The Bat and Ball pub, opposite the Broadhalfpenny Down ground – the original hallowed turf. It is well worth a visit if you are interested in the history of the game. The walls are lined with artefacts, pictures, scorecards and copies of the early rules written within those very walls, and the owners are knowledgeable about the collection and happy to share what they know. Kind of like the Lord's museum, only with beer.

rain stops play

On whether or not

Cricket is an absolute slave to the weather.

Heavy fog, frost or snow will stop most outdoor games, but the majority can cope with a little drop of rain.

It's got to rain pretty damn hard for a golf tournament to be cancelled. (Remember Tiger's 81 in a howling gale at Muirfield in 2002? That's proper golf that is, young Tiger m'boy.)

Rain is fine for football and good for rugby, aiding the slippy sliddyness and general lets-get-all-muddy-ness of it all.

But cricket is up there with tennis in the water-averse stakes. It's positively hydrophobic. During the season, especially when the weather is as bad as it's been in recent years, there are precious few fixtures that are not in doubt right up to the toss.

It really doesn't take very much rain at all to make a cricket field a pretty miserable place to be. Footing is difficult, whether you're batting, bowling or fielding, and a wet ball quickly becomes heavy, reluctant to get off the square, difficult to bowl and like a bar of soap to catch.

Rain stops play. It really does.

I imagine this is probably fine if you live in a country where the climate suits a game best played in the warm and the dry. I imagine. I don't actually know, of course. Maybe people in Australia, or South Africa, or the West Indies, or Ind... hang on. Maybe people who live... *everywhere else that cricket is played* could tell us what that's like. No wonder they all beat us.

It is odd that so much of a game that relies so heavily on dry weather should be played in a country that has so much rain.

But it is. And that makes all of us slaves to the weather, and therefore, slaves to the weather forecast.

The relentless march of technology means accessing up-to-date weather forecasts becomes easier all the time. Unfortunately, the relentless march of technology has clearly offered no help whatsoever in improving the accuracy of the actual weather forecasts themselves.

Now, I'm a big fan of the BBC. Big fan. A fan of its licence-fee structure and public-service mission as a general principle, and specifically a fan of its news, sport and arts programming on both telly and radio, as well as on its labyrinthine and in-all-respects excellent website. (Enforced cuts to BBC budgets and licence revenues, incidentally, on a mildly political hobby horse here for just a second, amount to nothing short of cultural vandalism to a unique and irreplaceable national treasure, and should make us all, as a nation, deeply ashamed.)

So naturally enough, BBC weather is usually my first port of call on the web. There are two major aspects of BBC weather that the regular user will notice. The first is that, to a staggering degree, it is almost always wrong. They would surely arrive at more accurate predictions by simply looking out the window and having a guess. Alternatively, perhaps they could do worse than to go ahead and consult the experts at the Met Office, then publish more-or-less the opposite of what they tell them.

(At the time of writing, The BBC is considering not renewing its contract with the Met Office, who have been doing their weather for 87 years. They put the contract out to tender ostensibly to ensure "best value for money". Presumably that would involve a level of accuracy somewhere in excess of 'none at all'.)

The second thing you notice is its tendency to be excessively pessimistic. Not just wrong, but cheerfully predicting wetter, windier and gloomier conditions than usually come to pass. So much so that I suspect the people who run it are either cricketers (and therefore predisposed to gloominess about the possibility of rain) or they harbour a passionate hatred of cricketers and want them to be miserable.

The beeb are not the most pessimistic precipitation predictors though. No, that accolade rests with the good people of Apple, via the weather application in OSX's 'dashboard' and on the iPhone. They clearly don't do it out of spite towards cricketers, as they are from California and therefore neither know nor care what cricket is. Their pessimism can be more believably attributed to the fact that most people in California think it rains in England pretty much all the time. Which, on the basis of the last few years at least, is understandable.

So in search of better news I'll go to other sites, one after another, my desktop cluttering up with windows full of weather. Metcheck, The Met Office itself, Will it Rain Today? The Weather Outlook, Weather Maps. Most if not all of them, presumably, get their raw data from the same place, so you might assume their content would all be broadly similar. You'd be wrong though. Even the beeb and The Met Office are not consistent, despite the well publicised fact that one gets its information directly from the other. They are often wildly different, some offering bright sunshine, others torrential rain.

I wouldn't mind if forecasts were presented with at least the passing possibility that they might not be accurate. On TV, radio, print and the web, tomorrow's weather is presented in absolute terms: it WILL do this or that. Not might. WILL. They are possessed of the same laughable certainty as rabid creationists.

In the same way that if you get all the colours in a paint set and mix them all together you end up with a dirgy sludgy brown, if you take a rough average of six or seven weather forecasts, you end up with the sort of dirgy sludgy day that passes for summer in England. Some rain, some sun, some wind, some cloud, bad light.

True, you could easily have arrived at that conclusion without wasting your time fiddling about on the internet by simply looking up. But where's the fun in that?

Checking the sites is an almost daily ritual, the intensity of which doesn't seem to change regardless of whether the prognosis is good, bad or indifferent. It's an unhealthy preoccupation, a turbo-charged combination of the Englishman's famous obsession with the weather, and cricket's absolute slavery to it.

There comes a point of course, when all the forecasts are

irrelevant, and that point is the morning of the match.

I live a couple of biggish sixes away from our ground – I am by far the closest to it. The phone calls the morning of a game can begin as early as nine o'clock.

Saturday morning, if we're lucky, our girls will get themselves up, sneak downstairs, get themselves some milk and happily ensconce themselves in front of the telly for a couple of hours. This is our lie in. At nine o'clock we'll be lying there, dozing, wondering which one of us is going to crack, (it's always me,) get up and make the tea to bring back to bed with the paper that's sitting on the mat, waiting patiently to be read.

Then the phone will ring. Soph will groan, mutter something along the lines of "Here we go," and pull the duvet up over her head.

On a Saturday, one of them will definitely be captain Mark. He lives ten miles away down near the coast, so his weather and our weather are often completely different. It could also be any of the rest of the team, several of whom also live a way away. It could well be one of the tea-ladies to see if they need to bother making sandwiches, and it could be the opposition. The most conducive conditions for excessive calls are when it's a bit drizzly, and looks set to remain a bit drizzly, even though yesterday's forecast was optimistic. On days like these, it's quite likely they'll all be on the phone.

I think the record was eight different individuals, though several of them rang more than once, so it was comfortably into double figures before I'd finished the sports section.

I often get multiple "What's the weather like?" calls even on days I'm not playing. "What's the weather like?" calls are, of course, all leading up to a pitch inspection. That's the real question, and we all know it, though we have to dance around "what's the weather like?" before we get to "have you gone and had a look at the pitch yet?" because, at nine in the morning, they know damn well I've done no such thing. So after a while "what's the weather like?" actually transforms into "Oh, just get out of bed and go and have a look."

Pitch inspection sounds quite grand. On the telly, you'll see Botham and Nasser and whoever kneeling down on that scorched almost bare bit of earth, seeing if they can get 50p pieces into the cracks. They look and sound knowledgeable about how it will behave, whether it will be hard and bouncy, soft and slow, a batsman's delight or a batsman's graveyard; will it deteriorate or get better as the game progresses?

Rather than predicting bounce or deciding whether to play two spinners because it's going to break up in the second innings, pretty much the entire pitch inspection process in village cricket is based around whether or not we're actually going to be able to play at all.

Usually I'll wander over the field at about half past ten to meet Derek.

Derek is sixty-something, retired, and an unbelievably dedicated volunteer groundsman. He does it for fun, this is his hobby. He gives up his time because he enjoys doing it – just as we give up our time because we enjoy playing cricket. It just so happens that Derek's hobby directly affects ours. His TLC gets us out playing when many other grounds in our area are unplayable. We are enormously grateful and extremely lucky to have him.

Unusually for a groundsman, he was never a cricketer himself. He doesn't know or care about the rules, other than those concerning the pitch itself. Usually groundsmen are guys who get roped in to do it because they know a bit about ground preparation, or ended up doing it because no-one else would and otherwise it wouldn't get done, and, although they don't really want to do it, it's either that or not play. Often they are captains or 'senior' players (which in pro cricket means 'experienced', and in village cricket means 'old') who are martyrs to their cause and do it begrudgingly rather than enthusiastically.

But Derek does it for the love of it.

He's completely self taught, and has put a great deal of time and effort, not just into doing it, but into researching how best to do it. He spends ages on the web, finding out tricks for this and that and buying bits of stuff from eBay and the like.

His sport is F1. He used to work on race cars, and his mechanical skills and knowledge of engines have not been wasted. Likely as not when I go out and meet him on a mizzley Saturday morning he'll be sitting on an ancient Benford 2-75 twin road roller. He replaced its noisy, smoky, reluctant diesel with an 8hp Honda petrol engine he rescued from an old cattle feeder he got for £40. With this and various other modifications to its drivetrain and pump, it now operates perfectly. This is a typical bit of improvisation.

Derek is rarely without a roll-up about his person, either in his mouth or behind an ear. I'll wander out to meet him on the square, and he'll spot me and turn off whichever machine he's on, and pat his pockets, looking for a lighter. The worse the weather, the longer the conversation. If the ground is relatively dry and doesn't look like raining anymore, he'll confidently declare we'll be fine. Sometimes he won't even bother to turn the engine off, then I know we're in good shape. Often, in borderline cases, his line will be "As long as it doesn't rain anymore, you'll be okay." This is the cue for three hours of anxiously peering out the window while repeating that mantra to whoever is on the phone again.

Different teams will have different attitudes to playing in poor weather, and different reasons, too. If you're playing a side in the league who only need a couple of points to secure promotion, they are likely to declare their swamp of a wicket playable after a morning monsoon.

Similarly, if you are due to play a side who don't fancy their chances against you, or can't raise a side and therefore risk forfeiting points, you might get a call the morning of the match to call it off on the basis that there are some ominous looking clouds on the horizon.

In the midweek league this year, one Wednesday afternoon I had a call from the opposition captain to ask after the condition of our ground, on which we were due to play them that evening. I assured him it was fine. Was I sure, he pressed, as it had been raining pretty heavily where he was. I sighed inwardly, and said I'd go and check again, then call him back.

I was working from home that day, so just before four I wandered over the road, through the pub car park to the pitch. There was Derek, sat atop his trusty old chugging Benford, rolling the square.

He didn't turn it off.

It's fine, he mouthed. It was the previous weekend's wicket which he'd touched up to use again, as is usual for a Wednesday wicket. It was wet, and so was the outfield, but we've certainly played on wetter. Derek would not give his blessing if he thought it would tear up his square too much, so if he says yes, the answer's yes.

I called the chap back and told him exactly that. He wasn't happy, and clearly would rather we called it off. He and three or four of his team arrived at the ground just before six and went to inspect the wicket, then walked around the boundary. He insisted that the outfield was too wet, and that he was worried about players slipping up and injuring themselves. In the end we called it off, as we're not an aggressive bunch, and we'd rather retreat to the pub than argue with another captain about his reasons for not wanting to play. That evening everyone got into the pub in plenty of time for the Champions League match that was due to start at seven. Not that I would dream of suggesting for one moment that a game of football on the telly that half his side desperately wanted to watch would have anything to do with the game being called off. Heaven forbid.

Other times we've played in horrible conditions. We played Compton Chamberlayne at our place right at the end of the season, so it didn't matter about damaging the ground as Derek was going to tear it up when he prepared it for winter anyway. It was a friendly, so the result didn't matter, we all just wanted to play.

It was drizzling when we started, and it didn't actually stop raining for the whole game. Sometimes it reduced to almost a fine mist, hanging in the air, like playing cricket in a cold sauna. Or inside a cloud. During tea, it really came down properly, the leaky gutter in front of the pavilion pouring a steady waterfall onto the grass, sounding like an enormous, endless, al fresco wee.

But we got back out there, ripped up bits of old towel tucked in everyone's waistband in a futile effort to keep the ball dry.

I remember batting and being able to hear the squelch with each foot movement. I had spare socks in my bag, and changed into dry ones to field, but they too were wet through in minutes. I don't think I've ever had feet that wet for that long. Despite the work of a whole bottle of Febreeze, my shoes never recovered.

Compton enjoyed it though, and there was a beer festival in the Compasses that night, for which several of them stayed on, wet feet and all. In fact they enjoyed it so much that they awarded us 'Friendliest Friendly' at their annual bash, an accolade we were delighted with, but I think we can safely say was achieved in spite of, rather than because of, the weather.

The obsession with the weather is a constant thing throughout the season.

The odd thing is that come October, it just stops. From May to September, if you ask me what the weather's going to be like at the weekend, I won't just have an opinion on it, I'll have six or seven expert opinions on it (at least three of which will be wrong) from which I will have drawn my own conclusions.

But when the season ends, so does the reason to see if it's going to rain, and the obsession comes to an abrupt halt.

I play golf in the winter, and I don't really care what the weather's going to be like as I am not a fair weather golfer. The opposite, in fact. Golf in shorts in Spain is very pleasant, but give me a choice of that or wrapped in woolly hat, thermals and waterproofs in a bitter three-club wind on a cliff-top classic like Perranporth, and I'll take the winter links every single time, thanks.

Sometimes I actually get weather obsession withdrawal, and go and have a look just for nostalgia's sake, or to see if they're getting any better at it, and laugh at their failure to predict alpine snow dumps.

Of course, it's generally easier in the autumn and winter, when the blanket assertion that the weather's going to be rubbish is almost certainly true, and everyone's so pleased when it isn't that the fact that the weather men comprehensively failed to predict it passes everyone by. Certainly me. As far as forecast addiction is concerned, apart from the odd stumble, I get half a year off.

The wilderness years

For a dozen or so years I was an average everyday London media tosser, living in an eye-wateringly overpriced suburb, working in the West End and complaining about the commute.

I spent my days trying to think up interesting new ways to sell stuff, and I had a girlfriend who spent her days doing cunning things with numbers.

There were millions of couples like us on thousands of trains into town every morning. We belonged.

We both worked long hours and did a fair bit of drinking with colleagues and 'entertaining' (drinking with colleagues on expenses). 'Work hard, play hard' they called it. I think at the time it might not even have become a cliché yet. No of course it had, who am I kidding; I just wasn't personally tired of it yet.

Life was sociable, fun, fast and boozy. We liked it. What's not to like?

In 2002 we had a little girl. Six months later Soph went back to work and Izzy went to nursery all day. 'All day' means quite a different thing in child-care terms than it does in work terms, and the discrepancy meant one of us was always 'late' into work, and one had to leave 'early'. Whoever wasn't on pick-up duty worked even later to make up for the times when they wouldn't be able to. Soon we were hardly seeing each other, let alone Izzy.

One day, during a row along the well-worn lines of how life had somehow shifted to being the worst of both worlds rather than the best of both worlds without our permission, Soph flounced dramatically that we should just chuck it all in and move to France.

It was quite a random notion, but it stuck.

Gradually it began to make more and more sense. We didn't want to scale back, or move to an even more heroically expensive suburb, or compromise any of our other already compromised compromises any further. It wasn't working, so surely it was better just to stop it, and make a clean break. Before it broke us.

Life had changed. We had changed. This wasn't fun anymore. It wasn't working anymore.

So we did it.

We left our jobs, rented out our house, and spent a year and a half in south-west France, an unspoilt, unhurried, unbelievably beautiful place which is, for all practical purposes, in the middle of nowhere.

I unreservedly recommend it as a venue if you ever get to the point where you really need to chill out, sit back, take stock, smell the roses, and the myriad other things like that which we all know we should do but never find the time for.

It takes a lot longer than you'd think. It took me a good six months to properly relax.

We did bits of work here and there for people back in England and after a while, we had quietly become self employed, working remotely.

When we came back we knew for certain that we wanted to live in the countryside, within striking (but not commuting) distance of London, and easy reach of family and friends on the south coast.

We found what we were looking for in a little village of a few hundred houses, a couple of churches and a pub.

Behind the pub there's a cricket field.

chapter 12

cricket and me

On how I had it, and how I lost it, before I found it again

I grew up with cricket. Playing in the back garden with a bald old tennis ball and a blue plastic bat while Kirsty from next door made daisy chains behind the stumps. Watching the West Indies thump us in the Tests on BBC2, catching Ashes scores on scratchy longwave radio on summer holidays in Cornwall.

I have a memory of the car park at Marizion near St Michael's Mount burned on my brain like a snapshot that was never taken: Dad sprawled under the dashboard of an old Morris Oxford, trying to nurse reception long enough to get through another Jonners anecdote until he got round to mentioning the score. That's how we experienced Botham's Ashes.

I was back there not long ago. The sandy grass car park is utterly unchanged 30 odd years later, exactly as I remember it. Other universal constants are the dreadful 198 longwave reception, and the ever-increasing sighs of irritation from the passenger seat because you won't turn the bloody thing off.

As I got a bit older, the back-garden-cricket got a bit more serious. No-one was allowed to make daisy chains anymore, that was for sure. It wasn't a large back garden. I grew up in Hedge End, which was then a small village six miles outside Southampton and is now a sprawling retail park off the M27 by the Rose Bowl.

Pretty soon came proper willow bats, which I was desperately excited about, and fanatically over-oiled, despite warnings not to, until any middle they might have had was drowned. Then came the real cricket balls, and with them, inevitably, came gloves and pads.

If you have ever been hit on the shin by a cricket ball, even one bowled under-arm in the back garden by a benevolent Dad who is doing his best not to hit you, you will understand the need for pads. I have never had a glove-less finger caught in the vice between ball and bat handle, largely because I have a fertile imagination which shrinks, whimpering, from the very thought of it. From about eight upwards, I wore gloves.

Besides, I liked the gloves. I liked all the paraphernalia, and still do. There is much pleasure to be found in kit. (So much in fact, that, as you may have already discovered, the whole of chapter 8 is devoted to it.)

With cricket kit came, I think perhaps for the first time, the thrill of new stuff.

The excited feeling of something up-to-the-minute – and the idea of newness as an appeal in its own right – characterised by the unmatchable smell of treated wood and leather. It is a wonderful, heady, joyous smell. Ask anyone who's ever had a new car. All of my life since, from BMX through guitars to golf to Macs, whatever it is I have been involved in, I have always been an incurable equipment junkie. That smell, or at least what that smell represents, has cost me a small fortune over the years.

We had an unusual scoring system for back-garden-cricket, based around not hitting stuff that people didn't want us to hit.

All scoring shots had to be along the floor. We had a couple of broken old scaffold boards which were propped up against some stakes. One at cover, one at midwicket. Not that I knew at the time what cover or midwicket were. These boundary boards cannot possibly have been more than 15 yards from the bat. Probably ten. Depending on what devious variation he intended to bowl, the bowler could choose which board was four and which was six. Actually physically running was not allowed, as this would have done too much damage to the one bit of lawn where we could play. If you hit the boards without bouncing you were out, caught. Anything that ended up in the flower beds was a dot ball, regardless of what it had hit on the way. If you hit the shed it was -4. If you hit the house, you were out. If you hit Mrs Mac's fence, you were out. If it went *over* the fence, it was game over for the day.

Maybe even a few days, until we could be sure the old witch was out so we could sneak round and get it back.

Theoretically, this system should have bred good habits. My placement should be exquisite. I should be an accomplished player of slow skiddy spin. I should rarely if ever hit balls in the air. All these things are manifestly not the case. In fact, the only legacy from these formative years seems to be a lingering disregard for the art of running between the wickets, my ineptitude at which continues to reach heroic lows.

Dad followed Hampshire and England pretty closely. We used to go to the old Hampshire County Ground at Northlands Road a fair bit when I was a kid. One of his older sisters was a serious Hampshire fan and had season tickets.

The loos in the pavilion were the same for members and players, and Dad remembers having a pee standing next to Michael Atherton. An odd thing to remember, but I imagine it would stick in the mind. Though possibly not for Athers.

I got Gower's autograph (no, not in the toilet,) and Marshall's, I think. I've probably still got them in a box in the loft somewhere. Attempting to get Dennis Lillie's, I remember running on to the pitch with a pen and a scoresheet between overs, which in those days was perfectly normal and acceptable behaviour. These days a twelve-year-old who tried that would be wrestled to the ground by four security people with walkie talkies and green hi-vis jackets, get a life ban from the ground and be arrested under the terrorism act.

Anyway, Lillie wasn't in the mood to sign autographs right then, though I think I did get it from him the next time. The reason I remember that gruff "No mate, not now," (poor bloke was probably having a stinker) was my Dad's reaction when I told him. "I'll have strong words with him if I see him in the bar," he said. At the time it seemed perfectly reasonable to me that a father might be miffed enough on his son's behalf to take one of the meanest fast bowlers the game has produced to task over an autograph. In hindsight, doubtless Dad made that comment with his tongue firmly in his cheek, but the mental image of him spilling Lillie's pint, squaring up to him and teaching him some manners remains hard to shift.

Dad was a teacher, and by the time I was old enough to be aware of it he didn't play much, bar the occasional staff game for his school. I played in one of them when they were really short at the last minute. I was about nine or ten, too young to do more than block a hole in the field. I remember Dad took a sharp slip catch, and I remember the pub afterwards, his serious friends being far from serious, the beer, the banter, the jokes I didn't understand. I liked it.

I'd always known that Dad's Dad had been pretty good. Vic White died a few years before I was born, so I only ever had family folklore to go on. Another vivid childhood memory is of talking to his brother, my (great) uncle Cecil at some family do, probably around the same time as I'd filled in for Dad's teachers' team. Uncle Cecil was a great fan of his late brother's cricket, and told me stories of it in the corner of a crowded sitting room between sips of sherry, leaning forward in his deep armchair with doilies on the arms, occasionally putting his glass down to swish an imaginary bat, still seated.

According to him, Vic was a pretty classy cricketer. Beautiful player, he was. Stroked the ball, Cecil said. "Yeah, my Dad plays cricket," I told him. "Yes, but not like *his* Dad did. He was gooood." It is the only conversation I remember having with Cecil.

Over the last few years, because I've got more and more into my cricket again, I've asked my Dad about his Dad. He's got some old newspaper clippings of him playing what was known as 'Parks' cricket, played on the big public parks in central Southampton between St Mary's Place and Above Bar. My Great Grandfather, Fred White, was also a pretty serious cricketer it seems, as was his brother, whose first name I'm not sure of, and the clippings only refer to as D White.

The paper supports the family folklore: "V. White gave a delightful batting display for the winners, his 70 not out containing six fours…" And later, under the headline 'The Great White Way': "The family White had a day out in the Parks on Saturday… playing in the first division of the Southampton Public Grounds League, D. White made 70 and V. White, his nephew, made another 70 not out…"

Those are from the Southampton Daily Echo in 1934 – a decade before my old man was born. From 1927 there are obituaries for Fred in several local papers, and one from a national, the Daily Mail, which notes that the 'veteran Southampton parks cricketer' had his coffin born by six team-mates wearing whites.

Now, that's heavily into cricket, that is. I know a few guys who are pretty into their cricket, but cricketing pallbearers? That's proper hardcore.

Showing me these cuttings, telling me about his Parks cricket, Dad went on to tell me that he and his sisters had scattered Vic's ashes on the No1 square at the Parks in 1965. For the first time in many years it made me wonder about my cricketing Grandad, and wish I'd known him. I resolved to visit those parks before too long.

On a fiercely bright and warm day in early October (one of those days a few weeks after the end of the season that makes you wonder fleetingly why it stops so early,) I found myself with a spare hour on my hands in Southampton. If I'm honest, part of the reason I'd gone in there in the first place was so I could make sure I'd find myself with a spare hour on my hands.

As I walked down from the ancient Bargate I could see the distinctive lighter colour of the roped-off squares on the park through the trees. The squares are wide, there must be nearly a dozen wickets on the bigger of the two. The pitches themselves are not large though, bordered on all sides by footpaths or main roads. I don't imagine those criss-crossing footpaths were there in Vic's day, but other than that I doubt the ground itself has changed much. Pre-war Southampton would not have had a lot in common with its twentyfirst century counterpart though, and I was struck by how different the world around the ground would have been 75 years ago.

I sat on a bench between the two pitches, squinting behind sunglasses in brilliant sunshine, and beyond the afternoon throng of students and shoppers, saw the spectre of flashing 70 not outs.

I played cricket for my school. This wasn't as impressive as it might sound as it was hardly a cricketing stronghold. I was okay rather than good, batted middle order and bowled mediocre medium. It was fun, we had a laugh and we got to visit other schools in a rickety minibus. I didn't play that much; I can only picture a couple of away grounds, though there may have been more.

We played in the 'rec' occasionally in the summer, too. Not formal games, just a dozen or so kids. Away from the sobering effect of consequences that teacher supervision brings, the game became a more feral, unpredictable, dangerous affair.

This was before helmets, even in the professional game. So a borderline psychotic 12 stone 15 year-old with industrial quantities of testosterone pumping through his newly muscular frame hurling bouncers at you really was potentially lethal.

Jonah Wheatley is a name that leaps to mind. He was the son of the vicar in the next village over. In later years we became friends and drinking buddies, and even shared a stage together – he was the green haired singer to my pink haired guitarist in *Shakespeare's Testicles* at the highlight-of-the-year *Rock Against College* gig.

But at the time, he was a thick-set rugby-playing maniac not averse to a bit of intimidation. Basically he was Merv Hughes without the moustache, and he had no reason whatsoever to like the tall lanky kid with the bad haircut. I did not enjoy facing him.

He wasn't alone either, there were a couple of kids who could really wang it down. Steve Wood was another one. He was a good friend, but that didn't stop him trying his hardest to knock my head off with a cricket ball. It's an odd game like that.

Occasionally, whether through malice or mistake it was never quite clear (is it ever though?) it would be beamers rather than bouncers. Fortunately, none of them were that accurate, so being hit was probably a lot less likely than it seemed.

It was through them, not through school, that I first experienced the curiously inclusive thrill of playing *with* a scary fast bowler. Your side hasn't got enough runs, and the other side look like getting them easily. Then the fast bowler comes on and no-one can hit him, and the measly three-an over they need starts creeping up. You can feel belief begin to seep back around the field, spreading like an airborne virus. Then, you see, someone hittable like me comes on to bowl, but they need runs quickly, and they make mistakes – usually they hit you in the air – and the chances come. Quick bowlers don't always take wickets, but they make the other guys more likely to get them. Economy is the true weapon of the paceman. I would not have expressed that thought then, but it is perhaps when I first understood it.

There was one guy who was quick, accurate and nasty. Tony Wright was probably the quickest of the lot, but he didn't bowl bouncers so much as back-of-a-length balls that rose up into your ribs or jagged into your legs.

I don't remember him playing outside school – he was way too busy being a Mod to hang around with losers at the weekend. I'm sure he must have played for the school, though I don't remember playing with him. He was certainly more than good enough. What I do remember is him bowling in the nets in the sports hall. I remember the bruises on my left thigh, sure, but mostly I remember a particular occasion when I was in the same queue as him waiting to bowl in the nets. He'd zipped a few down and was warmed up, when he announced with a calm, mirthless grin to his fellows in the queue: "I'm gonna hurt him now." The next ball lifted off the matting into the batsman's ribs. The poor guy dropped his bat and staggered around holding his side, half grimacing, half grinning, making light of it. Wright smiled and shrugged, went to the back of the queue. I was horrified that someone would deliberately set out to hurt a classmate under cover of a game. I was a gentle soul, and it seemed like just another form of bullying to me. Like in rugby, when the big kids were not only allowed, but *encouraged* by ruthlessly sadistic – or possibly just bored – PE teachers to flatten the little kids. (It was during this period, unsurprisingly, that I developed my life-long inclination to shrink from the very concept of rugby, to the point that I remain stubbornly ignorant of the rules.)

Now though, I think I would think of it quite differently. That kind of ability to get the ball to rear at a batsman off a length is rare, and one of the chief skills required in a proper fast bowler. The difference is that a proper fast bowler would only ever bowl like that at a batsman good enough to deal with it. That is, in essence, what the Spirit of Cricket means, and it is all that separates a nasty schoolboy with a vicious streak from a really good quick.

Then at fifteen I was seriously put off cricket, I thought at the time for life. Yes, I was hit. But not by a bowler. I wasn't even batting.

In the indoor nets in the sports hall at team practice after school, I was messing about at the back of the hall waiting to bowl with the others, merrily committing the most cardinal of cricket net sins: not watching the bat when the ball is bowled.

Even now in the nets, people not paying attention fills me with the urge to run over and explain the risk they're running, scolding them like an old woman. Mostly I resist. Sometimes it gets the better of me.

David Whiting, his name was. This is the only thing I remember about David Whiting, other than the fact that his name was always directly after mine on those sheets of exam results pinned to school notice boards at the end of term.

I never saw the shot, but it must have been sweetly middled, as it was hammered back over the bowler's head and zeroed in on mine. Someone shouted "HEADS!" and I turned round just in time to greet the ball with my right cheekbone.

I was knocked off my feet and unconscious for a minute or so, during which time the PE teacher in charge, Mr Palmer, must have been truly crapping himself.

I remember the relief on his face when I came round, and imagined the 'BOY KILLED IN CRICKET NETS' headlines dissolving from his mind.

He can't have been that worried though. When it was established that I was not dead I remember getting changed, phoning for a lift and wandering off outside to sit on the low wall surrounding the pale green fibreglass monstrosity of the swimming pool building, waiting for Mum to pick me up, and deciding that I was probably done with cricket.

Had this incident happened to a 15-year-old today, he would doubtless be in hospital for observation and see a councillor or sports psychologist to make sure his rehabilitation went successfully.

I was never a sporty kid anyway, and cricket was the only game I ever showed any interest in, so this moment marked a hiatus in my sporting life until pretty much ten years later, when I first picked up a club during a trip to Ireland and was irrevocably bitten by the golf bug.

To be honest, there was every chance I would pretty soon have drifted away from cricket anyway, even if I had been paying attention that day in the nets. Puberty had begun to kick in in earnest; I'd started to play the guitar; had stopped screwing up my face in disgust at the bitter taste of beer; and would very shortly discover the awesome power of the most intoxicating and addictive phenomenon known to man: woman.

I continued to follow the game, if with waning enthusiasm. In the early nineties, me and my housemates in a grotty four-bed-semi in an even grottier London suburb had scraped enough together to get Sky Sports. My Dad came up to stay, drinking beer and eating crisps through the night with us, watching England lose to Pakistan in the World Cup Final at the MCG.

The arrival of Warne and his Ball of the Century broke through the apathy, as did Lara and his various record-smashing knocks.

But mostly what prevailed, like a bluebottle half-heartedly trying to get out of a distant window, was the background hum of England's perennial woes. And though I kept half an eye on them, they concerned me less and less deeply.

Early on, when I wasn't whining about the pointless tyranny of tedious dead-end jobs, I was too concerned with playing guitar and having long hair to worry too much about what was happening on England's green and pleasant fields. Later, work became more consuming, weekends became more precious, and golf increasingly became the only sport I paid any attention to at all.

Even in golf though, my judgement of distance is based on cricket. The proportions of the game are so deeply ingrained that I will judge a chip to be about 50 yards on the basis that it looks like it's about two-and-a-bit wickets worth. This system is remarkably accurate.

In my first job in advertising, my creative director, who was actually younger than me, was a cricketer, and would go on cricket tours with his mates and come back lobster red and heroically hungover, plainly in need of a holiday to recover. This sounded like fantastic fun, but it didn't even occur to me to play cricket in London. It's only in hindsight, and in the light of my involvement in village cricket, that it's become obvious to me that many thousands of Londoners play cricket every weekend.

Oddly enough it did occur to me to play while living in France. There was an expat team near us, and while I didn't know any of them, a friend-of-a-friend was asking around for players as they were short, and I actually got quite excited about the prospect. But it never happened.

So as it turned out, that ball that hit me in the face after school in the sports hall in 1984 was the last one I touched for a long, long time.

In the two decades that followed, I played no cricket at all. Neither did I much miss it.

A chance pint

Not long after we moved to the village we went to some fair or fete or somesuch in the village hall.

It may well have been the Duck Race, the annual highlight of the village calendar, where several thousand plastic yellow ducks are released to race a mile or so down the river. It may have been. It doesn't matter what it was, what matters is that at some point during this afternoon, I found myself in conversation with a chap from the village.

It was an odd time, those first few months. We didn't know anyone. These days, going to these twee little villagey things comes with the reassuring safety net that there will definitely be at least a few people there to have a chat and a beer with. Back then, we knew no one, so they could be strangely intimidating, and came attached with an oh-god-do-we-have-to trepidation.

The guy I met that day was Chris Stott. He was, and remains, excellent company, always worth having a beer with. Though I hardly see him these days, as he moved away a few years later.

After ten minutes or so of polite so-you've-just-moved-in small talk, he asked nonchalantly, "You don't play cricket, do you?"

I hesitated. Looking back now I get an odd feeling of just how pivotal this question was for me, how many friendships and days standing around in a field it would lead to. I might easily have just said no, but I suppose it seemed as good a way as any to meet people.

I was right about that. If you'd told me that day in the village hall that within a year I'd be fairly deeply involved in the running of a village cricket club, I'd have assumed you'd mistaken me for someone else and bidden you a haughty good-day.

"Not for years."

"That doesn't matter. Fancy getting out there again?"

"I won't be any good. It's been at least 20 years, and I wasn't really any good then."

"Well that certainly doesn't matter. Tuesday night."

"Evening game, eh? What is it, this new Twenty20 thing I keep hearing about?"

"Something like that. Bar's open. Fancy a pint?"

"I think I do, yes."

chapter 13

steve harmison's 90mph inswinging yorker

On science, stupidity, and net worth

Suddenly I'm awake. I'm staring at the cciling, trying to pick out the lampshade in the almost-black. Swimming on the edge of my vision the green glow of LEDs on the clock say it's nearly three in the morning.

I am dimly aware that I'm covered in sweat. I am profoundly aware that my left foot is throbbing like a cartoon thumb hit by a cartoon hammer.

Soph is breathing deeply beside me. I lie there for a bit, trying to convince my subconscious that the best thing to do is go back to sleep. My subconscious is having none of it.

I sigh melodramatically, swing my feet to the floor stand up.

This is a bad move.

I'm never quite sure what happened next. It's possible that putting my weight on the foot was so painful I just blacked out. I find this hardest to believe in retrospect, though the theory carried most weight at the time. If you see what I mean. Perhaps it refused the weight, buckled under me and I fell on the floor. It's more likely that I got up too quickly and went a bit dizzy. Most likely of all is that I just fell out of bed, a beer or two worse for wear and still half asleep. Anyway, whatever happened, next thing I know Soph's leaning over the side of the bed, peering down at me.

"Are you all right?"

"I… don't know."

"What's going on?"

"My foot hurts."

"But what are you doing?"

"I don't–"

"–come back to bed. It's three in the morning."

It's six hours later and my foot really bloody hurts now. The whole of the top of it has gone blue and it's all swollen. I can walk on it, but it hurts like hell.

Maybe it's broken? I suppose it could be.

I've never broken a bone. I came close lots of times when I was a kid, falling off bikes and ladders and walls, and out of lofts and barns and go-karts. Oh, no, hang on: not that long ago I cracked a rib coughing, does that count? The doctor said it's quite common and there's nothing you can do about it, you have to give it six weeks to heal. Yes, I know, it's hilarious – so funny I've done a rib. Didn't half hurt though. Couldn't swing a golf club or anything.

Having never *properly* broken a bone, I have nothing to compare it to. But it definitely bloody hurts.

Yeah. Maybe it's broken.

Sod it, I'm not working this morning. Lets pay Salisbury A&E a visit. I haven't been to the hospital since we moved here, (this will shortly change when Maddie arrives,) so this can serve as a recce. These are the terms I couch it in to myself, as on some level a disconnected part of me is wagging my head and tutting at myself disapprovingly, aware that I'm probably making a fuss about nothing.

I wince to the car. On the way there I flinch at every gear change, whimpering every time I depress the clutch, wishing it was an automatic. Or at least wishing the clutch was hydraulic.

I sit in A&E feeling sheepish for an hour until a bloke about my age comes and calls my name. We walk through a corridor to an exam room. He watches without comment as I limp-whilst-trying-not-to-limp so as not to make a big deal out of it.

"So, what have you done then?"

"Well, it's my foot. It's probably nothing, but I thought I'd get it checked out, y'know, just to be sure."

He smiles. "What did you do?"

Cricket is a very difficult game to practice. In order to practice properly, to hone the crafts of batting and bowling, there's no real alternative to actually playing cricket.

To really practice batting, you need to do so against a bowler who is protecting his figures (ie has a vested interest in you not scoring,) and is focussed on getting you out. And not just him, but his whole team, with a field set for you particularly.

Similarly, bowling to a batsman who doesn't care if he gets out or not is fundamentally unhelpful. If he tries to wallop everything, it's very difficult for you to know if you're getting it right or not.

Unfortunately however, there aren't always two dozen people hanging around outside your house waiting to help you practice, like when you were thirteen. And even more irritatingly, from October to March (and often for a fair proportion of April to September as well) the weather's just too rubbish for playing cricket in this country. So it's nets or nothing.

Many believe nets are worse than useless – a breeding ground for bad habits.

There is much evidence to support this belief. People batting in the nets have a tendency to swing at everything. To try and smash the ball back past the bowler every ball. And if you miss it or edge it, it doesn't matter. You can hit it in the air without consequence, and get into the habit of just hitting it anywhere, without trying to place it or avoid fielders. You rarely see anyone play a considered leave or defensive shot in the nets, largely because you've got 10 minutes each to bat, regardless of whether you're out or not, so why waste time defending?

Defence is what most of us spend most time doing in the middle, and least time practicing in the nets. In a game, get it wrong once, and that's you done until next week. In the nets, you can swish and miss as often as you like.

And when you do whack the ball in the nets, it's blind. Was there a fielder there? Did the bowler take note of your tendency to cut and move point up, then feed you that ball so you'd smash it straight into his lap?

Nah. Four!

Is that someone lurking on the deep midwicket fence, just waiting for you to mis-time that wild mow?

Nah. Six!

It is the cricket equivalent of going to the golf range and hitting 200 balls as hard as you possibly can, smashing ball after ball, not even looking where they're going. Absolutely pointless. (Unless you've had a really tough week and just need to hit something as hard as you can. Then it's quite useful.)

For bowlers, nets are undeniably useful for grooving your action by simple repetition. But there are still dangers. Complacency is one, (No ball. Wide. Half volley. Wide. No ball: no one cares,) but bounce is the big one. I can get quite excited by the bounce. On the hard springy 'wickets' in the nets, I can get a topspinner up into your gloves, no trouble. The same ball on a Hampshire village pitch in May will sit up like it's on an eighteen inch tee, asking politely to be swatted to the boundary.

The same for the quicks. Back of a length in the nets will have balls climbing into your ribs or even over your head. In real life in southern England, it probably won't get above stump height until midsummer, and even then only if it hasn't rained for a month.

No, the nets are not perfect, and some people justifiably avoid them altogether.

For the rest of us, they're better than nothing.

But what's even better – yes, even better than better than nothing – is the machine.

At Hurn, near Bournemouth Airport, there's a slightly tatty warehouse with the rather grandiose name of The Dorset Cricket Centre.

90% of the building is one room, about 60 by 100 feet, fully carpeted in tough green astro-turf-like stuff. During the early part of winter it houses endless indoor cricket leagues for every age group imaginable. From February onwards the room is divided up by five nets, which take up the whole space. This, in spring, is where we practice.

The rest of the building is composed of a viewing gallery and an office upstairs, with a changing room below. Behind the changing room is a long thin scruffy room draped in sheets and nets and old rolls of carpet like a haberdasher's stock room, with a set of beaten up aluminium spring-back stumps at one end and a bowling machine at the other. The bowling machine net.

It's shorter than 22 yards, so you can't bowl properly in it even without a run up. The machine doesn't need a run up. With it almost up against the back wall, it delivers from about 18 yards. A touch shorter than the real thing, but only a touch.

In the first half of winter you can't get a normal net for all the indoor leagues going on, so if you want any sort of practice, the bowling machine is it.

It's become a regular haunt for me in the last couple of years. Apart from me, Henry is the other Damerhamite least able to cope with the sudden and cruel cessation of cricket in September. It takes us a couple of weeks of mourning until, towards the end of October, we'll venture to the 'BM net'. Once the seal is broken we're in there once a week at least. As the winter deepens sometimes Clive comes, or Dave, or Joel, but often it's just me and H. I'm not sure if it actually helps your batting, but facing balls at the rate of one every 10 seconds or so in 15 minute stints for two hours is at least a decent work out, and infinitely preferable to the gym.

Tinkering with the bowling machine itself is as much fun as batting against it. You can vary line, length, swing and of course speed. You can set it up to repeat a shot you want to practice, whether it's one you're good at or one you're bad at, or mix up line length and speed every delivery. Henry and I are both weak on the leg side, so we'll often have a fair proportion of those, trying to nonchalantly turn balls off the hip or whip them off our pads. It's odd that in the professional game even the tail-enders will punish anything that strays onto leg, but in the village game you rarely meet anyone who deals with quick balls swinging into the pads comfortably.

We've discovered many things from the machine, but two of the most important ones are: 1.) 'Fast' in village terms, is anything above 60 mph. H himself is the benchmark here, as we rarely if ever face anyone quicker than him. Comparing him to the machine, I would say he bowls somewhere around 65; he might touch 70 with his real effort ball. 2.) It's not about speed, it's about length. Half volleys at 80 mph are relatively easy to hit. Yorkers at 50 are not. Who'd have thought?

65-70 mph is laughably ponderous in international cricket terms. In fact some spinners (Shahid Afridi leaps to mind) have quicker balls faster than that. But on a village green, believe me, 70 is rapid enough to get people backing away to leg and calling for a helmet. Most bowlers we face in games will be between 40 (spinners) and 65 (quicks), so this range is where we concentrate most of our efforts.

When you first start using the machine, there's a temptation to whack it up fast to see how you deal with it. This is fine, and fun enough, but not very useful.

What you find is this: there is a length that's comfortable for you. You don't often get a chance to rationalise it when you're playing in a game, but there is a certain type of perfectly good ball – and it'll be different for everyone, depending on how tall you are, your reach, and so on – that will rarely trouble you, even at international opening bowler speeds. This is good to know.

Here's another plain truth: properly fast, short-pitched bowling requires a certain type of reflex to be able to score off it, and we simply don't have it.

I don't say 'we' lightly – believe me I don't wish to tar Henry with my rather third rate brush. To be clear, H is a better cricketer than me in every conceivable respect: he's young, fit, can catch a fly with chopsticks, bowls full fast and straight, and if you bowl in his slot he'll hit you for six every time. But when it comes to bouncers he is every bit as clueless as me. To borrow a ridiculous affectation from Geoffrey Boycott, he is no more capable of pulling a fast half tracker off his eyebrows than my Mum. His instinctive reaction to such a ball is the same as mine: get out of the way.

The smooth roll of the swivel pull through backward-square is something we're only ever likely to see on television, or from 100 yards away in the stands.

In every sport you play you will sooner or later butt up against the reality of the gulf between your abilities and those of people who get paid to do it. In snooker and golf it's obvious for all to see – they keep getting the balls in the holes. In football and rugby it's physical, and more about the marriage of strength and skill. In cricket, for batsmen, it's about reactions. It's about the speed with which the message gets from the eyes to the bat. Back/forward/ drive/defend/punch/clip/cut/pull/leave/duck/hook – in a tenth of the time it just took you to read that list, you must have made your decision, and done it.

Now, as they say in all the best shampoo ads: here comes the science bit.

A helpfully round number, this: 90 mph equates to 44 yards per second. So that's exactly half a second for the 22 yards between wicket and wicket. Except a bowler's hand will be a few yards in front of the stumps at the point of delivery, and the batsman in his crease is 4ft in front of his wicket, so the actual distance between ball and bat at the moment of release is more like 19 yards, so a bit less than half a second then.

Even less if what you're measuring is the time elapsing between the ball leaving the bowler's hand and the ball hitting the deck, which is the time you have to select your shot. For a 90 mph bouncer, this will be something like a fifth of a second.

Those who study these things under laboratory conditions often make sweeping (and rather self-defeating) observations like this one: "Some aspects of high-speed ball games such as cricket are effectively impossible."

There is simply insufficient time for batsmen to respond to really quick bowling, apparently. I for one am happy to agree that hooking 90 mph bouncers is indeed impossible, but only for me. Clearly it's not impossible for some people. I've seen them do it, I've watched it happen live in front of me, and been part of the applause.

Given the success with which cricketers routinely perform the impossible, it's not surprising that scientists have attempted to measure their abilities.

In controlled lab tests as well as analysis of high-speed film taken during games, international cricketers rather surprisingly demonstrated no better than average reaction times.

Other tests showed that professional cricketers take roughly as long as casual players to pick up 'ball flight information' from a ball coming towards them.

So much for such useful advice as "See the ball early," eh, Mr Boycott?

These two sets of findings suggested to one set of researchers twenty years ago that the dramatic contrast between the ability of professional and non-professional batsmen to act on the basis of visual information "does not lie in the speed of operation of their perceptual system, but in the organisation of the motor system that uses the output of this system."

In other words, we see it just as quickly as the pros do. But in us this knowledge provokes the reaction to duck – or, just as likely, stand there like a rabbit in the headlights and let it hit us – and in excellent batsmen, the information they receive translates into them playing the appropriate shot, effectively instantaneously.

Now, clearly I'm no expert, but it still sounds rather like it's all about reactions to me then – if they don't pick the ball up any faster than I do but they still manage to react so quickly that it looks like they've got time for a quick G&T before they swat it away, that makes it even more impressive doesn't it, not less?

Anyway, apparently that old research is all cobbler's. Which is why those quotes are not credited, to save blushes, and possibly lawsuits. I only mention it because until fairly recently, it seems to have been the accepted wisdom.

Then some actual honest to goodness *SCIENCE* came along to trample all over accepted wisdom of all kinds.

The celebrated scholarly journal, *Nature*, in a paper published in 2000, conducted experiments with head-mounted eye cameras which effectively disproved the oldest bit of batting advice of all: keep your eye on the ball.

We all think we watch the ball 'all the way onto the bat', but according to *Nature* we do no such thing.

Know what a saccade is? Neither did I. Saccades are rapid movements of the eyes as the fovea (the central part of the retina that does all our sharp focussing) moves from one fixation point to another. We do it all the time – you're doing it right now, as you read this, for example. Saccades are apparently the fastest movements the human body is capable of producing.

This is what happens when you bat.

You watch the ball very closely out of the hand, and your gaze is steady on it for a period after delivery as you establish its path.

Then: saccade! The fovea flicks down to below the ball, close to the part of the pitch where you anticipate it landing. In a nice little phrase, the fovea is thus said to 'lay in wait' for the bounce. 'Anticipatory saccades' like this are seen in other high speed sports like squash, tennis and ping pong, too.

Here's a sentence from *Nature* that I like very much, but don't understand: "The vertical counter-rotation of eye and head (presumably driven by the vestibulo-ocular reflex) kept gaze direction roughly level for a period before and after the bounce."

What I glean from this is that the second oldest bit of batting advice at least is still valid: Keep your head still. Phew. Don't rip up the text book just yet then.

Then your eyes jump back to the ball, but ahead of it, 'leading the ball' by about five degrees. By the time the ball bounces, the gaze and the ball are within one degree of each other. The gaze tracks the ball closely after the bounce, right up to just before you hit it.

Rather importantly though, *Nature* concluded – quite differently from previous tests – that the better the batsman, the faster his eyes.

Less skilled batsmen did not anticipate the ball as quickly, and waited until it had completed a larger part of its journey to the bounce point before starting the saccade.

Such 'catch-up' saccadic behaviour is adequate if the bowling is slow, but not for the really quick stuff. If a ball pitches a fifth of a second after delivery (like that 90 mph bouncer we started with) the lesser batsman would either not have started his saccade yet, or the bounce would have occurred at mid-saccade, during which 'saccadic suppression' would briefly suspend his vision – he would simply not see the ball.

By comparison, even with very short, very quick balls, the saccade of very good batsmen reaches the bounce point a full tenth of a second before the ball does. Even at that ridiculous speed, the really good player has still got time.

So Geoffrey was right after all, dammit. (It's annoying when the pugnacious old curmudgeon is right, but in matters of batting he so often is.) It really is all about seeing the ball early.

What *Nature*'s study does not delve into is whether these

superior response times are purely nature, or can be nurtured. Is it got-it-or-you-ain't talent, or can it be learned? No indications either way, but I strongly suspect the former. World class opening batsmen and fighter pilots: born, not made.

Facing the bowling machine is made particularly difficult by the fact that you have very little warning of what's coming. There's no doubt it's more difficult than facing a real-life bowler.

When a bowler bowls at you, he runs in. Arms pumping, huffing and puffing. Or maybe he runs in smoothly, like he's gliding on rails, without breaking a sweat or changing his breathing. He may come in straight, maybe he runs in at an angle. His front arm probably comes up first as a sighter-slash-counterbalance for the delivery arm. Maybe he's square, chest on, or maybe he's completely sideways. Whichever, he'll usually leap into his delivery stride, front foot landing as his arm comes over, face twisted with the effort. The arm itself, the angle it comes through at, the way he holds the ball, the seam position, the angle of the wrist. Every detail will be different with every bowler.

All this tells you stuff.

With the bowling machine, there's a hole in the top where you drop the ball in.

So that you've got some idea it's coming, convention has it that the 'bowler' – the guy operating the machine – raises his arm directly over the hole. He pauses at the top, and then smoothly lowers his arm, releasing the ball into the hole at the last moment.

Like so much cricket practice, it's better than nothing, but nothing like the real thing.

In a very different kind of test, which I read about but can't remember where, (this will be the last anecdote masquerading as 'science', I promise,) cricketers were shown film of bowlers from a batsman's-eye-view, which was frozen at the moment of release, and asked to predict what sort of ball it would be. With remarkable accuracy they foresaw line, length and even swing. Even amateurs were uncannily good at it.

Clearly there is all kinds of subtle information that a bowler gives a batsman before he lets go of the ball, whether either are aware that they're giving or receiving the information or not, and we react to this instinctively.

Instinct is behaviour arising from knowledge provided by one or more of the five senses, but below the threshold of awareness: we know something without consciously realising how we know it. It's not foreknowledge or a 'sixth sense', though sometimes it may seem like it. This innate capacity to respond unthinkingly is the product of millions of years of evolution. It's primal. These are the animal instincts that shaped the human race and made us what we are. It's also how lions hunt, and how antelope get away; they don't have thought-through strategies or empirical knowledge, they don't examine or question their own behaviour, they just do it.

And I think (yes, I'm claiming this particular bit of pseudo psychological armchair theorising as my own,) that this is why we love it so much.

Those instincts, sharpened by patient necessity through countless generations, are these days just left to blunt themselves quietly behind so many desks.

There's not much call for them in modern life, is there? Not much call for that quicker-than-thought fight/flight reflex to swing into action when you're sat at a computer chewing a pen with a phone tucked under your chin.

We don't use them in 'real' life – unless of course you spend your real life in a war zone. Most of us only get them out and dust them off for sport.

Those instincts are why anything from driving fast to skiing to batting is so much fun. It awakens the primitive in us, makes the blood pump hot and fast in our ears, makes us aware of how quick we are – or how quick we're not.

It's what life felt like before we got soft. When dinner was something you had to skin, rather than unwrap.

It's a reminder of just how capable the human machine is, and it feels fantastic.

It didn't take long for us to stop trying to kill each other with really short fast balls from the bowling machine. The thrill wears off quickly, the bruises do not.

When we started regularly doing BM sessions, there'd be more bruises most weeks than convincing pull shots. So we reined it in, if only in order to allay the suspicions of our other halves that instead of going to the nets we'd joined Fight Club or something.

Swing, at least in the bowling machine, is relatively easy to spot early. This probably has something to do with how it's achieved. The machine is driven by two horizontal wheels going in opposite directions, just far enough apart for a ball to squeeze between them. The ball is dropped in and spat out the front. If one wheel is going faster than the other, the ball will rotate on its vertical axis in the air, causing it to swerve. (This is of course quite different to why real cricket balls swing when bowled by real bowlers – see 'swing' in the glossary. Real swing tends to be more subtle, and happen later in the ball's path than bowling machine swing.) The effect can be quite pronounced, and means you must aim quite wide of the mark for the ball to end up on target.

A favourite of ours is the outswinger that starts on the stumps and swings away to off. It's easy enough to pick up, far less easy to deal with. Simplicity itself to nick. The opposite can also be tricky; the hooping inswinger that starts off looking like an off-the-strip wide and ends up taking middle out.

But the undoubted king of the bowling machine is the yorker. It does it beautifully.

Other than short balls, the most difficult deliveries to pick up are the ones where it's hardest to anticipate the pitch, and if a ball is going to bounce right below you, under your eyes, triangulating it is particularly tricky.

You're much more likely to have to deal with a yorker in a game too, as they'll work on any surface at any speed, whereas it's very unusual to find either the bowler or the pitch capable of really fierce bouncers at village level.

The problem with the yorker is, as TV commentators are so fond of telling us, it has to be pinpoint accurate. Over pitch a fraction, and it's a full toss. Not quite enough, and it's a half volley. Most amateur bowlers – many pros, come to that – can hope for maybe a one in five strike rate.

For all its faults, the machine can put a ball in the 'blockhole' time and time again.

This is very difficult to not-get-out to.

If you survive a perfect yorker in a game, you feel like you've done pretty well. You also feel like you now have the advantage, because the chances of the next one being a perfect yorker as well are pretty remote.

The machine will keep hurling them down ball after ball, like some sort of, well, like some sort of goddam machine.

We've experimented with what style of yorker is most effective, and there are three that are particularly good at being basically unplayable.

The first and perhaps greatest of these, is the inswinging yorker. At first it looks like it's going to be wide of off stump, inviting the drive. But then in it comes, homing in on middle-and-off. By this time your weight is forward and your arms are too far out, and getting back to defend is very tricky. Darren Gough and Steve Harmison both had real beauties in their heydays at around 90 mph. For us, 65 mph is quite quick enough to make this ball an absolute killer. I have been clean bowled by four of these in a row, and it's not like I can pretend I didn't know the next three were coming after the first one.

In our BM sessions, the 65 mph inswinging yorker has earned its own name – it's taken so many scalps, it has become known as 'The Legend'. As in "Yesssss! The Legend strikes again!" yelled unsympathetically from behind the machine.

Another brute is a simple, fast, Flintoff-like full ball hitting the base of leg stump. This needs to be a touch faster. 70 mph for this one will probably guarantee the hollow clang of the spring-back stumps.

The third of the machine's arsenal of yorkers is the 'Reverse Legend' – a 65 mph awayswinger, starting outside leg and swinging across you to splay middle and off.

It, like its brethren, is an absolute corker of a ball. I've never encountered one in a game and I hope I never do. But if I do, all I'll be able to do is give it the full 'Bambi', and hope I survive.

The 'Bambi' is a unique shot I have personally developed especially for the yorker. It is full of style and poise, and is as visually pleasing as it is effective.

The style is Disney's baby deer that has kindly given the shot its name. The poise is that of said animal attempting to get up for the first time, whilst wearing roller skates. When I say visually pleasing, I mean 'funny'. And when I say effective, I lie.

Here's how the Bambi shot is played: immediately you recognise the yorker line and length, forget all you know about orthodox defence. Instead, turn square-on to the ball, which is now spearing in towards your feet. Jump, attempting to get both feet as far out of the way as possible, spreading your legs and landing in a semi 'splits' position. Lastly, smack your bat down where your feet just were, whilst emitting a girlish yelp. Your balance is now dependent on your bat as most of your weight is on it, like the middle leg of a tripod.

If you're lucky, your bat will make contact with the ball, and people will just point and laugh at how ungainly and ridiculous you just looked.

If you're not, you'll miss it, and the ball will comprehensively uproot at least one of your stumps.

If you're really unlucky, you will mis-time it all so badly, that even your best splits attempts will not be sufficient to stop the ball hitting you full on the toe.

This is still out, obviously, plumb LBW. But that is nothing next to the pain.

All the bruises I ever got in the nets pale into insignificance next to the pain of ball meeting toe at 65-70 mph. It is excruciating.

It really is like being hit with a hammer.

This off season, the toes really came in for it. The Legend was perhaps over zealously employed, or maybe getting hit a few times made us more wary and thus more prone to being hit, in a vicious and painful toe/ball circle.

And this, it has to be said, is a strictly bowling machine based problem. I have never been hit on the toe whilst actually playing cricket. Thighs, yes. Gloves, pads, arms, stomach, chest, lid. But never toes. This is probably simply down to the frequency and quality of fast, accurate yorkers you find in village cricket.

Whatever the reason, our feet were really taking a battering at the hands of The Legend this year.

Why not just stop bowling it, you may ask? Now look, where's the fun in that? We have to beat it! Since we stopped the really silly speeds, the game is to get the other guy out using cunning. And The Legend. No-one has yet survived a whole session against the machine without being bowled at least once. In fact I don't think anyone got away with just once. And the delivery that gets you is almost always The Legend. To take it away would be… well just not cricket.

Henry took to bringing some size 12 steel toecapped workboots along to the nets, and these were very effective, but a little bit like trying to bat in… well in size 12 steel toecapped workboots, really.

Clive and Joel both soldiered on in trainers, despite both having been Legend-toed.

I looked online for cricket shoes with toe protection, and found precisely none at all. Over a pint with Clive he assured me that boots back in the day were made of stiff hard leather, and naturally offered some level of protection. (Not that Clive is old. Just older than me.)

He reckoned the best bet might be to try and find my Dad's old boots in the loft or something. Which is not a bad plan except for Dad's strict non-hoarding policy: he jumble-saled all his cricket kit years ago.

It's certainly true that cricket footwear today has more in common with flimsy running shoes than sturdy boots.

They're made of breathable fabric, and are basically lightweight trainers with spikes. They offer as much protection against the missile-like yorker homing in on your toes as the average sock does. Protection-wise, you might as well wear flip flops.

Bowling boots are slightly more robust, but only in terms of support around the ankle for the fast bowler who comes pounding in. Being a sedate leggie with a four stride 'walk up', I don't have to worry about any of that nonsense.

Finding no mention of toe protection in any of the blurb from the major manufacturers, I emailed four or five of the big online cricket retailers, explaining I had a broken big toe (this may have been a slight exaggeration, but it may not have been – I was limping for two weeks, in pain for six and I made quite a fuss) and was looking for batting spikes with some sort of protection.

To my surprise and their credit they all emailed back within 24 hours. There was a touch of resigned exasperation in their replies, which amounted to: no, sorry, you're not the first to ask, we've asked them all and none of them make anything like it any more, or have any plans to.

On a web forum, someone looking for the same thing had a theory that protection in batting boots had gone out of fashion due to people being given out caught off the foot, as with hard protection, ball-on-boot sounded very much like ball-on-bat.

Hmm. I found several industrial footwear companies who make trainers with toecaps, and that would be fine for the nets, which is really the only place there's a problem. But they were about £50, which seemed excessive for a little bit of yorker-proofing.

I could feel a project coming on.

I searched eBay for steel toecaps, but nobody seems to sell them. So I bought some rather ugly blue suede shoes with toecaps in them for 99p. When they arrived I cut them open with a Stanley knife, kept the caps and discarded the shoes. Next I found a pair of 'unwanted gift' cricket shoes two sizes too big for me. Another steal at £3.90. Then a trip to my local hardware store to ask about how best to bond steel to fabric. Their advice was Gorilla Glue, which is one of the oddest substances I've ever encountered. Also one of the stickiest. I was still picking bits of its foaming oddness off my fingers weeks later. But boy does it stick. I now have my very own BM shoes with inner steel toe protection: total cost about £15, including postage. Probably wouldn't want to run in them, but probably I'll never have to.

And my toes are safe, even against The Legend. Next year. Next year will be the off-season I get through a whole two-hour BM session without the mocking clang of the knackered old aluminium spring back stumps. Next year I will tame The Legend.

But let us go back now. Way back. (Cue dreamy, wavy, wibbly-wobbly flashback transition, with harp music and everything.) Back to my first ever encounter with a bowling machine.

There were three of us. Me, Chris Stott, and Mark Matthews. We messed about with the machine, experimenting. We all had a bat, though not a long one, as it took us a while to get the hang of the machine.

We had the net for an hour, and at the end of it I decided I couldn't leave without finding out how quick 'quick' really was. With no-one in the stumps end, I cranked the machine up to 90mph. Its hum rising steadily, I fired down a few experimentals, and zeroed it in to pitch up near the crease, swinging in to clip the outside of off stump.

What I would learn in the future but didn't yet appreciate, is that while the machine is pretty good at landing ball after ball on an area the size of a beermat, it is prone to the occasional aberration. The whole thing judders horizontally when it fires a ball, especially when it's set at the upper end of fast, and it will stick on its rubbers every now and again and its aim will go awry, firing the odd ball down a foot or two wide of the mark. Sometimes it takes another ball or two to get it to sit back properly where you've aimed it. All bowlers lose their radar. Even machines.

I take up position in front of the stumps, with a guard outside leg, so I'll definitely be safe. Just want to see what it's like to face Steve Harmison. Try and defend it. Keep his spearing inswinging yorker away from my off stump.

Okay, I nod to Chris at the controls. Do it. His hand rises above the machine, displaying the ball. He lowers it smoothly, dropping it into the slot.

An orangey blur streaks towards me, not unlike a tracer bullet.

Simultaneously, and rather distractingly, someone shatters the outside of my left foot with a 20lb sledge hammer.

The doctor is still smiling. He picks up my left foot, feeling it gently. "That hurt?"

I nod stoically. "A bit." He feels underneath, applying steady pressure to the arch of my foot with both thumbs. I wince.

"You're fine."

"Eh?"

"You're fine. If it was broken you'd have gone through the roof when I did that."

"Oh."

"It's just a really nice bruise. It's going to go some lovely colours. Put an ice pack on it, keep it up on a chair. Try and keep off it for a week or two."

"Chair. Keep off it. Right."

"And, it goes without saying…"

"Mmm?"

"I'd give that Steve Harmison a wide berth if I were you."

Ashen skies

Thursday 15 April 2010. La Manga, south-eastern Spain. We're due to fly home today, but when I take the car back to the car hire place, the blonde girl who switches between any of a dozen languages for each new conversation tells me we might struggle to get back to England because a volcano erupted in Iceland last night.

They're hilarious, the Dutch, aren't they? Or maybe she's German. No, Scandinavian definitely. Probably. Hilarious anyway. A volcano in Iceland! What's that got to do with anything? I smile and agree with her.

Six hours later the volcanic ash cloud has shut down every airport in northern Europe and it seems somewhat less funny. We've spent most of the intervening time on hold with Ryan Air. Their call centre is brilliant. You're in a queue. We're charging you a fortune for this call. Please hold. We're charging you a fortune for this call. Please hold. We're charging you a fortune for this call. Ooops– we've cut you off.

Repeat ad nauseum. We never do get to speak to them. Presumably their theory must be that if their customer service is that terrible, why give people the opportunity to shout at them? They're on the list now, along with Talk Talk and Tesco: we solemnly vow that they are never getting another penny out of us. That'll teach 'em.

In the meantime we're stuck. We've checked out of our villa. Our luggage is piled up expectantly at the taxi place. We're in the 'Sí!' bar overdosing on coffee while the kids run riot outside mainlining mint-choc-chip. It looks unlikely there'll be any flights tomorrow. We have work commitments on Monday. More importantly, Saturday is our nephew's eighth birthday party, which the kids have been looking forward to for months. More importantly still, Sunday is the first cricket game of the year, which I've been looking forward to for months. Seven whole ones, in fact.

Are we gonna let a little volcano stop us? We are not. We are resolved. We are driving. It's either that or stay here haemorrhaging cash in the five-star resort hotel.

We struggle to get through to car hire places, in more ways than one. Those we do manage to speak to on the phone seem to have great difficulty grasping the concept of hiring a car in one country and dropping it off in another. Avis: "No. You can't do that. You just can't." Finally, with the help of a friend in the UK calling a UK office, we have a car booked at 8pm from Alicante airport to be dropped off 24 hours later in Paris. Hertz see the potential for exploitation here, and consider that journey to be worth over £1200. We'll take that car, but after that they're going on the list.

On the way it slowly emerges from their indecipherably obtuse website (with the help of my sleepy sister in the UK in the middle of the night) that the Eurostar from Paris idea is one everyone else has had too, so the new plan is the Caen ferry. We drive through the night, phone poised for 8.30 when the Brittany Ferries booking line opens. At 8.31 an actual real-life person answers the phone and chats pleasantly while selling us tickets for the 'sleeper' ferry for £97 for the whole family. There are no cabins or even chairs. It's standing room only, but they can get us on. (Brittany Ferries are the only company to emerge positively from our little adventure.)

The kids are awesome. 24 hours straight in a people-carrier jammed to the roof with suitcases and golf clubs, and they're fantastic. No whinging. Plenty of toilet breaks, but no whinging. I am less awesome. We're sharing the driving, and I'm really struggling to keep my eyes open as identikit motorways blur into each other.

We drop the car off exactly 24 hours and 1839 kilometres later at Hertz in Caen. The two taxis (one for us, one for the luggage) to the ferry terminal cost more than the ferry tickets.

The ferry is rammed full of good natured spirit-of-the-blitz Brits with stories similar to ours. We drink warm rosé with ice and the four of us sleep curled up on a landing by a staircase; the steel floor throbbing beneath our heads as the massive diesels fifty feet below rumble their steady, well-worn path across the channel.

A couple of thousand pounds and a day and a half later, we've all had a great time at the party and I'm on the cricket field.

It's a beautiful cloudless day (everyone is quick to point out how the weather in England has been better than Spain for the last week) the cornflower blue sky eerily unbroken by the normally ubiquitous vapour trails, as it will remain for another week.

I tell the story I've just told a dozen times, though mostly it's the short version: "Yeah we got stuck, yeah. Drove. Couldn't miss this, could I?"

It's good to see them all again. No matter how much you might try to keep up with beers in the pub over the winter, it's not the same. Never the same as the beers after the game, when there's the dissection how brilliant/mediocre/rubbish we just were, and the unique pleasure of alcohol wiping out any good the exercise just did.

In the second over I'm standing at point, and the ball is cut hard, but straight at me. I'm about to get my first touch of a cricket ball in anger since last September. I'm down to it, side-on, kneeling, body behind it. Four feet in front of me it hits a bump in the field and leaps left, avoiding everything I've carefully placed in its way and racing on towards the boundary.

Amidst the jeers and the 'never-mind's and the 'next-time's, I can't help grinning as I trot after it to retrieve it from the long grass beyond the rope. Two grand I paid for this.

"Worth coming back for, Si?"

"Every penny."

glossary and jargon buster

Let's call a hand held manually operated portable soil excavation and relocation device a spade, shall we?

abdominal guard ludicrously demure euphemism. See 'box'.

across the line to play across the 'line of the ball' (qv) – ie perpendicular to its direction of travel – is to dramatically increase your chances of missing or edging it. Good players rarely do it. Only bad ones and exceptional ones make a habit of it.

action the manner in which a bowler delivers the ball, the way his arms coil and release, his posture during delivery. Though broadly similar – their arms windmill over – the detail of a leg spinner's action makes it a completely different animal from that of a swing bowler. Each bowler's is unique, like a fingerprint or a golf swing. Some are elegant and fluid, some ugly and stilted. Either can be effective. The basic nature of the bowler's action must be announced to the facing batsman by the umpire at each change of bowler, or if at any point the bowler chooses to change his action. This tells you simply which hand he will deliver the ball from, and from which side of the wicket he will approach. Examples are "left arm round" and, by far the most common, "right arm over". An umpire might also announce to the batsman: "New bowler, same action," or "Same bowler, new action: he's coming around." See also 'over, 2' and 'round the wicket'.

aerial of a shot – played in the air. Can be deliberate – to chip the ball over the infield (qv) for instance, or a six, of course – or unintended, being played 'uppishly' instead of along the floor, offering catches. See 'in the air'.

agricultural functional, inelegant heave. A full blooded, cross batted (qv) wallop, usually to cow corner (qv). In village cricket, often performed by farmers without a hint of irony. See also 'slog' and 'yahoo'.

air of a spinner, to give the ball air is to toss it up, as opposed to 'firing it in' (qv) so it rises above the batsman's eye-line (qv). This has the twin effects of making it more difficult to judge the length (qv), and giving the ball more chance of landing softly and spinning.

all ends up for a batsman to be beaten all ends up is for him to have very little idea of where the ball just went or how it didn't bowl him, because he didn't really know too much about it. See 'beat the bat'.

all out once a batting side has lost ten wickets in an innings, they are all out (the eleventh batsman cannot bat on his own), and it is their opponent's turn to bat. In limited overs cricket you never want to be all out, because your side won't get as long to bat as your opponents. Unless you're all out going for the umpteenth six off the final ball, in which case it looks like you've paced (qv, 2) your innings nicely.

all-rounder A cricketer who bats and bowls well enough to get into the side on the merits of either discipline. There are four types: a batting all-rounder is an excellent bat who bowls a bit, a bowling all-rounder is the opposite, a 'genuine' (qv) all-rounder excels at both. Very rare. As opposed to a village all-rounder (qv), which is not even slightly rare. An all-rounder who succeeds at both disciplines in the same game is often a match-winning difference.

all the toys of a spin bowler, to have lots of variations (qv). The two greatest spinners of recent times (some would argue ever,) only really had two each. Murali had his ripping off-spinner (qv) and his doosra (qv), and Warne, who was famous for all his different deliveries, never mastered the googly (qv) so hardly ever used it. He really only used two: his big spinning leg break (qv) and his slider (qv), which was really a variation on a top-spinner (qv), as was his flipper. No-one really knew what a zooter was, and there was much speculation that a lot of the new variations Warne claimed to have developed were entirely fictional, and all just part of the mind games. Which didn't make them any less effective, of course.

all three given that a set of stumps are nine inches across and cricket balls are under three inches in diameter, it is not possible for one to hit all three stumps. It is possible for it to hit one stump into another though, and leave them thoroughly splayed or even uprooted, looking like they've been attacked by a wrecking ball. Balls that leave stumps this comprehensively disturbed are said, often not without glee, to have hit all three. Also descriptive of an LBW shout that is so 100% plumb (qv), that simply to say it is out seems insufficient.

anchor a batsman who settles in to bat the duration of the innings and play conservatively, while others can come and go around him, being more aggressive.

appeal To shout "Aaarrrrrgggghhhhhh?!?" whilst pointing menacingly at the umpire is to appeal. To enquire of the umpire whether in his opinion a batsman is out. See 'how's that'.

area 'to bowl good areas' is one of cricket's hoariest old clichés. All it means is to bowl line and length (qv) – that awkward shall-I-go-forward-or-back length and shall-I-play-or-leave line. To bowl well, in other words. Because of stump microphones, when he was standing up (qv) to Warne, you could hear pretty much everything Adam Gilchrist said to him after every delivery. Almost without exception, what he said was some sort of variation on the theme "Awwwww – Nice area, Shane!"

arm short for throwing arm. The praise "Good arm!" means 'that was an excellent throw'. See 'take on the arm'.

arm ball a spinner's variation (qv) that goes 'straight on with the arm', ie does not turn. From a habitually big spinner of the ball, the one that doesn't turn can be very effective, often getting wickets LBW or bowled. From less prodigious spinners, the arm ball is often indistinguishable from all the other balls in his formidable arsenal.

around the wicket see 'round the wicket'.

asking rate see 'run rate'.

attack (1) The bowlers a captain has at his disposal is referred to as his attack.

attack (2) An attacking field is one set to try and get wickets and not worry about the batsman scoring runs. An attacking bowler similarly is always after the wicket-taking ball and is not worried about conceding runs. An attacking batsman wants runs all the time and plays aggressive shots, showing little regard for the protection of his wicket. The confluence of all three makes for a riveting passage of play.

average (1) A batsman's average is calculated by dividing the number of runs he's scored by the number of times he's been out. (Not getting out is therefore an excellent way to boost your batting average. Who'd have guessed?) So the higher the better. Over 30 is good. Over 50 is excellent. A bowler's average is the number of runs scored off his bowling divided by the number of wickets he's taken, and equates to how many runs each wicket costs. So the lower the better. 35 is good. 20 is excellent. An all-rounder (qv) with a batting average higher than his bowling average is clearly doing a few things right.

average (2) To be a village all-rounder (qv) is to know the meaning of mediocrity.

back see 'field back'.

back and across see 'backward defensive'

back away an often involuntary retreat into the legside, to avoid fast bowling. A natural self-preservation instinct, it is never a good idea. Either the bowler will 'follow' you, and bowl at you, or he'll aim at your unprotected stumps, which you must now play across the line (qv) to defend. Either way you're in trouble. If you're not 'in behind' (qv) quick bowling, it's that much harder to hit.

back cut a cut (qv) shot played late (also called a 'late cut') when the ball has already passed the batsman, so that the ball goes finer, backwards of square (point). Back cuts will generally race through the slips or gully area to third man, and are particularly effective if there's no one there – see 'vacant'.

back foot The foot of the batsman nearest his stumps: the right foot for a right hander. Back foot shots are played to short (qv) balls, and the batsman steps back towards his stumps with most of the his weight over his back leg. This gives him more time to react to short-pitched balls, either to defend them if they're straight (see 'backward defensive') or to drive (qv), cut (qv), or pull (qv).

back-of-a-length of fast bowlers, to bowl just short of a length (qv), so the ball rears towards the ribs. Very difficult to score from if straight, prone to cuts (qv) and pulls (qv) from better players if not. See also 'heavy ball'.

backing up (1) of the non-striking batsman, to advance down the wicket in preparation for a quick run. Vital to avoid run outs (qv). Beware the Mankad (qv).

backing up (2) of a fielding side, to get behind the stumps on the line of a throw, to cover in case the bowler or wicket keeper miss it, or in case the fielder is 'having a go' at the stumps; trying for a direct hit run out (qv). See also 'overthrows'.

backlift raising the bat in preparation to hit the ball. There is a great variety of methods, and no set way to do it. Brian Lara had a huge flourishing backlift which was rarely less than vertical. Others hardly seem to move the bat back before it comes forward at all, like a Bruce Lee one-inch punch.

backward anywhere behind the bat on the field. Thus, level with the bat on the legside is 'square leg'. Just behind level with the bat is 'backward square leg'.

backward defensive a shot played off the back foot (qv), to a short (qv) or back of a length (qv) ball, with a vertical bat. Designed to stop the ball – on the basis that it might hit the stumps if left – not to score off it. Orthodox action is for the batsman to step backwards in his crease and across to cover the stumps ("back and across") and get in behind the ball with his bat up high to get on top of the bounce and play it down.

bails two four inch bits of wood that sit atop the stumps (qv, 1) to form a wicket (qv, 2).

bakerloo predominantly commentator (rather than player) slang for when a batsman plays down the wrong line. See 'line of the ball'.

balance (1) See 'front foot' and 'back foot'.

balance (2) the balance of a good side is determined by the specialists within it. A typical Test match line up would be five batsmen, an all-rounder, a wicket-keeper (effectively making seven specialist batsmen) and four bowlers. (Five, with your all-rounder. See how useful he is?) A typical village line up would be two or three guys who bat and don't bowl, and eight village all-rounders (qv).

ball (1) hard and solid, cricket balls weigh about five and a half ounces, and measure about nine inches in circumference. (Less for women and children.) They're made of cork, tightly bound with string, and encased in four pieces of leather. Pairs of these are shaped and sewn together (inside) to form hemispheres, which are then stitched together externally to form the 'seam' (qv). They are mostly red. White balls are used for limited overs (qv) professional games under floodlights. Orange balls are increasingly common for village (qv) evening games where floodlights are not an option. Pink balls have also been experimented with, potentially for use in First Class (qv) games under lights.

ball (2) another term for a delivery. There are six balls in an over.

'ball' (3) contraction of 'good ball'. See also 'bowled'.

ball of the century Also known as 'The Gatting Ball'. The young, brash, inexperienced Shane Warne's first ball in an Ashes Test, at Old Trafford in 1993. It is the perfect legbreak (qv). It starts dead on middle stump, then drifts (qv) incredibly as it dips (qv), pitching maybe eighteen inches outside leg. Gatting, an excellent player of spin, follows it and plays forward to defend, bat angled to smother the spin. But the ball turns sharply, passing the edge and sending the off bail spinning in the air. Even with repeated slow motion replays it doesn't look possible. It marked the start of a decade and a half of psychological domination from Warne himself and Australia in general, and revived the almost dead phenomenon of the attacking, aggressive spinner who strikes fear into the hearts of the very best batsmen in the world.

ball tampering Thorny issue at the highest level, but if you play at anything less than first class or international level, you can safely ignore it. In the longer forms of the game, a ball is used for 80 overs before a new one is due. In order to reverse swing (qv) the ball needs to roughen up, get scuffed and lose its sheen. The Laws say that artificially altering the state of the ball is illegal, yet every fielding side in top class cricket will do their best to help it happen, from purposefully throwing the ball in 'on the bounce', so that it scuffs on the hard square before reaching the keeper, to bowling 'cross seamers' (qv) to 'fielding' the ball with their spikes, to picking at the seam with their fingernails. Or bottle tops, in one famous case. Other ways to make it swing include sugary saliva, from boiled sweets or mints, to make the shiny side even shinier, and vaseline or suntan oil. All are against the Laws, all are done all the time. Many pundits take the view that the contest is so much in the batsman's favour these days, anything the bowlers can do to make it more difficult for them should be allowed, and the Laws should be changed. What you are allowed to do, is 'maintain' the ball, ie shine it, but without any assistance other than spit and polish. The Laws as they stand are ambiguous and uninforced, and their blurry edges often seem as much a mystery to the players and officials as they are to the rest of us.

bang it in of fast bowlers, to bowl short (qv). Usually a verb, but can also be an adjective to describe an individual: "He's a bang-it-in bowler". See 'back-of-a-length', 'bouncer' and 'heavy ball'.

bat the objects of much debate and much affection. A good one might last a lifetime. But what fun is only ever having one? Modern bats are bigger and heavier than ever, with thick edges and massive middles. There is no limit on weight in the rules, and some have chosen to take this as an invitation; many are enormously powerful, promising huge sixes, but at nearer 4lb than 3lb, too heavy for most normal people to wield effectively. Bradman's was 2lb 2oz. The old adage about workmen and tools applies most emphatically.

bat all the way down many village sides will claim to bat all the way down, which means in essence that little or no variation in the ability of the batsmen is discernable anywhere in the batting order (qv). This can of course be a good or a bad thing, depending on the general level of that ability – whether they're all cavalier Botham-esque all-rounders, or are all equally unsure as to which way up to hold the bat.

bat deep a more realistic claim than 'bat all the way down' (qv), meaning that a team has a good few all-rounders, and therefore a very short tail (qv).

bat-pad (1) sitting down? This is complicated. To a spinner or slow bowler, a batsman is likely to defend (qv, 1) the ball with his bat and front pad very close together. This throws up possibilities for wickets that means the umpire needs to be paying very close attention indeed. In a televised game, you may see the third umpire (qv) using snicko (qv), Hawk-Eye (qv), and hot spot (qv) all for a single delivery. What needs to be determined is whether the ball hits the bat, the pad, or both, and if so in what order. If it hits the bat and then the pad, the batsman can be out caught, but can't be out LBW. If it hits the pad only, he can be LBW but not caught. If it hits the pad and then the bat, he can be either. How's that?

bat-pad (2) fielding position set specifically for a bat-pad (1). Very very close on the leg side, between a very short leg and a very silly mid on. Rare in village cricket – if you drop it short the pull (qv) could have murderous consequences – common for world class spinners.

'Batsman in' said by someone on the fielding side to alert his team to the arrival at the crease of a new batsman. The response is applause; the simple, polite, sporting recognition of an opponent before battle. Right and proper. Ignored by cads.

bat time to stay in; to not get out. To be more concerned with not getting out than with getting runs. To 'occupy the crease'. Often happens when most of a team are out following a collapse (qv) and whoever's left needs to consolidate and really get 'in' before they do anything rash, or when a team is batting for a draw. See 'gritty'.

batting knickers briefs or shorts with a built in pouch to hold your box (qv) securely in place. See also 'jockstrap'.

batting order the order in which batsman come out to bat, after the openers (qv). Conventional wisdom has it that a side's best batsmen bat at 3, 4 and 5. 6 and 7 are usually a wicket-keeper and an all-rounder, the rest bowlers. In casual cricket there is unlikely to be an order set in stone, and the captain decides who bats where, often at the last minute. Even in professional cricket, especially Twenty20, captains are increasingly delaying their decisions as to who goes in when depending on the kind of player (a big hitter or a strokemaker) they're replacing. See 'tail' and 'balance' (2).

batting partner batting is done in pairs, one facing the bowling, the other waiting to face. The two batsmen run between the wickets to score runs. Successful partnerships are vital to scoring well, and an understanding with the guy at the other end is always important. See 'call'.

BB or 'best' a bowler's best bowling figures. Wickets count as more important than runs, so figures of 8-250 are better than 7-1.

BCCI The Board of Control for Cricket in India. Indian cricket's governing body. As that is these days where all the money is, arguably it has effectively, if not officially, overtaken the ICC (qv) as the real power in the world game. See also 'MCC'.

beachball see 'football'. The same, only even better, bigger, easier.

beamer a fast full toss that goes straight at a batsman's head. Very dangerous, as batsman will be looking for the ball pitching on the wicket, so often won't see it till it's too late to react. Usually a mistake by the bowler and followed quickly by an apology to the batsman.

Automatically a no ball (qv) as it's above waist height. Because they are so dangerous, deliberate beamers or repeated accidental ones are not tolerated at any level of cricket. After two warnings, the umpires can direct the captain to "take the bowler off forthwith".

beat the bat of a bowler, to bowl so well that the batsman can't 'lay a bat on it'. A 'play and miss' is a world away from a considered 'leave' (qv). A batsman repeatedly trying and failing to hit the ball is probably getting pretty close to it in the process, and is therefore very likely to edge (qv) it sooner or later. Usually prompts "Oooo"s from the slips – if a bowler is routinely 'passing the edge' you'll almost certainly have slips in place, unless the game is at the death (qv). Often, a good bowler repeatedly beating a lesser batsman in the corridor (qv) can psychologically finish him in the space of an over, prompting Fred-Trumanisms such as "That were wayysted on thee, lad," and irony-laden commentary like "He's not quite good enough to edge those." To beat the bat is a moral, if not actual, victory for the bowler.

beehive a tv graphic, courtesy of Hawk-Eye (qv) showing from the bowler's-eye perspective the grouping pattern of balls as they reached the batsman. Usually either for a particular bowler, or all balls to a particular batsman, allowing analysis of an individual's or a team's plans. Or lack of them. Often the balls are coloured differently on the graphic to indicate if they were left, attacked, dots, runs, wickets, etc. So called because the patterns tend to be roughly beehive – or pair – shaped. See also 'pitchmap'.

behind (1) the wicket-keeper is behind the bat, as are slips, gully, etc. At these fielding positions (qv), the ball comes quickly, any contact with the bat often adding to the bowler's pace.

behind (2) not scoring quickly enough. See 'run rate'.

behind the bowler's arm see 'sightscreen'

belter a very flat (qv) pitch, offering no glimmer of help for the bowlers. Presumably so called because the batsmen will spend all day belting the leather off the ball.

bend your back of fast bowlers, to make an extra special effort, either for a one off effort ball (qv), or in a continued concerted effort to try and wring some kind of life out of a dead, flat (qv) belter (qv) of a pitch.

big mo see 'momentum'

blade a bat *(n)*. Often preceded by the adjective 'flashing'. Specifically, the front of the bat, the flat(ish) part designed to make contact with the ball.

block any defensive shot. In some situations, all that's required, for a while at least, is that you stay in and don't get out. The forward defensive is your friend. See 'bat time'.

blockhole where batsmen take guard (qv) on the crease (qv). Where a yorker (qv) lands: right up on your toes. A delivery with every chance of creeping under the bat, and very little chance of being scored off – leaving the batsman with no option but to block – is in the blockhole. Or perhaps named after the little trench made by the constant tapping of bat after bat: holes made by blocks.

Bodyline the cricket tactic that changed the game, entered folklore, and conceded the moral high ground to the Australians. During the 1932-3 Ashes tour to Australia, MCC (England) captain Douglas Jardine instructed his fast bowlers – most notably the super-quick Harold Larwood, alleged to be one of the fastest ever – to bowl not at the wickets, but at the batsmen. Jardine called the tactic 'leg theory' and set a ring of close fielders around the bat on the leg side for the ball that pops up in the air as the batsman desperately defends his head and body. As a tactic to combat the run-machine that was Donald Bradman (qv), Bodyline could be said to have failed, as he still averaged over 50 in the series. What it succeeded in doing was hospitalising several players, sparking an international incident, cementing the rivalry between the two countries (England won the Ashes using the tactic), prompting changes in the laws of cricket ('dangerous or intimidatory bowling' and 'no more than two fielders behind square on the leg side'), popularising the phrase "it's not cricket" and spawning countless books and an excellent TV mini-series. See chapter 5.

bottom edge an inside edge (qv) but when the bat is horizontal, either playing a cut or a pull. See also 'chop on', 'drag on', 'chinese cut', 'edge', 'outside edge', 'nick', 'feather', and 'walk'.

bottom hand the hand closest to the blade of the bat – the right hand for a right hander, left for a lefty. Bottom hand shots, or shots said to contain 'a lot of bottom hand' tend by dint of simple anatomy, to be across the line (qv) and therefore into the leg side, and will almost invariably be in the air. Can be very effective if used wisely. Batsmen with only bottom hand shots in their locker will be out caught in the legside fairly shortly if the fielding captain has any nous at all. Unless they're a big enough hitter to repeatedly clear the cow corner (qv) fence, of course.

bounce lively or unusual movement off a pitch, usually extracted either by a tall fast bowler, or by a spinner with a top-spinner (qv).

bouncer A fierce delivery from a fast bowler that pitches short (qv), usually about halfway, so that the ball bounces up towards the batsman's head. See 'hook' and 'duck (2)'.

boundary (1) the edge of the field of play. Marked by flags, a painted white line or a rope.

boundary (2) to hit the ball over the boundary (1) is to score a boundary (2). If the ball has not bounced on the way, it's worth six runs. If it has, it's worth four.

boundary ball a poor ball that deserves to be swatted to the fence. See also 'long hop'.

boundary rider a sweeper (qv).

bowl to 'deliver' or propel the ball from one end of the 22 yards to the other, towards the batsman at the striker's end (qv) where he will defend his wicket (qv, 2). The difference between throwing and bowling is essentially that a bowler does not bend his elbow, and all the power comes from the rotation of the arm from the shoulder. (Though strictly speaking this is not true – see chapter 7). Also see 'chuck'. There are many different kinds of bowling and bowler, see 'fast', 'slow', 'leg-spin', 'off-spin', 'left-arm orthodox', 'chinaman', 'swing', 'medium', 'dibbly-dobbly', 'pace off' and 'military'.

---

bowled (1) if a delivery hits a batsman's stumps and removes the bails, he is out, bowled.

'bowled' (2) contraction of "well bowled". Shouts of encouragement and approval from the fielding side to their bowler. Occasionally even from the batsman to the bowler.

---

box the hard plastic case one keeps one's balls in. Also known by the hilarious euphemism 'abdominal guard', or a 'cup', if you're American. Whatever you call it, it's the one indispensable piece of cricket kit that every player, even if he only plays one game a decade, should own. You want your own. It's not something you want to borrow, any more than you'd want to borrow your mate's Y-fronts. But borrowing is better than going commando, where boxes are concerned at least. To bat or keep wicket without one is to invite a world of pain. Being hit down there is unbelievably painful, even with a box. Without one, frankly, doesn't bear thinking about.

Bradman Sir Donald, 1908-2001. Australian cricket legend. Widely accepted as the best batsman the game has ever known. In his final Test he needed four runs to average a staggering three figures, and was out for a duck. Career average 99.94. A genuine phenomenon, the chasing pack of his nearest rivals are nearly 40 short of him. The Australian $100 bill is still known as a 'Don'. See 'Bodyline' and chapter 5.

---

buffet Bad bowling, easy to score off, is buffet bowling: help yourself.

build to build or construct an innings is to proceed serenely, carefully, cerebrally. To be patient, to defend the good balls, punish the bad ones, take few risks. To see where the runs can be made and which shots not to play – not today; not in these conditions. As opposed to just going out and having a thrash. Both methods of course can be as successful or disastrous as the other, and which you choose is as much about personality and temperament as situation and technique.

bump ball a ball hit straight down into the ground. It often happens so fast that it looks like it might be a catch, especially from a good distance away, but a caught bump ball of course cannot be out, it can only ever be tidy fielding. See 'crowd catch'.

bumper little-used, rather old fashioned term for a bouncer (qv)

bunny see 'rabbit'

bunsen rhyming slang (bunsen burner) for a turner (qv).

Burrough's Law see 'shit gets wickets'.

byes when a ball misses everything – bat, pads, body – the batsmen can still run. Byes count towards the batting side's total, but not towards the individual batsman's score. See 'extras'. They don't count against the bowler's figures either, but they do count against the wicket-keeper, who is, not unreasonably, expected to stop anything that misses the batsman, his bat, and the stumps, but isn't a wide.

call to shout to your batting partner (qv) to indicate whether or not you should run. The general rule of thumb is, for the first run, if the ball goes in front of the batsman, it's his call. If it goes behind him, it's his partner's call. For subsequent runs, the call should be made by whoever is running to the danger end (qv). Calls are usually 'Yes', 'No', or 'Wait'. Sometimes all three, occasionally with 'Sorry' added on the end. Judging a run is a skill in itself, and depends on the speed of both batsmen, the field (a long or wet outfield will slow the ball down considerably) and fielders. 'Taking on the arm' (qv) of a good fielder can be fatal, and often results in a run out (qv). The author is not a great judge of a run, but derives solace from the fact that many a better batsmen than he is are truly appalling at it. Current and recent England players Bell and Shah leap to mind; classy bats both, prone to reckless, suicidal singles.

captain a cricket captain has an awful lot on his mind. Who's playing? Who's got a wedding this weekend? What's the batting order? Who shall I bowl and when? Defensive or aggressive field? Slips? Third man? Perhaps most crucially, heads or tails? (See 'toss') There's so much to it, chapter 9 is devoted to it.

captain's innings an innings a captain plays where he gets runs or digs in and defends when the team really needs it. An innings where the captain as a batsman turns the course of the game.

carry (1) *n* the distance a ball stays in the air after it has passed the batsman on it's way to the wicket keeper or slips. Hard bouncy tracks have 'good carry', and the keeper and slips can stand well back and still be able to take catches. On slower wickets they must come in closer, or the ball is likely to bounce before it reaches them.

carry (2) *v* of a catch, 'to carry' is to make it all the way into the fielder's hands without touching the floor. If it does touch the floor of course, the batsman is not out.

carry (3) the chief duty of the twelfth man (qv) in professional cricket is that of a waiter: to carry the drinks onto the field.

carry your bat a batman who opens the innings and remains not out at its conclusion is said to have carried his bat.

cartwheel of a stump. To be hit by the ball, usually near the top, with such force that it is uprooted and dances end over end towards the boundary, sometimes even past the wicket-keeper. There are few more joyous sights for a fielding side, and none more satisfying for a fast bowler, than a cartwheeling off stump.

catch see 'caught'.

'catch!' the yell, usually issued from either the bowler or the wicket keeper, indicating that the batsman has hit the ball in the air and someone really should think about catching it, please.

catches win matches splendid old cliché spouted as enthusiastically by 8 yr olds with tennis balls as by gnarled international coaches. At every level it is fundamentally true – if every half-chance is snaffled by spectacular reflex catches, you are very unlikely to lose. Drop half a dozen sitters, and you are very unlikely to win.

caught (1) if a batsman hits a ball in the air and a fielder catches it, he's out, caught. In both professional and amateur cricket, roughly three quarters of all wickets are caught. Being caught on the boundary going for your sixth six in the over is a glorious way to get out. Being caught at midwicket having flapped at one like a pansy is not. Catches can rebound off other body parts, protection, other players or even umpires, but must be taken with bare hands. Any taken in hats or gloves are not out. The exception is the wicketkeeper, who may wear gloves. (And you are unlikely to meet one who doesn't.)

caught (2) To tell your wife you're having an affair, only for her to turn up at the ground and discover you playing cricket instead.

caught and bowled a bowler taking a 'return catch' off his own bowling, so it reads in the scorebook 'Caught: White, Bowled: White'. (I still have that scorebook.)

century a hundred runs scored by a batsman in an innings. A century in any form or standard of cricket is a real achievement. Only good players get them.

chance the possibility of a wicket. Nearly a catch, nearly a stumping, nearly a run out. What could have been. A dropped catch is a chance that went down.

charge see 'dance down the pitch'.

chase (1) if a ball passes a fielder and there is no sweeper (qv) beyond him, he must chase the ball in an attempt to stop it reaching the boundary. Sometimes, if balls are hit very hard or timed very well, the ball will win the contest before it's begun. Other times the fielder wins it easily. The best contests are when the issue is marginal, and some terrific feat of athleticism is required to halt the ball and return it to the middle, prompting praise all round of "Great chase!"

chase (2) to bat second in a limited overs game, is to chase (a target).

cheap to be out without scoring many is to be out cheaply. For a bowling side to dismiss several batsmen for few runs is for them to get cheap wickets.

check drive a check (or checked) drive is almost a defensive shot, with little or no follow through, but with sufficient timing to see the ball race off the bat.

cherry a (red, obviously) cricket ball, especially a new one. As in "Anderson gets the new cherry." Also a delivery, bowled with a new ball. As in "That's a terrific cherry from Anderson." Also descriptive of the red marks the ball leaves on the bat.

chin music bouncers (qv). Especially a series of them, or a sustained spell of bowling containing a lot of them.

chinaman a left handed wrist spinner, whose stock ball spins in to the right hander like an off-break. Occasionally, it's bowled as a variation by left arm orthodox (qv) spinners. (Allegedly, the first exponent was of Chinese extraction.) A chinaman googly is a left handed wrist spinner's wrong'un. Moves from leg to off like a leg break. It's another variation for the left armer, making it harder to pick (qv) – essentially it does the same as an orthodox left arm spin delivery, but *looks* like it's going to go the other way. Confused? Don't worry. They're pretty rare. The last chinaman bowler with all the toys (qv) worthy of note was Sir Garfield Sobers.

chinese cut an inside edge (qv) that narrowly avoids chopping on

(qv) and squirts away down towards fine leg (see 'fielding positions').
Also known as a 'Harrow drive'.

chirp to keep the banter and encouragement up in the field. Cricket
can be quite isolating if you're not careful, the team being necessarily
spread thinly across the field, making conversation difficult. It is
important to keep the communication flowing, even when there's
nothing to say. Anything from a simple 'well bowled' to such irony
as 'bowl him the quicker one now' after your quickest bowler has
whistled down his effort ball. Observations like 'they're all in the air
boys, a catch is coming,' are a world away from 'this guy's a talentless
loser and his wife is ugly'. (See 'sledging'.) If you can keep smiling and
keep talking, you're all more likely to keep focussed. Besides, this is
supposed to be fun, isn't it?

chop on (v) to hit the ball on to your own stumps with your bat,
usually off an inside edge (qv). Sometimes 'play on'. See 'drag on'.

chuck a bowler who bends and then straightens his bowling arm
during his delivery action is deemed to be throwing, or 'chucking',
not bowling, and the delivery is deemed a no ball. Being no-balled
for throwing – being branded a 'chucker' – is effectively being told
you're cheating. Famously, Muttiah Muralitharan ('Murali') was
repeatedly no-balled for throwing in the 1990s, by no-stranger-
to-controversy Darrell Hair, among others. Slow motion cameras
and motion capture were used in a very close biomechanical study
of Murali's unique action, only possible as a result of an inherited
deformity in his arm. Unexpectedly, the tests proved that actually
ALL bowlers flex their arm when bowling, and as a result a limit of
15° was set as an allowable amount for the elbow to bend and Murali
was exonerated. He took his last Test wicket with his final ball in his
final game, making his tally 800, 92 more than his great rival Warne.
See chapter 7 for more about chucking and Murali's action.

circle a series of white discs on the ground forming a circle (actually
an oval) usually 25 or 30 yards from the wickets. This area is used for
fielding restrictions in the shorter forms of the game, so that during
specified times only a certain number of fielders are allowed outside

the circle. See 'power play'.

clap in see 'batsman in'.

class a batsman who looks good and plays all the shots with effortless grace is a classy bat. If he can score runs while he's doing it, so much the better, but it's certainly not a prerequisite for the epithet. You can spot class from further away than you can read a scoreboard.

classical of a batsman's technique. Well-schooled. Nothing across the line (qv), nothing flashy or risky. See 'textbook', 'top hand', 'straight bat', 'elbow' 'elegant'.

clean bowl or clean up: to hit the stumps without anything else (bat, gloves, pads, body) getting involved.

clip a shot, usually played off the pads (qv) through square or midwicket, which is timed with an economy of movement and minimum of effort, rather than swung at.

close to field anywhere within about 20 yards of the bat is close. Close fielders are attacking (qv, 2) positions. See 'silly' and 'crowd (2)'.

close the face turning the face of the bat in towards your body as an aid to guiding the ball through the leg side. Usually a wristy, nonchalant flick or clip (qv) off the pads. Looks very easy. Isn't. Beware the leading edge (qv).

collapse when the majority of batsmen in a side are out one after the other for little or no score. Depressingly familiar to all England supporters.

consolidate if a side lose wickets quickly (see 'collapse'), the next batsmen in are forced into a position where they can't afford to be out, and must take their time to get 'in' (qv, 3) before taking any risks with aggressive shots. So if a batting side are reduced to, say, 10-3, the batting pair next in need to be careful to avoid a total collapse. At

100-3 they've rebuilt pretty well, are probably both well set and have a healthy partnership going. They have consolidated.

construct see 'build'.

County Championship domestic first class (qv) competition in England and Wales, officially since 1889, though the earliest known inter-county match was 1709. Currently contested in two innings four day games by 18 counties over two divisions.

correct of a batsman's technique. Well-schooled. Nothing across the line (qv), nothing flashy or risky. See 'textbook', 'top hand', 'straight bat', 'elbow', 'elegant'.

coming on on hard, quick wickets on sunny days, the ball seems to race off the surface when it bounces, almost like it's gaining speed off the pitch. This is not physically possible, of course, the pitch will only ever slow the ball down, but sometimes it feels like it. The ball bounces fast and true, it's easier to time, (see 'timing') and seems eager to find the middle (qv 1). In these conditions – beloved of batsmen everywhere – the ball is said to be 'coming on' to the bat.

conditions weather. Generally, though not always, if it's cloudy or close, the ball will swing and the conditions favour the fielding side. If it's warm and sunny they favour the batsmen. If it rains or gets dark, it doesn't do anyone any favours.

corridor the 'corridor of uncertainty', made famous by the Yorkshire drawl of Geoff Boycott on TMS (qv), refers to the area just on and outside off-stump. Bowling here consistently on a good length makes it difficult for a batsmen to know when to attack (qv), when to play defensively (qv), and when to leave (qv). See also 'fourth stump'.

count towards see 'extras'.

cover drive The best looking of all cricket shots. A top hand (qv) shot played off the front foot (qv) into the covers (qv, 2) with a high elbow (qv). Usually preceded by sumptuous adjectives like 'silky', 'smooth' and, er, 'sumptuous'. Looks good even when done badly. Done well, can reduce cantankerous old men rarely short of a comment to wordless dreamy sighs.

covers (1) Effectively, an umbrella for a cricket pitch. Large portable apparatus brought onto the wicket (qv, 1) to keep it dry when it rains. Cheap ones are just big tarpaulins, expensive ones are like a pitched roof on wheels. Insanely expensive ones are hovercraft, so as not to damage the hallowed Lord's turf with anything as plebeian as wheels.

covers (2) The area of the field in front of a batsman on his offside, from about 45° to about 90°. See 'fielding positions'.

cow corner where most agricultural (qv) shots are headed – the ones a batsman connects with, that is. Around midway between square (qv, 2) and straight back behind the bowler. Officially: deep midwicket / wide long on. See 'fielding positions'. Some might contest it gets its name from the fact that no proper cricket shot would ever be headed there, so cows could safely graze there. In the author's experience, it is more likely to be named after the favourite area of hefty farmers and farm hands.

cramp for a batsmen suddenly to have no room to play, as the ball turns, seams, swings or jags back in on him, meaning suddenly there's not enough room to swing the bat and he's tied up in knots.

Cricinfo .com – since it merged with Wisden online, the home of cricket on the web. With commentary, comment, essays, results, and the career stats of just about everyone ever.

crease painted lines on the floor of the wicket. The stumps are on the batting crease. Four feet in front of that is the popping crease. This is the important one, the one part of the batsman or his bat must be behind in order for him to be 'in', and some part of the bowler's front foot must be behind in order for his delivery not to be a no ball (qv). The return crease runs perpendicular to these two at the ends, 8'8" apart. The bowler's back foot must be inside the return crease (not touching or 'cutting' it) at the moment of delivery too, or it'll be a no ball.

cross if batsmen pass each other in the process of attempting a run, they are said to have crossed. Important because, in the case of a run out, the batsman nearer the stumps that are broken is the one who is out. Also, in the case of a catch, if the batsmen cross while the ball is in the air, even though the run doesn't count, the new man in is not on strike, and so gets the opportunity to have a look at the bowling before he has to face it.

cross bat to play with the bat parallel to the floor. Many orthodox back foot shots require this, especially to short or wide balls – cut (qv), pull (qv), hook (qv), sweep (qv), etc. To play cross batted shots to full, straight balls is to invite disaster. See 'across the line'.

cross seam of a quick bowler, to bowl the ball with his fingers across the seam, rather than parallel with it. He might do this a) to make sure a delivery does *not* swing, b) for variation; if it lands on the seam it's likely to get up (qv) or if it hits a smooth part it might be a shooter (qv), or c) to hasten the deterioration of the ball's condition. See 'swing' and 'ball tampering'. See also 'scrambled seam'.

crowd (1) anyone watching a game, whether the time-honoured one-man-and-his-dog, or 100,000 paying punters. As in 'he's hit that into the crowd' – a six.

crowd (2) to crowd the bat is to bring all the fielder's in close. A field often seen to spinners at the death (qv), when wickets are needed but runs are not important, or just to batsmen who are clearly having difficulty playing a spinner and keep popping potential catches up in the air. See 'close' and 'silly' and 'field up'.

crowd catch a catch off a bump ball (qv), which looks from a distance like it's a wicket so the crowd reacts accordingly, but the players all know is not out.

cut a cross bat (qv) shot played off the back foot (qv) to a short (qv) ball outside the offstump. It has two arcs: the big one from the shoulders, and then at full extension the bat is swung in a flat arc with the handle as its fulcrum, all in one flowing movement. As elegant and effortless as a coverdrive when done properly, the cut uses the bowler's pace, and if timed (qv) will race to the cover boundary more often than not.

cut in half see 'straight through'.

cutter a fast bowler's variation (qv). By running his fingers down the ball at the point of delivery, he takes pace off it and imparts spin, so that it jags back in to the right hander, like an off-break (off-cutter) or away from him, like a legbreak (leg-cutter).

daisy a daisy bowler is one who is unplayably brilliant some days, completely innocuous on others: some days he does, some days he doesn't.

daisy cutter a delivery that rolls along the floor, or bounces more than twice. (Either of which these days makes it a no ball.)

dance down the pitch if a batsman advances down the pitch, he can turn what was going to be a good length (qv) ball into a half volley (qv). To advance in this manner, one must shuffle one's feet, much like a quickstep, hence the expression. Of course, if you dance down like this – it's usually done to spinners, so the keeper will be standing up (qv) – and you miss the ball, you'll almost certainly be out, stumped (qv).

danger end the end – either the bowler's or wicket-keeper's end – where the ball is most likely to be returned by the fielder, and therefore the end a run-out is most likely. If the ball is 'down the ground', ie hit straight, it will probably come back in to the bowler's end, as it will be 22 yards closer. The batsman running to the danger end should be the one to call (qv) the next run. All things being equal, if the ball is square of the wicket either side and nobody has called for it (shouts of "keeper's" or "bowler's" will do it) the fielder will usually default to returning it to the wicket-keeper, as the man with the gloves is the man in control.

dart a spinner's quicker ball (qv) darted in at the feet. See also 'fire it in'.

dead ball the ball can be dead for many reasons: when a boundary is scored; after a batsman is out; if the ball gets trapped in protective clothing; if the bowler drops it on his way in to bowl; or loses his run up (qv) and pulls up short of the crease; if a batsman backs away from his crease before the ball is bowled indicating he is not ready; or when it's finally settled in the bowler or wicket-keeper's hands after a run has been made or attempted. A lost ball is automatically dead. All it means is that for now, you can't score or be out, the game has effectively paused, and will not resume until the bowler begins his run up to bowl the next ball. There are technical restrictions on what precisely constitutes a dead ball, but everyone who plays cricket intrinsically understands when a ball's dead and when the game's afoot.

dead bat to play the ball with soft hands (qv) and a loose grip so the bat absorbs the ball's momentum and it falls harmlessly at your feet.

death the last few overs of any limited overs game, when the batting side are reckless in the pursuit of runs, and the bowling side are desperate to keep the score down. Death bowling requires economy (qv) above all, often features yorkers (qv) and slower balls (qv) and frequently decides games. Death batsmen need to be able to score off deliveries meant to be as difficult to score from as possible, and are known as finishers (qv).

decision review system see 'third umpire'. And chapter 7.

declare in a two innings game (I suppose it could happen in a limited overs game, but it would be deeply patronising), a captain may end his team's innings and invite the opposition to 'reply' (have their go) before his men are all out, thus declaring his opinion that they've got enough runs.

declaration bowling deliberately poor bowling from a fielding side – often from the batsmen within it, in fact – to allow the batting side to score runs quickly and declare. Usually only seen in County Cricket.

deep to field deep is to be nearer the boundary than the bat. Generally defensive (qv, 2) though not necessarily – if for example, you deliberately bowl short on leg stump, inviting the hook (qv), the man at deep square leg (see 'fielding positions') is attacking (qv, 2).

defensive (1) a defensive shot is one a batsman plays to a good ball in order to protect his wicket. Can be played off both the front (qv) and the back foot (qv); hence 'forward defensive' (qv) and 'backward defensive' (qv).

defensive (2) a defensive field is one set to stop a batsman scoring runs, and has few if any catching positions to try and get him out. A defensive bowler similarly is not trying to bowl wicket-taking balls, he's just trying to be economical (qv). A defensive batsman is one uninterested in scoring runs, his only aim being to protect his wicket. The confluence of all three can be deeply soporific.

delivery to bowl a ball is to deliver it.

demons in the pitch an unpredictable, two paced (qv) minefield (qv).

diamond duck a wicket taken the first ball of an innings, or more specifically the first ball of a match. Can also refer to being run out without facing a ball. There are many regional variations – sometimes a ruby or platinum duck mean the same thing. A Royal duck also means to be dismissed first ball of an innings, after the Prince of Wales, later to become Edward VII, was out first ball of the innings (though not the match) opening the batting against The Gentlemen of Norfolk on 17 July 1866.

dibbly-dobbly a rather less than flattering way to refer to medium (qv) pace bowling. Can actually be very effective though – see 'pace off'. See also 'military'.

dig in (1) as in to dig yourself into an entrenched position. To defend. See 'bat time' 'stonewall' and 'gritty'.

dig in (2) of fast bowlers, to drop the ball short (qv). See 'bouncer' and 'back of a length'.

Dilscoop see 'ramp shot'

dip of a spinner's delivery, to drop suddenly in flight towards the end, so that it pitches shorter than the batsman thought it would. Can be a result of topspin, as well as all manner of other types of sideways spin.

direct hit a throw from the outfield (qv) that hits the stumps. Almost invariably, direct hits mean run-outs.

distraction no player may deliberately distract a member of the opposition, whether he be batting or bowling. To the extent that, a batsman distracting a fielder attempting to catch him out, whether physically obstructing him even simply by shouting "drop it!" will be given 'Out, obstructing the field'. See 'obscure ways to be out', and 'penalty runs'.

doing "is it doing anything?" or "doing much?" means 'how is the pitch behaving?' Is the ball seaming (qv), swinging (qv), turning (qv), or just 'straight up and down' (qv).

dolly a very easy catch. Could be as simple as 'child's play'. Though is perhaps more likely to derive from a colonial era Anglo/Indian word meaning a gift of free food (itself derived from 'doolie', being a food cupboard) offered on a tray. Harder to refuse than accept. Or to put it another way: handed to you on a plate.

done too much a ball that spins or swings or seams so much that it misses – the edge or the stumps. A delivery that does so much of what is asked of it that it's actually too good.

doosra Urdu and Hindi word that roughly translates as 'the other one'. A doosra is a delivery from an off-spinner that turns away from the righthander – effectively a leg break bowled with an off spin action. Pakistani off-spinner Saqlain Mushtaq is credited with its invention, and wicket-keeper Moin Khan with its name, as he would loudly encourage Mushtaq from behind the stumps to 'bowl the other one'.

dot a dot ball is a ball that is not scored from, so called because it is marked with a dot in the scorebook. Dot balls, especially at the death (qv), can be priceless.

dot ball pressure felt by a team that is not scoring like it needs to be. See 'run rate'.

double hat-trick taking four wickets in successive balls. Achieved only once in international cricket, by Sri Lankan super slinger Lasith Malinger in the otherwise largely dire 2007 World Cup. See 'hat-trick'.

double teapot a wordless expression of extreme disgruntledness, which simply means to stand with both hands on hips, resembling a teapot with two handles. Most usually performed by a bowler who wants to make it clear to everyone that he feels extremely hard done by. Whether because the streaky (qv) batsman just edged yet another one through the slips for four, or marmalised (qv) a perfectly good length ball for six, or because one of his team mates just dropped an absolute sitter off his bowling. An extremely lucky batting pair might be treated to a whole fielding side double teapotting at them in incredulity at their sheer gall. Why the expression is not 'a sugarbowl', which already has two handles and doesn't need the 'double', is unclear, though it's probably a sign of falling standards.

down the ground see 'straight bat', 'v', and 'over' (3).

drag down of a bowler, to release the ball too late in his action, so that it pitches far shorter than he intended to, turning the delivery into a rank (qv) long hop (qv). Often happens to spinners when they're trying to give the ball a real rip (qv).

drag on if a batsman hits the ball onto his stumps he has 'dragged it on'. Almost invariably an inside edge which was otherwise missing the stumps, creating the illusion that he has helped out the bowler by guiding the ball to his own demise.

draw in a two innings match, when the game has reached the end of its allotted duration (3-5 days) before anyone has won. Sounds dull, and sometimes it is, but sometimes it's thrilling. Close draws, when all three results are possibilities until right near the end, can be edge-of-the-seat spectacles.

drift if a spinner gets a lot of revolutions on the ball, as it dips towards the ground, it will move in the air in the opposite direction to which it will spin when it pitches. This effect is so counter-intuitive, that it's almost impossible for a batsman to resist following the ball to its pitch, which effectively doubles the turn. In physics it is known as the Magnus Effect. Look it up by all means, knock yourself out. See 'ball of the century'.

drift down leg of a bowler, to have a tendency to stray towards or outside leg stump, which is generally easier for the batsman to hit. An LBW appeal where the ball is thought to be missing just wide of the leg stump is said to be 'just drifting down leg' or 'going down' (qv).

drinks drinks are brought onto the field for all the fielders, the not-out batsmen and the umpires at regular intervals in all forms of cricket. This is both right and proper.

drive (1) a straight bat (qv) shot played in front of the wicket, often more or less back along the line of the ball (qv) or in the 'v' (qv), though sometimes squarer on the offside (qv). It requires the full face (qv) of the bat and good timing (qv). Can be played off both the front (qv) and the back foot (qv). The most pleasing of shots, both the play and to watch. See also 'cover drive', 'top hand' and 'elbow'.

drive (2) to offer team mates a lift to away games.

drop (1) a catch that was not taken. Generally speaking, if you get a finger to it, it's regarded as a drop.

drop (2) to be left out of the 11 in the playing side, having been in it the previous game, is to be dropped. Other than death in the family, the worst news you can get on a Saturday. See 'twelfth man'.

duck (1) *n.* to be out without scoring is to be out for a duck. You knew that. And yet you looked it up anyway. But here's something you might not know: the term is thought to have come from the shape of a duck's egg, being a big fat zero. The same source is also thought to apply to 'love', meaning nothing, in tennis, being a contraction and Anglicisation of the French l'oeuf.

duck (2) *v.* prudent reaction to a bouncer (qv), the only really viable alternative to the hook (qv).

Duckworth-Lewis method of recalculating a run chase (qv) in limited-overs games (it was initially devised for the 50 over format) after a rain delay. The formula itself is so devilishly complicated that even most mathematicians just shrug and say 'yeah, sounds about right'. Can throw up ridiculous equations, such as the semi-final of the World Cup in 1992, when the big screen proudly declared the revised target after a rain break as '22 runs needed from 1 ball'. "Farcical" is a word not uncommonly ascribed to D/L affected games. The rise of T20 has further added to the problem, as the rhythms of the shorter form are quite different, and one big quick innings can win a game very quickly with what always seems to be a very low revised total. D/L often favours the chasers in T20, so the new wisdom is to bat second if it looks like rain. A bit like democracy, it's really not a very good system at all, but it's currently the least bad of a pretty poor set of options.

ECB The England (and Wales) [my brackets] Cricket **B**oard, in 1993 when it took over the role from MCC (qv), the governing body for, you guessed it, cricket in England and Wales, both 'Professional' and 'Recreational'. Based at Lord's (qv). Its main responsibilities are the direction and selection of the England side, at which it has recently been highly successful, and the control of money into and out of all levels of the game, which is a lot more contentious. The decision to deny the public any cricket whatsoever on free-to-air telly in return for filling its coffers with hundreds of millions from Sky is undoubtedly its most divisive yet. The game may be richer, in purely financial terms, but it has lost its mass audience. Many cricket fans, especially children, can't afford or simply refuse to pay Rupert Murdoch £30 a month for the privilege of watching cricket. See chapter 10 for more on cricket media.

economical of a bowler, to concede very few runs. See 'economy'.

economy a bowler's economy rate is the rate at which the opposition score runs off him, calculated simply by dividing runs by overs. The shorter the game, the higher the economy rates of even the best bowlers. An economy rate of 6.00 in Tests is terrible, but in Twenty20 it's brilliant.

edge to only just hit the ball, with the edge of your bat. Sometimes so lightly that it hardly deviates. Often goes to the wicketkeeper or slips. See 'nick', 'feather', 'walk' and 'snicko'.

effort ball a fast bowler's effort ball is one he bowls as fast as he possibly can.

elbow in a correct (qv) top hand (qv) shot like a drive (qv), the (right handed) batsman's left elbow will be high in the air – above his head even, in his follow through (qv) – helping to keep the bat straight (qv) through the ball, and play the ball down, along the ground. Looks effortlessly elegant (qv).

elegant a term applied to batsmen, both village and professional. Like the word itself, it is difficult to satisfactorily define, but easy to spot when you see it. It's all very well to describe a batsman's technique as dignified, graceful, simple, effortless and economical, but they're empty words until you see it. Sadly, I suspect it is probably something you can't learn – you either have it or you don't.

expensive of a bowler, to concede lots of runs. See 'economy'.

extras any runs that don't come off the bat. They count towards the batting side's total, but not towards the individual batsman's score. Examples are: wides (qv), no balls (qv), byes (qv) and leg byes (qv). Wides and no balls count against the bowler, whereas, byes and leg byes don't. Though byes (not leg byes) are held against the wicket-keeper, who is, reasonably enough, expected to stop anything that misses everything else and isn't a wide.

eye a batsman with a good eye is one who can hit most balls, often without even moving his feet (qv). A natural gift, rather than practiced skill. Strangely, 'He's got a good eye' is often said by purists as a kind of veiled criticism of a batsman's lack of classical technique, much like one might comment of a less than beautiful girl, 'she's got a nice personality', but such public school snobbery is slowly fading. The combination of both a good eye *and* classical technique is most unfair, and to be found chiefly in international top orders (qv).

eye-line most deliveries will travel from the bowler's hand down towards the pitch, then bounce up towards the bat. Slower bowlers and spinners, however, can release the ball in an upwards trajectory, so that the ball goes above the batsman's eye-line, which makes judging the length of the delivery that much harder.

fall of wicket (FoW) the score at the point each batsman gets out.

farm the strike of a batsman, to face most of the bowling. Or of a pair, to control the bowling, so the senior or better bat, or the one who is 'in', does most of the batting. See 'rotate' and 'nick, (2)'.

fast the definition of fast bowling varies hugely depending on the standard of cricket. At international level, anything above 85mph is considered fast. A handful in the world can touch 95mph, which is considered very fast. At village level this would be considered attempted murder. A casual cricketer bowling at 70mph is properly quick. See also 'medium'.

feather the tiniest edge (qv). Even less so than a nick (qv). See also 'walk'.

---

feather bed a dead, batsman-friendly pitch. See 'flat'.

---

feet a batsman must move his feet to be in the correct position to play a shot. Whether to move closer to the pitch of the ball, or to back away to allow more room to cut it – if you stand rooted to the crease, batting is a lot harder. Once a batsman is in and seeing the ball well, he will move his feet unconsciously. While he's still thinking about it is when he's most vulnerable. See also 'footwork', 'dance down the pitch', 'forward', 'back foot' and 'front foot'.

---

fence (1) *n.* the boundary (qv, 1)

---

fence (2) *v.* to prod the bat out, in the hope of connecting with a quick ball outside off. To tentatively engage in the manner of one wielding an épée, rather than a bat.

---

ferret a batsman purported (rather cruelly,) to be even worse than a rabbit (qv). Because the ferrets go in *after* the rabbits.

---

field (1) *n.* another name for a cricket ground or pitch.

---

field (2) v. to field the ball is to stop it, collect it, catch it, return it to the wicket-keeper or bowler, to prevent or minimise runs, and get wickets caught and run-out (qv). Some fielders are so good at it, that they almost warrant a place in the side for that alone. (Paul Collingwood and Jonty Rhodes are recent examples.)

---

field (3) *n.* the fielding positions (qv) the captain and/or bowler decide upon. As in 'an aggressive field' or 'a defensive field'.

---

field back when fielders are mostly on or near the boundary, the field is back. A defensive (qv, 2) field, set (qv, 2) to a batsman who is scoring boundaries freely.

---

field up when fielders are mostly closer to the bat, 'on the one' (qv), the field is up. A more attacking (qv, 2) field, set either to a batsman who is not getting the ball away, or when conceding runs is less important than getting wickets.

fielder any of the eleven guys on the fielding side, including the wicket-keeper and the bowler.

fielding circle see 'circle'

fielding positions illustration for a right-handed batsman.

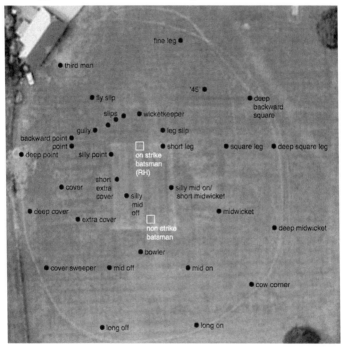

(You are, of course, only allowed nine at a time, taking a bowler and a wicket-keeper as read.) There are countless variations on these. Take a position, say midwicket. Push him squarer, he's square midwicket, straighter, he's wide midwicket, closer he's short midwicket, further away he's deep midwicket. (Soon, pictures will form in your mind when Henry Blofeld describes a field on TMS.)

Further away *and* straighter, he's deep wide midwicket. (Which is actually cow corner (qv), but Henry Blofeld would never sully TMS with such a vulgarity.) Usually, people just point. And shout. More often than not two or three people at once, all contradicting each other. Whenever you move a fielder, the ball will go where you just moved him from. This is an immutable truth. Fields should be set by the bowler and captain together. It can be hugely important in how games pan out, and imaginative or pedestrian fields can win or lose matches. Depending on a batsman's strengths, sometimes you might leave an area open for him to hit into, inviting him to try it while bowling in a certain way that makes that area difficult to reach; for example leave midwicket open and bowl well outside off, or leave the covers open and bowl into his pads. There is no right way to set a field, but there are wrong ways. The rule of thumb is to set a field for how you want to bowl, not so it can rescue you when it goes wrong: don't set it for the bad ball, set it for the good ones.

fielding side   the bowling side; the team not batting; the team 'in the field'.

fifty   50 runs scored by a batsman in an innings. A landmark, often called a half-century. 50s are, naturally enough, far more common, and not as impressive as a century (qv) but still not an achievement to be sniffed at.

fine   if an imaginary line was drawn between both sets of stumps and is extended to the boundary behind the batsman, anything close to it would be referred to as fine: a fine cut (qv) is one that is only just wide of the keeper on the off side; a fine glance (qv) is the same but the on side.

finer   see 'squarer'.

finisher   a middle-order batsman with a fantastic eye (qv) who can score off just about anything, whose job it is to do so quickly at the death (qv), with little regard for his own wicket. Indian captain MS Dhoni is probably the finest proponent of the art.

finger the umpire's index finger, usually on his right hand, which is raised to indicate that a batsman is out, in response to an appeal (qv) of 'how is that' (qv).

fingerspin using the fingers to impart spin on a ball. See 'offspin' and 'left arm orthodox'.

fire it in of a spinner, to bowl quickly, denying the ball a real chance to grip and turn. The occasional, surprise 'quicker ball' is an excellent idea, but some spinners, especially when nervous or under pressure, resort to speeding up, which is a bit silly, and is more like bowling cutters (qv). If you want to bowl medium pace, you might as well take a run up.

first class cricket at a very high standard. There are many delineations in the cricket playing countries, but generally it covers two-innings 3-5 day matches, not limited overs (qv). Test matches are first class, ODIs and T20s are not. In England, other first class matches are the County Championship, Oxford, Cambridge, Durham and Loughborough universities, or MCC vs any first class county or touring team.

five-fer a bowler taking five wickets in an innings is said to have got five-fer, as in 5-20 (five for twenty). It's often given an indefinite article – a bowler gets *a* five-fer. See 'michelle'.

flash to bat aggressively, to swing the bat hard. As in 'flashing blade'. The old adage "If you're going to flash, flash hard", means if you're going to have a go, then throw the bat (qv) at it, so any chances will come that much faster and harder.

flat a pitch which does nothing: doesn't seam (qv), swing (qv), turn (qv), or bounce (qv). Consequently, lovely to bat on, dull to watch.

flat six a ball hit so hard that it travels at about head height all the way out of the ground.

flat throw a throw that seems hardly to arc at all, and comes in hard and fast, six inches over the stumps like a guided missile. Fielders with really good arms (qv) flick the ball out of the hand, rolling the fingers down it, imparting backspin to help keep it flat through the air. This robs the ball of velocity, so don't try it unless you've got a rocket arm or you'll look even more pathetic than you really are. Exclusively available to the under-40's.

flat track bully a big powerful top order batsman – Matthew Hayden leaps to mind – who is devastating and merciless on a flat (qv) pitch.

flick wristy (qv) shot off the pads (qv, 2)

flight (1) *n.* the path of a spinner's delivery. Includes tossing the ball up above the batsman's eye-line (qv), dip (qv), and drift (qv). To 'beat the batsman in the flight' is to deceive him with length, rather than turn.

flight (2) *v.* to give the ball air (qv).

flight and guile often said to be the spinner's two main weapons. Well, for those spinners who can't get the two big ones – turn and bounce – (qv) anyway.

flipper a legspin (qv) variation (qv) which goes straight on and stays low.

fly slip a deeper slip, between conventional slips and third man. See 'fielding positions'.

follow on if the team batting second in a two innings game are substantially behind after the first innings, they may be asked, at the discretion of the captain of the team batting first, to follow on – to bat again immediately. (To 'enforce' the follow on.) The magic number to 'avoid the follow on' is 200 in Test matches, 150 in 3 or 4 day matches. The advantage of enforcing the follow on is that you may have the opportunity to win by an entire innings, or restrict your opponents to a very slim lead before you bat again. It is a very powerful position to be in. The disadvantages of it are primarily that your bowlers may very well be tired, and secondly you may have to bat last, chasing a tricky little total on a worn, increasingly unpredictable pitch.

follow through (batsman) the position a batsman ends up in having played a shot. Some finish with the bat horizontal, some almost wrap it around their necks. Like a golf swing, no two are the same, but all good ones are perfectly balanced.

follow through (bowler) the position of a bowler's body after having released the ball. Some bowlers continue down the pitch almost to the batsman in their follow through, others hardly have one at all. What they are prohibited from doing is following through onto the middle of the pitch, where the ball is likely to land on a good length when bowled from the other end. If they do, they can be warned and then taken off by the umpires.

football when a batsman gets 'in' (qv), he becomes more comfortable with the bowling and the conditions, and the game gets, temporarily, progressively easier for him. He seems to see the ball earlier, and it seems bigger and easier to hit. At this stage he is said to be 'seeing it like a football'.

footwork the movement of a batsman's feet to get him into a favourable position to play the ball comfortably, negating or allowing for spin or swing, and getting to the pitch of the ball (qv). Done well, you hardly notice it. Glaringly obvious when missing. The subject of much pontificating by coaches and pundits. See also 'feet', 'dance down the pitch', 'forward', 'back foot' and 'front foot'.

form To be in form is to play at the peak of your powers, when everything comes together. To be out of form is to go through a patch were you continually fail to live up to your potential. Many casual cricketers live out their cricketing lives in this state. Garfield Sobers, one of the game's finest ever all-rounders (qv), summed it up for everyone, good bad or indifferent: "Form is temporary. Class is permanent."

forward any shot that involves the batsman advancing his front foot, so his weight is over it, and he's leaning forward.

forward defensive a shot played forward (qv), to a length (qv) or full (qv) ball, with a vertical bat. Designed to stop the ball from hitting the stumps, not to score off it. The first shot any player learns, and usually the first one he forgets.

four see 'boundary (2)'

fourth stump pace bowlers will often aim at an imaginary fourth stump, next to the off stump, when they are trying to bowl a line to make the batsman play and induce an edge in the corridor (qv) outside off. Sensing it is likely to miss the stumps, batsman will often elect to leave (qv) such deliveries. Thus, a 'fourth stump line' can also be very economical (qv).

free hit in professional limited over games, the penalty for a front-foot no ball is not only a penalty run and an extra ball, but the extra ball is a 'free hit'. For this delivery, the striker can only be out under the circumstances that apply for a no ball – basically he can be run out, and that's about it; caught, bowled, stumped etc do not count, so he can go for broke without risk. If the striker is the same as for the no ball that preceded it, no change in the field is permitted, but if the batsmen changed on the no ball, the field may change as well. If the free hit delivery is another no ball (of any kind, not necessarily front foot) or a wide, then the next delivery will become a free hit for whichever batsman is facing it, and so on. Got it? Honestly, the offside rule is just *nothing*. The harsh nature of this penalty – it very often results in boundaries – has dramatically reduced the number of front foot no balls in top flight limited overs cricket.

free your arms any delivery wide enough of the batsman to give him room to take a full blooded swing at it is said to have allowed him to free his arms. Aggressive players may also step away from straighter balls, exposing their stumps but allowing them to give the ball a good whack.

front foot (1) the foot of the batsman nearest the bowler: the left foot for a right hander. Front foot shots are played to full (qv) balls and those on a length (qv). The batsman steps forward with his balance over his front foot and leans into the shot, using his weight to add power.

front foot (2) the lead foot of a bowler (the left foot for a right arm bowler) some part of which must land behind the line of the popping crease in his delivery stride, in order for the delivery to be legal and not a no ball.

full a ball pitched up nearer a batsman's feet is a full delivery. See 'half volley' and 'yorker'.

full face to show the bowler the full face of the bat, or 'show him the maker's name' is to play very straight (qv). Very correct, it's a sign of solid technique.

full toss a delivery that reaches the batsman without bouncing. Much easier to hit, more often than not dispatched to the boundary. A fast full toss passing above the striker's waist height is a no ball, as is a slow one passing above shoulder height.

furniture stumps (1). As in 'rearrange the furniture' – to be comprehensively bowled. See also 'all three'.

gap a gap in the field is where fielders are not. Can be found by luck (see 'streaky') or by judgement (see 'placement').

gardening of batsmen, to prod at indentations or spike marks on the pitch with the toe of the bat between deliveries. No-one is quite sure what it achieves, but everyone does it. It's quite compulsive. Especially when you've just been beaten by a shooter or one that really rears off a length. Or even just an excellent ball. The implication being that whatever went on there it was the pitch's fault. Not yours. Heavens no.

genuine perhaps the most over used word in cricket commentary.

Everything, from an edge to an all-rounder to a chance to a fast bowler will be described as genuine. Its use as an emphatic has become so ubiquitous as to be effectively meaningless.

get big to bounce high off a length. See 'get up'.

get off the square (1) to hit the ball any distance. If a batsman cannot time the ball for whatever reason (lack of form, lack of talent, hangover) or if the ground or ball are very wet, he will lament, often loudly, his inability to get the ball off the square.

get off the square (2) of groundsmen and cricket club members, to shout angrily at youngsters, dogs or tourists to please leave their hallowed turf unmolested.

get up A ball that bounces unusually high, rearing up into the batsman's gloves off a length, will be said appreciatively by the fielders to have 'got up'.

glance a delicate shot played to a ball bowled on your pads (qv) or down the leg side. Only needs the merest of deft touches, and uses the pace of the bowler, rather than the force of the shot. Requires sweet timing and is much harder than it looks.

gloves batting gloves are heavily padded on the outside to protect a batsman's fingers from the ball hitting him as he holds the bat. Both the gloves and the padding are technically regarded as part of the bat whilst he is holding it – so runs taken off 'gloved' balls are runs, not leg byes (qv), and catches taken off gloved balls are out. The wicket-keeper (qv) is the only fielder allowed to wear gloves, though his are padded on the palm side, to protect him against the ball as he catches it.

going down abbreviation of 'going down the leg side', in relation to an appeal for LBW, a ball that is deemed to be missing the wicket wide of leg stump is said to be 'going down.'

golden duck To be out first ball, and therefore obviously without scoring, is to be out for a golden duck. Yup. You waited all week for that.

---

good length see 'length'.

---

googly a delivery from a legspinner that spins in to the righthander like an offbreak, the opposite of his normal or 'stock' ball, the leg break (qv), which turns away from him. Often called a wrong'un (qv). Archaically called a 'bosie' after Bernard Bosanquet, an English cricketer playing around the dawn of the twentieth century who is credited with its invention. The word 'googly' itself may have its roots in a Maori word after MCC's 1902/3 tour of New Zealand, but this is disputed, as it is said to have been in use in Australia (who felt the brunt of it) in relation to Bosanquet's delivery before that. More likely it derives from 'googly-eyed' as in 'bamboozled'. Like all spinner's variations, the point is to deceive the batsman, so it is most effective when bowled with a very similar action to the standard leg break, making it difficult to 'read' (qv). It varies between proponents, but usually it is bowled with a leg break action, but then flipped between the second and third fingers out of the back of the hand at the instant of release.

---

good toss to lose see 'toss'.

---

greentop a wicket covered in live green grass. Likely to jag (qv) and seam (qv, 2) and bounce (qv) and generally be helpful to fast bowlers and not batsmen. The kind of track that captains will often elect to bowl first on.

---

grassed a dropped catch. Also a verb: "It was an easy chance but he grassed it."

---

grip (1) of a spin delivery, to find purchase on the surface. To turn.

---

grip (2) the different techniques bowlers use to hold the ball, or batsmen use to hold the bat.

---

grip (3) the rubber tube covering the handle of the bat. Used to be very straightforward, but as one of the few customisable things on a bat, there is now a vast range of colours, designs and textures available. Some people prefer a thicker handle, and will have two, three of even four grips fitted at once. Some prefer a thicker area at the base of the grip, others a large bulge at the top, so they can feel where the handle ends without looking. Others take so little notice of it that the grip has to actually perish and fall off in bits before they'll bother to replace it.

gritty As in the John Wayne movie *True Grit*. Usually of a batsman, generally of one under pressure in a rearguard action trying to save a draw in a Test match. Solid in defence. Determined not to get out, to protect his wicket at all costs. Obdurate, steadfast, stubborn, staunch, impassive, immovable, indomitable. In the modern English game, epitomised by the Geordie grit of Paul Collingwood, who was also often credited with the Australianism 'nuggety', a weird but definite form of compliment.

ground (1) another name for a cricket pitch. As in "He's hit that out of the ground."

ground (2) The crease (qv). A batsman is in his ground when his foot or his bat are 'grounded' behind the popping crease. In which case he cannot be out stumped or run out. If he gets back behind the line of the crease before the fielding side can break the wicket after a run, he has 'made his ground'.

grubber see 'shooter'.

guard to take guard is to mark the ground at the crease (qv) to tell you where you're standing in relation to your stumps. Some take middle, some leg, some halfway between the two, which is known as 'two'. Why these are not simply painted onto the ground with the crease is a mystery which may never ever be solved.

half-century a fifty (qv).

half-tracker a bouncer (qv).

half-volley a gift ball that bounces just in front of the batsman, so he doesn't even have to move his feet to hit it. Has its own adjective: 'juicy'.

handled the ball one of the ways to be out that rarely if ever happens. Michael Vaughan was given out handled the ball on the India tour of 2002-3, becoming the seventh batsman and second Englishman (Graham Gooch was the first) to be dismissed in this manner in Test history. In village cricket, it's accepted practice for the batsman to pick up the ball and toss it to a fielder if he is nearest to it and it's quite obvious to everyone that the ball is dead (qv). This action is unfailingly met with a polite and respectful "Cheers Bat, thanks." Technically though, in such circumstances the ball is not yet dead, and if the fielding side appealed, the batsman would be out. Though it's unlikely he would be given out on most village greens, and rightly so. The Law was initially intended to stop a batsman from interfering with a fielder attempting to catch him out, which was apparently common practice in the game's infancy. These days though, it is among cricket's more silly laws. See 'obscure ways to be out' and 'out'.

hang the bat out often followed by 'to dry'. To waft (qv) airily at a ball outside off-stump. More hopeful than purposeful. See 'fence' (2).

Harrow drive see 'chinese cut'.

hat-trick three wickets in consecutive balls by the same bowler. Hat-tricks are reported form the game's infancy in the mid seventeen hundreds, but the first recorded hat-trick was by H H Stephenson in 1858. From either start point the legend has several endings. One is that a hat was passed around among the spectators, and the player was awarded the collected money. Another is that the collection was used to buy him a hat to mark the occasion. Another is that such a feat was deemed worthy of a special kind of hat awarded to him by his own club. Whichever it was, the term became popular towards the end of the 19th century and was adopted by hockey, football, rugby, baseball, etc. Wickets can be split across overs and even innings. The splendidly moustachioed Australian Merv Hughes has probably the most unusual hat-trick to his name, being so far the only one achieved in three separate overs in the same match. (Worked it out? 1st wicket: last ball of an over. 2nd wicket: first ball of his next over, but the batting side's 10th wicket, so the end of the innings. 3rd wicket: first ball of his first over in the second innings. See?)

hat-trick ball after two wickets in two balls, the next ball is known as the hat-trick ball, and a very aggressive 'schoolboy field' (qv) is often set, just for that one delivery, to have the best chance of making the hat-trick. Hat-trick balls are actually pretty common (there will be one after most golden ducks.) Hat-tricks are not.

Hawk-Eye the computer simulation software used in TV coverage to track the actual and probable path of a ball. It works by using triangulation data from a minimum of four and up to 30 high speed cameras (the more there are the more accurate the results) at different points around the ground to precisely plot a ball's path. In tennis it is extremely effective, as its job is simply to determine what happened: was the ball in or out? In cricket, as ever, it is a little more complicated. It does simple ball-path plotting for things like pitchmaps (qv) beehives (qv) and wagon wheels (qv), but its most contentious function is to use the data to extrapolate the likely path of the ball after an interception – specifically, is the ball likely to have hit the stumps following an LBW shout. Though better than nothing, and undeniably entertaining whether right or wrong, it is still nothing more than an educated guess. Its use by third umpires (qv) at the top level grows ever more contentious, as they, the public and the pundits gradually forget that it is not fact they are dealing with, but conjecture, by definition.

hit out to play aggressively, in order to up the run rate (qv).

hit out of the attack see 'target' (2).

"hit out or get out" muttered under one's breath or yelled – depending on the severity of the need – at one's own team-mates, or by supporters to their own team, when it's clear that a point in the game has been reached where quick runs are more important than preserving wickets: get on with it, or get out so someone else can.

hit the deck A bowler who hits the deck is one keen on dropping the ball short, usually from a great height (ie he's tall, and his action is straight). See also 'heavy ball' and 'back-of-a-length'. The phrase is also used as an adjective, to describe such players, as in "He's a hit-the-deck bowler."

hit wicket if a batsman hits or treads on his own stumps in the process of playing or attempting a shot he is out hit wicket.

heavy ball tall fast bowlers who bowl back-of-a-length are often said to bowl a heavy ball, as they hit the splice of the bat hard, the impact reverberating up the bat like a bell hit by a sledgehammer. Often though, the term is simply a synonym for knee-weakeningly rapid.

helmet see 'lid'.

hole out to be caught in the outfield, in front of the wicket, playing an attacking shot (as opposed to being caught behind or off a top edge).

honest good tidy bowling, sharp, focussed fielding that gives nothing away, no sloppy mistakes, means the batsmen have to play well in order to score any runs at all. This is keeping the batsmen honest.

hook similar to a pull (qv) but played in front of the face, to a bouncer (qv). An aggressive shot to an aggressive ball, hooks can be spectacular and often go for six. It is thrilling to watch a fast bowler trying to knock a batsman's head off and being smashed into the crowd (you don't see too many hooks in casual cricket) over square leg. Requires exceptional reflexes, confidence and bottle. Apart from the obvious danger of a cricket ball in the face, it's also very susceptible to a top edge (qv) if you don't get through the shot quick enough.

hoop to swing (qv) the ball prodigiously. "He's hooping it about."

hot spot tv innovation; an infra-red camera that shows up the heat of impact marks on bats and pads, to help determine if a batsman is out. Or just to marvel at how beautifully he middles it.

how's that? the question a bowler and fielding side nominally ask the umpire to enquire whether, in his esteemed opinion, the batsman is out or not. Most modern appeals bear no resemblance to the actual words anymore, and sound roughly like the noise you can imagine making if someone were to pass an electric current through your genitals using jump leads made for trucks. See also 'appeal' and 'shout'

hutch pavilion, dressing room, bench; especially one where rabbits (qv) reside. To be "back in the hutch" is to be out.

ICC The governing body of international cricket. Founded as the Imperial Cricket Conference in 1909, renamed the International Cricket Conference in 1965, and became the International Cricket Council in 1989. There are 104 member countries. The 10 full members are the Test playing nations (qv). Then there are 34 associate, and 60 affiliate members. The ICC organises all global tournaments, like the 50 and 20 over World Cups, and various lesser ones. Also appoints umpires and referees to officiate in Tests, ODIs and T20Is.

in (1) when it's you're turn to bat, you're 'in'. As in "Dave's out, who's in next?"

in (2) if a batsman is 'in' he – his foot, his bat, or any part of him – is behind the line of the popping crease (qv). If running, he has 'made his ground' (qv).

in (3) when a batsman has faced a good half a dozen overs and/or made 20 or so, he is said to be 'in'. That is, he is used to the pace and nature of the pitch, the bowling, the circumstances. He is settled. He should – and this is easy to say, rather harder to do – go on from this solid base to build a decent score. This is also known as being 'set', and as getting, or having, a 'start'.

in behind to get in behind the ball is to get your body in the way, so you play the ball compactly, close to your body, usually with both your eyes facing forwards, directly above your bat. To do so is to make the ball much harder to miss, particularly if it's quick bowling. See 'back away'.

in-ducker a ball that swings in towards the batsman late. See 'swing'.

in the air any ball hit in the air is a potential catch. Bowling sides don't mind the odd boundary if a batsman is hitting everything in the air, because it means the chances are a catch is coming sooner rather than later.

in the slot see half-volley.

innings (verb) a bat. The process of batting. Presumably derives from when one is 'in' as opposed to 'out'. Applied both to individuals and teams. As in 'Botham's wonderful innings' and 'Damerham's first innings total'.

inside edge the edge of the bat closest to the batsman's body, and the stumps. An inside edge is quite likely to chop on (qv). See also 'drag on', 'chinese cut', 'edge', 'outside edge', 'nick', 'feather', and 'walk'.

inside out a forcing shot that a batsman plays away from his body, with the bat swinging from inside its natural arc to outside of it, so it goes squarer on the off side.

inswing a ball that starts outside off and swings in to the batsman. See 'swing'.

IPL Indian Premier League. T20 tournament held for six weeks in March and April since 2008. Features the best short-game players in the world, hired guns who play for the highest bidder. Big players, big money, big league. See chapter 10.

jaffa an unplayable delivery. An absolute peach. A beauty. (Another expression with an unknown derivation. Jaffa means beauty in

Hebrew, apparently, but Hebrew is hardly cricket's first language. Jaffas are the best oranges? No, that's a bit lame. Could have something to do with them being seedless; jaffa is also slang for someone who's infertile, so maybe something around incapability? Oh I don't know.)

jag of a ball, to bounce or kick or 'seam' (qv) unpredictably off the pitch.

jockstrap an odd, strappy, contrivance, designed to go over your underwear but under your trousers and hold your box (qv) in place while batting, wicket-keeping or fielding close. See also 'batting knickers'.

jug if a bowler gets a fiver-fer (qv) or a hat-trick (qv), or a batsman makes a fifty (qv) or a century (qv) his team mates will – loudly – expect him to buy a jug of beer in the pub after the game for general consumption.

jug avoidance to get two wickets in two balls and then bowl a wide on the third, or to be out for 49 – and thus to appear to have failed in order not to have to buy your team-mates a beer. No-one ever actually does this, of course, and to accuse someone of it is simply a way to refocus attention from ineptitude to alleged tight-fistedness, which, for most of us poor talentless souls, is easier both to accept and make amends for.

juicy see 'half-volley'

king pair a batsman out for a golden duck (qv) in both innings of a two innings game has got a king pair (two ordinary ducks are just a pair). Really not his week.

knock an innings. "Good knock mate," is freely interchangeable with "Well batted."

late to play the ball late or 'under your eyes' is to wait for it to react off the pitch before committing. Requires lightning reflexes and sound technique.

late cut see 'back cut'

---

late swing a ball that is straight until right at the last possible moment. Very hard to play. See 'swing'.

Laws cricket does not have rules, it has Laws. They are overseen, written and updated by the MCC (qv) at Lord's (qv) and they govern all forms of cricket everywhere. They are available free online or in a nice little booklet for a few quid from www.lords.org/laws-and-spirit

---

LBW Law 36, the cricket law that makes football's offside rule look as simple as it patently is. LBW is tricky because it is a matter of opinion, not a matter of fact: it is about whether, in the opinion of the umpire, the ball would have gone on to hit the stumps had the batsman's body not been in the way. An amazing number of keen cricketers struggle to define it accurately; many are bafflingly happy to go out and umpire regardless. In essence, to be out **Leg B**efore **W**icket is to get yourself (usually but not necessarily your padded leg) in the way of a ball which would otherwise have gone on to hit the stumps. But not if it pitched outside the line of leg stump. Or hit you outside the line of off stump. Unless you weren't playing a shot, of course. Told you. Tricky. See page 7 for more. See also 'Hawk-Eye'.

---

leading edge an edge that goes forwards, anything up to 90° away from where the batsman intended. Often happens when trying to turn the ball to leg and closing the face (qv). Instead of hitting the blade (qv), the ball connects with the outside edge and shoots through the off side, or back towards the bowler. Will race for four as often as they loop up for easy catches.

---

lean (1) a period of poor form (qv) for a batsman when he can't seem to make runs no matter what he does. Whether he's aggressive or watchful, he always seems to be scratching around in single figures, unable to time the ball, never getting a break, getting out in stupid ways, almost in relief. This is a lean period.

---

lean (2) a sign of quality batting is to appear not to have hit the ball hard. Playing off the front foot (qv), with his weight forward, a batsman can appear to just lean on the ball, rather than do anything as crude and base as swing his bat at it. The ball will of course find the middle (qv) of the bat, and race through the off-side like it's been clubbed by a sledge hammer, as the artist holds the shape of his follow through (qv) and admires his work.

leave a delivery which is not going to hit the stumps but might be dangerous to hit, which the batsman elects not to play at. Leaving is an art in itself, requiring fine judgement. The hastily re-raised bat, lazy sway out of the way, or bat flourished sky-wards can be every bit as elegant as a shot at the ball. See 'shoulder arms'.

left arm orthodox identical in action to offspin, but bowled by a left handed bowler, so that the ball turns away from righthanders like a legbreak. Balls that turn away from you are generally harder to play well, so good left arm spinners, just like good legspinners, are highly prized. The perfect delivery, just like a legbreak, drifts wide of the stumps down leg and spins away to off when it pitches.

leg / legside the entire side of the field as defined by the side the batsman's legs are on at the moment of delivery. Also known as the 'on' side.

leg break a legbreak or legspin delivery is one that is bowled at the legs and spins away from the righthander. Balls that turn away from you rather than in to you are generally considered to be harder to play. The ideal 'leggie' pitches on or just oustide leg stump, forcing the batsman to play at it, then turns – either past the edge towards the stumps, or takes the edge. Usually bowled using a flick of the wrist to impart spin, rather than just the fingers, and consequently sometimes known as 'wrist spin'. Often described as cricket's most difficult art, it's very tricky to do consistently, as flicking the wrist when letting go will inevitably rob the delivery of accuracy, be it line or length or both. And no matter how much it turns, if it pitches short and wide it's easy to punish. Really good wrist spinners maintain accuracy whilst still giving the ball 'a real rip', meaning a lot of revs, and get turn even on the least receptive pitches where fingerspinners can find no purchase. But really good ones are once-in-a-generation rare. See 'ball of the century'.

leg byes when a ball hits any part of the batsman except his bat or gloves – his pads, body, even his head, helmet or not – the batsmen can still run (providing the umpire thinks a shot was attempted, or that the batsman was trying to protect himself, rather than just kick that ball away). Leg byes count only towards the batting side's total; they don't count towards the individual batsman's score, or against the bowler or the wicket-keeper. See 'extras'.

leg cutter see 'cutter'.

leggie (1) a legspinner – both the person and the delivery.

leggie (2) that 25-year-old fast bowling all-rounder's girlfriend.

leg glance (1) see 'glance'.

leg glance (2) see 'leggie' (2).

leg theory see 'bodyline'.

leg side see 'leg'.

leg spin see 'leg break'

leg stump the stump nearest the batsman's legs. See 'guard'.

length a 'good length' for a ball to pitch on varies with each bowler, pitch and the batsman he's bowling to. For a quick bowler it might be 7-15 feet in front of the bat, for a spinner maybe two. As a batsman, you know a bowler is bowling a good length if you're not sure whether to play forward (see 'front foot') or back (see 'back foot').

lid helmets in cricket were introduced during the Packer (qv) era and have been common since the 80's, and ubiquitous in the professional game for several decades, but many village players still resist them. They are a little cumbersome, and require a bit of getting used to. Under 18s must wear them in league cricket, and most adults will refuse to bowl to a kid without one even in casual games. As a rule, the better the batsman, the less need he has for protection. Thus Sir Vivian Richards, for example, can be forgiven his disdain for the idea, being one of the most naturally talented, swashbuckling men ever to wield the willow. If you are less gifted than Sir Viv, you might want to think about getting one, unless you're a big fan of unnecessary dentistry. Here's a humorous quote: "The box was first used in cricket in the 1870s. The first cricket helmets were used in the 1970s. It took a century of bollocks for cricket to come to its senses." See chapter 8 for more on lids and protection.

lifter a ball that gets up (qv). See also 'back-of-a-length' and 'rising ball'.

light short for bad light. To 'go off for light' or to be 'off for bad light' means the game is suspended because it is too dark to play safely. Test matches are suspended sometimes for heavy cloud. It used to be that batsmen were 'offered the light', and it was their decision whether or not to come off, but the modern way in the professional game if for the umpires to decide unilaterally. Village games are rarely if ever stopped for light. Many evening village games, especially in May and August, finish farcically in near darkness.

limited overs games determined by a pre-agreed amount of overs per side. Village league games are limited overs, as are the professional T20, Pro40 and ODI formats. First Class (qv) cricket – County, Test, etc – is not, being determined primarily by time elapsed, rather than overs.

line of leg stump the imaginary line between a batsman's leg stump and the stump directly opposite it at the other end of the wicket. Crucial in LBW decisions – a batsman cannot be out LBW to a ball pitching outside the line of his leg stump.

line of off stump the imaginary line between a batsman's off stump and the stump directly opposite it at the other end of the wicket.

line of the ball the path along which the ball travels on its way from bowler to batsman. This is not necessarily a straight line. See 'swing'.

line and length the ultimate combination. A bowler consistently pitching the ball around about the line of your off stump on a good length is maddeningly difficult to score off and very easy to get out to.

long barrier to field the ball crouched sideways, so both legs are coiled behind the ball, presenting as big an obstacle as possible, so if you don't get it cleanly with your hands, you'll still stop it with your body.

long hop a ball that pitches way too short (qv), and is nothing like quick enough to be a bouncer (qv), giving the batsman all the time in the world between when it bounces and when he swats it away to the boundary with all the contempt it deserves. Has its own adjective: 'rank'.

loop see 'flight'.

Lord's home of the MCC (qv), Middlesex County, the ECB (qv), the oldest sporting museum in the world, and the Laws (qv) of the game. Has a popular and very reasonable claim to being the home of cricket itself. A magnificent place, it embodies all that is good and bad about the game, past and present. The first Test of the summer at Lord's is among the best days out available to mankind. (See chapter 10.)

lose your run up if a pace bowler running in to the crease feels he's got his stride wrong and is likely to overstep the crease, he is said to have lost his run up. It is best to pull out of it and start again, rather than concede a no ball (qv).

lower order the bottom third of the batting order (qv), roughly slots 9, 10 and 11. The specialist bowlers, who are not expected to be great batsmen. See 'tail'.

magic ball In a frustrating conundrum, bowlers who are always looking for those unplayable wicket-balls often go for lots of runs. If you're always searching for that late outswinger or inducking yorker or ripping wrong-un, chances are you'll get it wrong much more often than you'll get it right, and while you're searching for it the batsmen are tucking in. Often, bowlers who concentrate on getting their stock (qv) ball right will have more success than those always looking for that one perfect delivery. But get that one ball right, of course, and all of a sudden it's a very easy game indeed. See 'ball of the century.'

maiden an over from which no runs are scored. (There can be byes, as these are considered the wicketkeeper's fault, or leg byes, as these are considered no-one's fault, but no wides or no balls, as those are definitely the bowler's fault.) The derivation is obvious: pure and unsullied.

maker's name to 'show the bowler the maker's name' is to use the full face (qv) and play with a very straight bat (qv). Correct. Solid. Textbook. Of sound technique.

manhattan a runs-per-over graphic resembling the New York skyline.

Mankad when the bowler runs-out the non-striker before delivering the ball. Named after Indian bowler Vinoo Mankad, who made a habit of the practice. The Laws have since been (wrongly, to my mind) changed so that the bowler may only attempt such a run-out before he enters his delivery stride. Which means these days the non-striker can back-up (qv, 1) almost half way down the pitch and get away with it.

marmalise a ball that is hit with perfect timing (qv) and serious ferocity may be said to be marmalised. The kind that close fielders perhaps don't try as hard as they might to get a hand to, for fear that it might turn their fingers into marmalade.

MCC The **M**arylebone **C**ricket **C**lub, founded in 1787. Based at Lord's (qv). Since 1788, the MCC has written, re-written and held the copyright for the Laws (qv) of cricket. The governing body of all cricket until 1993 when the ICC (qv) took over the global role, and the ECB (qv) took over the local one. Until 1977, the England cricket team officially played as MCC. A private club of 20,000 members with a 20 year waiting list, the MCC is stuffy, staid, condescending, inherently sexist and elitist. Or the guardian of the game's heritage, traditions, values and very soul, and the last bastion of defence against the corporate greed that now seeks to devour it and strip it of all that's decent and worthwhile. Depending on your point of view.

MCC Coaching Manual see 'textbook'.

medium Of bowling speed. Professional medium is 70-85mph, which is unplayably quick by amateur standards. On village greens a gentle 50-55mph is quite fast enough to be insulted by the term 'medium' and force the bowler to put his back into it. See 'military' and 'fast'.

michelle rhyming slang for the actress Michelle Pfeiffer. See five-fer.

middle (1) *n.* the 'sweet spot' area of the bat; *v.* to hit the ball solidly with this area of the bat. There are few better feelings. See 'timing'.

middle (2) the wicket (qv, 1). "To spend some time in the middle" is to play a longish innings.

middle (3) the central stump of the three. Sometimes called centre. See 'guard'.

middle order the middle of a batting order (qv), roughly slots 5, 6, 7 and 8. If you're lucky, consisting of a couple of specialist bats or batting all-rounders (qv), a wicket-keeper and a genuine or bowling all-rounder.

midwicket the area of the field in front of the batsman on his legside at about 45°. See 'fielding positions'.

minefield a terrible wicket to bat on. Usually uneven, lumpy and unpredictable, making decent cricket shots all but impossible. Matches are often called off if the pitch is too poor, as it can be dangerous for batsmen, especially if the bowling is rapid. Village friendlies are occasionally contested on minefields, because people would rather play than not. But it's not cricket. The opposite of a featherbed (qv).

military medium 'military' in this case is as pejorative and uncomplimentary an adjective as it's possible to apply to a bowler, implying that not only is he not quick, but also that he is tediously predictable and regimented, and entirely lacking in flair or imagination.

mis-field to fail to collect the ball cleanly, or indeed at all: to field ineptly.

momentum the upper hand, chronologically speaking. It has become something of a commentators' cliché to suggest that the side 'on top' has all the momentum, but it is undeniably a factor, even if it is an almost 100% psychological one. A side is chasing 40 to win off the last ten overs with one wicket left. If an hour ago they were 9 down chasing 200, it could reasonably be argued that the 'big mo' had begun to swing in their favour. On the other hand, if 10 minutes ago they had 40 to win from 12 overs with 8 wickets left, there's little doubt that they have lost any momentum they may have had. Just because it's a cliché doesn't make it any less true.

moving ball refers to lateral or sideways movement, not forward motion. See 'swing' and 'seam' (2)

natural variation little tiny variations of movement off the pitch for spinners and seamers – maybe it'll turn or jag, maybe it won't.

nets an oblong tunnel of netting supported by a steel cage used for practice by both batsmen and bowlers. The nets are simply so you don't have to keep stopping to chase after the ball. See chapter 13 for much more on the nets.

new ball at the beginning of the game, you'll start with a new ball. Sometimes, if you're feeling flush (match balls cost between £10 and

£80, depending on quality) or you're a professional, each innings will start with a new ball. In longer cricket, you get a new one every 80 overs. It is hard, varnished, shiny, bounces higher, and likely to swing. Almost invariably, fast bowlers will use the new ball, as it's unlikely to spin.

nick (1) the merest of edges (qv). See 'walk'.

nick (2) to nick the strike (qv) is to take a single off the last ball of the over, so you are facing the first ball of the next over too, and your partner doesn't get to bat.

nightwatchman in two innings (Test or first class) games if a batsman is out late in the day's play, with only a few overs to go, say, sometimes a bowler is moved up the batting order and sent in to bat in place of the next 'proper' batsman, to protect his wicket for the next morning. Personally, the practice has always mystified me. If you're in the team for your batting, get out there and bat, man. If Jimmy Anderson can survive six overs against Steyn and Morkel with the new ball, why the hell can't Kevin Pietersen, who's one of the best batsmen in the world? Why do top class international batsmen need 'protecting' from bowlers by their own bowlers? I don't get it. I've never got it. It seems thoroughly ridiculous to me. Get out there and bat.

no ball an illegal delivery. There are many reasons why, the most common being the bowler's front foot lands on or in front of the popping crease on delivery. In casual cricket, equally common is a full toss above the batsman's waist. The penalty is one run to the batting side (see 'extras') and the bowler will have to bowl another ball. See also 'free hit'.

non-striker's end The end the bowler is bowling from.

not out (1) to finish an innings with one's wicket intact.

not out (2) a call by the umpire, in response to an appeal (qv) from the bowler or fielding side, indicating that the batsman should continue with his innings.

nuggety see gritty

nurdle to nudge the ball around, knock it into gaps, and use placement (qv) rather than power, is to nurdle. Often done by a good batsman off a good bowler, while he waits for either a loose ball, or a change of bowler. Or by sides who know they can win it in singles.

OBO Over-by-Over coverage, usually written, a paragraph per over, in real time, on the internet. Typically features humorous asides from the writers and/or comments from readers via email, text, twitter, etc. The Guardian's is excellent at best, excruciatingly geeky at worst. Cricinfo (qv) is more straight-laced, and also covers games that don't involve England. The BBC, as ever, is probably the most accessible.

obscure ways to be out there are four of the 10 ways to be out (qv) that you will not see happen in village cricket, and will make back page headlines if they happen in a professional game. They are 'handled the ball' (qv), 'hit the ball twice', 'obstruction of the field', and 'timed out'. Timed out is simply a way to stop time wasting – in a T20 game, the outgoing and ingoing batsmen must cross on the outfield, in longer forms a few minutes are allowed, but it would take an umpire of extraordinary tetchiness to raise the finger to someone taken by surprise by a few quick wickets who was still strapping his pads on. The others are hangovers from the early days of the game a few centuries ago, when batsmen who had hit a ball in the air would not run, but chase after it, and attempt to stop a fielder from catching him out, to the extent of trying to grab the ball from him, or attempting to hit the ball away again with his bat, or even attacking the fielder with it. Now these practices no longer occur in the game, the rules that stamped them out have been robbed of their meaning, but remain enshrined in the Laws.

obstruction No player may deliberately obstruct an opponent. See 'obscure ways to be out' and 'penalty runs'.

occupy the crease see 'bat time'.

ODI One Day International. 50-over one-day game that took off after the Packer Revolution (qv), often 'Day/Night' games played under floodlights to maximise the crowd attendance and TV figures. Tend to have dull patches in the middle overs, but are often close with exciting finishes.

off/offside the entire side of the field as defined by the side the batsman's bat is on (the side his legs are not) at the moment of delivery.

offbreak see 'offspin'.

off-cutter see 'cutter'.

off the pads see 'pads' (2)

off stump the stump furthest from the batsman. What most non-spin bowlers aim at most of the time. See 'top of off'

offspin a slow, spinning delivery that pitches outside off stump and turns in to the righthander. Spin is usually imparted with the fingers, either by snapping them together or by rolling them down the ball as it's released. A perfect offspinner or offbreak pitches outside the line of off-stump and spins back in to the batsman, cramping him for room, taking the edge or bowling him through the gate (qv). Offspin is often particularly effective against left handed batsmen, as with them of course the offy's stock ball will turn away, searching for the edge, or straighten onto the stumps from around the wicket (qv), bringing LBW firmly into the equation. England's Graeme Swann has had much success with this tactic of late.

offy an offspinner – both the person and the delivery.

old ball any ball that's been used for more than around 20 overs is old. By that time most of the lacquer is gone and the ball will be scuffed up and much softer than a new one. It can be shined, to aid with conventional swing (qv) and may even begin to reverse (qv). Old, rougher balls are also more likely to spin.

on/onside the opposite of 'off' – another term for leg or legside.

on the one any fielding position, the main function of which is to stop the quick single.

on the pads see 'pads' (2)

on strike The batsman whose turn it is to face the bowling.

on the up / on the rise to hit a ball above about knee height that is still rising, rather than having reached the top of its bounce. Much harder to control. Batsmen who can do it comfortably are that much harder to bowl at.

one down another name for number three in the batting order, who goes in to bat when his side are one wicket down. It is often where the best batsman in a side bats.

one short see 'short (2)'

one-sided (1) of a batsman, to heavily favour shots to either leg (qv) or off (qv).

one-sided (2) of a game, to be a hopeless mis-match. Happens in Test matches as well as on village greens, and is no fun in either instance, either for those getting whooped, or those doing the whooping, or those sat around wondering if there's anything nearby that's been freshly painted, which might be marginally more exciting as an entertainment spectacle.

open the batting The two batsman that go out to start the innings for a side. In pro cricket, they are excellent, orthodox players, especially good at playing quick bowlers and the new ball (qv). In league cricket they'll be two of the better bats, and in truly casual cricket they are often just the ones who don't mind opening, so the rest can have a look and get an idea of how quick the opening bowlers are and if the ball is doing anything (qv).

open the bowling The two bowlers who bowl first, one at each end. Usually quicker bowlers who can exploit the hardness and possible swing (qv) of the new ball (qv). Increasingly though, especially in T20, at least one may be a spinner, so the openers have to hit out before they get 'in' (qv, 3) rather than relying on the pace of the quicks.

orthodox of a batsman's technique. Well-schooled. Nothing across the line (qv), nothing flashy or risky. See 'textbook', 'top hand', 'straight bat', 'elbow' 'elegant'.

out the end of a batsman's innings. There are ten ways to be out in cricket, but you can safely ignore the last four, certainly in village cricket, as they simply never happen: bowled (qv), caught (qv), stumped (qv), LBW (qv), run out (qv), hit wicket (qv), handled the ball (qv), hit the ball twice, obstruction of the field, timed out. See also 'obscure ways to be out'.

out of sorts of a batsman: out of form (qv). To be going through a lean (qv, 1) period.

outfield the outer part of a cricket field, nearest the boundary. Refers both to the area of the ground, and to the fielders stationed there.

outside edge the edge of the bat furthest away from the batsman's body. Outside edges are the most common form of catch offered behind the wicket, to the slips (qv) and wicket-keeper (qv). They tend to come very fast, often the edge adding to the bowler's pace, and they're quite likely to race through everyone for four. They're the favourite dismissal of outswing bowlers – the more the ball swings away from the bat, the more likely it is to take the edge. See also 'edge', 'inside edge', 'nick', 'feather', and 'walk'.

outside off the place to bowl. Good areas (qv). The Corridor (qv) of uncertainty.

outswing a ball that starts on the stumps and then swings away from the batsman towards the slips (qv), searching for the outside edge (qv). See 'swing'.

over (1) set of deliveries bowled by a bowler. Usually six, though used to be eight. Some evening competitions still use 8-ball overs.

over (2) to bowl with your bowling arm closest to the stumps is to bowl 'over the wicket'. As most people are right handed, the most common bowling action is 'right arm over'. The bowler must declare his action to the umpires – who will convey it to the batsman – before he commences. Bowlers may change their action whenever they wish, for example to a left handed bats, but must say so. See 'round the wicket.'

over (3) to hit the ball 'back over the bowler's head' is to hit the ball hard and straight and well. Bowlers dislike it intensely.

over rate overs bowled per hour. The longer the game, the slower the over rate.

overthrows a ball fielded and returned to the middle but not collected by the keeper or bowler, so it continues over the wicket to the other side and needs fielding again. The batsmen may continue to run. Often the result of direct hit (qv) run out (qv) attempts where there's no-one backing up (qv, 2), overthrows can easily go for four, in which case the four runs are *added* to the runs the batsmen have already run and count towards the on-strike batsman's score, which can lead to the unusual instance of batsmen scoring more than six runs off a single ball.

overpitched an attempted length (qv) ball which is a bit too full (qv), and turns into a half volley (qv).

pace (1) fast (qv) bowlers are sometimes known as pace bowlers. "Good pace", as encouragement from a fielding side to a bowler means "That's nice and fast".

pace (2) the rate at which an innings progresses. A well paced innings will usually accelerate in the second half, and pick up speed even further towards the close, as wickets become less important and runs more so.

pace off   not-particularly-quick bowling is often somewhat dismissively called dibbly-dobbly (qv), or military medium (qv). But it can be very effective on slower wickets, to 'take the pace off' the ball, forcing the batsman to take a slash at it, rather than be able to time it. When it's not offering much for the either quicks or spinners, the dibbly-dobbler comes into his own, and he becomes the one doing the dismissing.

Packer Revolution   Kerry Packer was an Australian TV mogul who got into a fight with Cricket Australia over TV rights to the game in the late 1970's. Basically he won, and the game hasn't been the same since. Helmets, coloured clothing, white balls, floodlights, superstar millionaire players, big money sponsorship, high-tech multi-camera TV coverage – all this is thanks to Packer and his 'World Series Cricket'. For good or ill, more than any player or coach, he shaped the modern game, both professional and amateur, turning a sleepy class-ridden anachronism into the global-audience money-spinner and ever-more-popular participation sport it is today. See chapter 10.

pads (1)   batting pads. Thick, lightweight, flexible protection worn on the legs.

pads (2)   the area of the crease where the pads – ie the batsman's legs – are. At a high level, for quick bowlers to bowl 'on the pads' is to invite trouble, as most top class batsmen are very strong 'off the pads', and will easily clip (qv) or flick (qv) anything offered there through the legside for four. This is not always true of amateur batsmen, and at a lower level bowlers can have some success with 'a legstump line'.

paddle   see 'sweep (1)'.

pair (1)   a batsman in a two innings game who is out for a duck (qv, 1) in both innings is said to have collected a pair. Best to steer clear of him for a while. See 'king pair'.

pair (2)   the two batsmen at the crease. "This pair are going well."

partnership two batsmen batting together; the score made by them. Games are built around partnerships. One good one can turn a match on its head, as can breaking a partnership – getting one of them out – at the right time.

part timer a batting all-rounder who's definitely more of a batsman than a bowler, and will only bowl as a fifth or sixth option. A dilettante spinner or medium pacer. (In the recent England set up, Trott and Pietersen are the part timers.)

pass the edge see 'beat the bat'.

penalty runs in addition to extras (qv) the umpires may elect to award either side five penalty runs if they consider underhand tactics have been employed. This may include ball tampering (qv), deliberate attempts to distract the batsman, obstruction of the batsman, deliberate attempts to distract fielders, time wasting, deliberately damaging the pitch, and stealing a run. So rare in professional cricket that it makes headlines if it happens. I've neither seen or heard tell of it in village cricket. Penalty runs can also be awarded to the batting side if the ball strikes unused equipment (usually a helmet, but might be a jumper, a hat, sunglasses or a water bottle) on the field of play.

pick to pick a delivery is for a batsman to accurately gauge which type of variation (qv) is coming his way from the bowler. See 'read'.

pick the gap see 'placement'

pick up a ball that a batsman recognises very early is going to be in his slot, and duly administers the full treatment to.

pie chucker a bowler, usually a dilettante spinner, of questionable skill. As is ever the case, often gets wickets because proper batsman think he's rubbish so every ball should get thumped. Perfectly illustrated by Kevin Pietersen's derogatory comments concerning the bowling of Yuvraj Singh, who continues to dismiss him many more times than he has any right to with evident delight. Also true of Pietersen himself, the self-proclaimed 'original pie chucker' who firmly asserts 'I can't bowl', yet has a knack of coming on for a few overs before tea and taking a vital wicket. Though, of course, neither of those world class cricketers is really a pie chucker worthy of any self respecting village green. See 'shit gets wickets'.

pill slang for a ball. Especially either a new one – 'new pill' – or one that has been well worked on, and now has one very rough side, and one very shiny side – 'that's a special pill, that is'.

pinch the strike see 'nick' (2)

pinch hitter a term borrowed from baseball, a pinch hitter is someone who bats in place of another – who has pinched someone's place in line. The idea in cricket originally was to promote lower order batsmen up to the top of the order so they could smash some quick runs, and if they got out it didn't matter because all the 'proper' batsmen were still to come. The tactic of aggressive openers has become so widespread in the shorter formats, that the term is now effectively redundant, as they're now just 'hitters' and are no longer 'pinching' anything.

pitch (1) another name for a ground (1).

pitch (2) another name for a wicket (1).

"pitch it up" advice and encouragement offered by team-mates to a bowler who is bowling too short.

pitch of the ball if your footwork (qv) is good enough to get you to the pitch of every delivery, so you are waiting for it there, turning it by your movement into a half volley (qv), you will have few problems batting. By hitting the ball so soon after it has pitched, you negate any swing (qv), seam (qv), spin (qv) or bounce (qv). Easy.

pitchmap another tv graphic from the Hawk-Eye (qv) stable. A bird's eye view showing where on the wicket a bowler is pitching his deliveries – wide, straight, short, a good length, full, etc. Like the beehive (qv), can be a graphic of one bowler against one batsman, all bowler's to one batsman, one bowler to left handers, etc. A useful analytical tool to demonstrate tactics and plans, for both batsmen and bowlers.

placement to purposefully hit the ball into areas of the field least covered by fielders. To pick the gaps, to split the field (hitting the ball directly between two fielders so that both must give chase). One of batting's finer arts.

'play' instruction from the umpire to the bowler that everyone is ready to start or continue a game after a break in play for any reason – from tea to someone tying a shoelace.

play and miss see 'beat the bat'.

play on (v) to hit the ball on to your own stumps with your bat, usually off an edge (qv). Sometimes 'chop on'. See 'drag on'.

plenty of batting to come see 'wickets in hand'

'plenty of time' what batsmen in the middle say to each other, especially when one of them is new to the crease. It is code for 'don't do anything stupid.'

plumb adjective to describe an LBW shout, as in it definitely was: exactly, utterly, absolutely; derived presumably from the use of a plumb-line to find absolute vertical.

point fielding position square on the off side, originally derived from being at the point of the bat, ie under the batsman's nose. The field has spread a bit since the game's early years: these days that would be silly point. See 'fielding positions'.

pop on particularly bouncy, worn or uneven wickets, the occasional ball will rear sharply or 'pop' off the surface, surprising the batsman and often inducing a top edge to point or gully (see 'fielding positions') as he tries to fend it off.

popping crease see 'crease'.

---

power play a specified period of a limited overs game – 5 overs, for example – during which only 2 or 3 fielders (the restrictions differ with the format) are allowed outside the circle (qv). Intended to increase scoring rates by reducing the number of fielders on the boundary, they often bring wickets as well, as batsmen feel the pressure to hit out (qv).

---

premeditated a shot that the batsman has decided to play before the ball is bowled, rather than playing the ball on its merits. Most typically precedes the word 'sweep' (qv).

---

procession see 'batting collapse'

---

pull a cross bat (qv) shot played off the back foot (qv) to a short (qv) ball. With a pull the batsman plays right across his body, hitting the ball hard more-or-less at right-angles to it's line, so it goes through the legside, usually roughly square (qv, 2). See also 'swivel pull'.

---

pudding a slow, soft, often wet pitch that's very hard to score on.

---

punch shot usually but not necessarily played straight (qv), off the back foot (qv), with crisp timing (qv) and minimum follow through (qv).

---

quicks fast (qv) bowlers are sometimes known as quicks.

---

quicker ball a variation (qv) for a spinner, a ball that doesn't spin but arrives at the batsman a lot sooner than he is expecting.

---

quota the maximum number of overs each bowler is allowed to bowl in a limited overs match. Typically the total number divided by five, or as close to it as whole numbers allow.

---

rabbit A rubbish batsman, easy to dismiss, a walking wicket (qv). Usually specialist bowlers. Named after the animal's frightened, nervous, clueless, always-on-the-verge-of-running-away demeanour.

Some bowlers have rabbits, or bunnies, who are proper batsmen that they habitually dismiss. Or at least taunt the poor chap that they do, having claimed to have worked him out. See also 'ferret'.

rain the perennial bane of cricket. See chapter 11.

ramp shot an invention of the T20 age, pioneered by Sri Lankan batsman Tillekeratne Dilshan, also known as the 'Dilscoop' in his honour. Played to length balls from pace bowlers, basically the batsman lays his bat almost flat in front of him, pointing at the bowler, so the ball runs up it like a ramp, and at the moment of impact flicks or 'scoops' it up, over his own head. Usually for six, straight behind the keeper. Much much much more difficult than it looks. Try it. In the nets. Wear a helmet.

rank see 'long hop'.

read to be able to read or 'pick' a bowler is to be able to tell which variation he's bowling as he bowls it. Jimmy Anderson's outswinger action looks almost identical to the action for his inswinger (see 'swing'), and Saeed Ajmal's off break (qv) appears identical to his doosra (qv) right up until the point at which it pitches. Being difficult or impossible to read is a big part of what makes them among the best bowlers in the world: bowlers who are very hard to read are very hard to play.

rearrange see 'furniture'.

rebuild see 'consolidate'.

referral a system in top flight cricket whereby players may refer decisions they think the umpire may have got wrong to the third umpire (qv). See chapter 7.

reply a side batting second makes their runs 'in reply' to the team batting first.

required run rate see 'run rate'.

retire of a batsman, to voluntarily stop batting, rather than be out. In friendly games it might be agreed before play that batsmen will retire at 25, 50 or 100, depending on the length and standard of game. The only other reason to retire is through injury, or 'retired, hurt'. In any instance, a retired batsman may come back in to bat at the end of an innings when all other batsmen are out.

return catch a catch a bowler takes off his own bowling. See 'caught and bowled'.

return crease see 'crease'

reverse order see T20x2R.

reverse swing with conventional swing, the ball moves in the air away from the smooth side of the ball and towards the rough side. With reverse swing, the opposite happens. When bowled very fast – above 80mph, so not available on the village green – old balls sometimes swing the other way, towards the shiny side. No-one is quite sure why, though there are lots of convincingly complex aerodynamic theories to do with airflow, turbulence, 'boundary layers' and keeping the ball very dry; it doesn't seem to happen when it's damp. For a fuller explanation of all sorts of swing and how much we don't know about it, see 'swing'.

reverse sweep the same as a sweep (qv, 1) but played with the bat reversed, so that the ball goes behind square on the offside, down towards third man. Unless you're Eoin Morgan, in which case it goes 20 rows back for six. See also 'switch hit'.

review see 'third umpire' and chapter 7.

ring field field set where everyone is in a circle up 'on the one', saving singles, and there's no-one out on the boundary.

rip of a spinner, to spin the ball as hard as you can, to get as much turn as possible: 'to give the ball a real rip'; of a delivery, to turn prodigiously: "Man, that ripped!"

rising ball short (qv) or back of a length (qv) bowling that is always on the up, towards the hands, torso or head. Hard to play well and keep down if it's straight.

road a very flat (qv) pitch.

rock back to have your weight on your front foot (qv), change your mind at the last minute and transfer it smoothly to the back foot (qv), usually for a cut (qv) or pull (qv).

rotate for a batting pair to keep scoring singles between boundaries, so that each faces a similar amount of balls in a partnership, is to rotate the strike. This is useful not only because it allows both batsmen to get their eye in, it also makes it that much harder for the bowlers to settle. The opposite is to 'nick' (qv, 2) the strike.

rough the area of the wicket that is scuffed up by the fast bowlers' feet. As games wear on this becomes more pronounced, and spin bowlers will try to land the ball there, as balls will tend to grip and turn out of the rough a lot more than normal.

round his legs about the coolest and cruellest thing a leg spinner can do to a right handed batsman. To pitch the ball so far down the legside that the batsman considers it no threat and leaves it, thinking it's probably going to be called a wide anyway. Only for it to turn so sharply that it comes back in and bowls him behind his legs. Simply wonderful.

round the wicket to bowl with your bowling arm furthest away from to the stumps. Often employed by left arm bowlers to give them a better angle into righthander's, or by right arm bowlers to left hand bats. See 'over (2)'.

Royal duck see 'diamond duck'.

run a batsmen scores a run by hitting the ball and running to the other end of the wicket, while his batting partner (qv) completes the opposite manoeuvre. That is one run. If the ball is still being chased, the batsmen may decide (see 'call') to run a second. In which case they both set off again to the other end. See 'run out'.

run chase the innings of the team batting second in a limited overs game, or last in a two innings game.

runner if a batsman is injured during the course of his innings, he may appoint a member of his side to run for him. The batsman stays still, having hit the ball, and the runner runs parallel with the wicket at square leg. When he's non-striker, the runner takes the batsman's place on the strip. Sound complicated? It is. It's always incredibly complicated and mixed up, and I've rarely seen a runner last long in an amateur game because everyone's so confused they usually get run out before too long. No longer allowed in international cricket.

run out while the batsmen are running between the wickets, if the fielding side manage to break either wicket with the ball before the batsman heading for that wicket has made his ground (qv) that batsman is run out. Said batsman will invariably be a) livid, and b) blaming his batting partner (qv). The author is famous for being run out. Though he would protest it is rarely his fault, he cannot deny that he is the only common factor in them all. See 'call', 'danger end' and 'take on the arm'.

run rate the speed at which a side scores, or needs to score, measured in runs per over. A side scoring 400 in a 40 over game would have scored at a run rate of 10. (They would also, incidentally, have done remarkably well.) The side batting second would start the game with a 'required run rate' or 'asking rate' of 10 runs per over. If the first four overs of their innings are maidens, however, the required run rate for their remaining 36 overs has already climbed above 11. And, lets face it, considering they conceded 400 and then started that badly, their chances don't look great.

run up the route into the wicket where a bowler runs in to bowl. Spinners and medium pacers will have short runs, but some quick bowlers have very long run ups to help get themselves in the right rhythm. Some of the West Indies pacemen of yore would start with their heels resting on the advertising hordings around the boundary.

Saturday League The proper stuff. The village cricketer's 'longer form' of the game. The Test match of the provinces. Usually between 40 and 50 overs a side. Starts at 2pm. Don't be late. Taken seriously.

schoolboy field an almost ludicrously attacking field, as might be set by an enthusiastic eleven year old. All crowding around the bat, or a packed slip cordon, hell bent on wickets, to hell with the runs. Often set for a hat-trick ball (qv).

scorers those responsible for recording the score in a cricket match. The most famous scorer was TMS's late great 'bearded wonder' Bill Frindall, who developed his own meticulous system of scoring, and elevated the position to something of an art, becoming a geek-hero in the process. Coloured pens – different for each batsman and bowler – can be used to record every possible permutation for the information. In village teams, the scorers, like the umpires, will often be members of the batting team who have yet to bat or are already out, and are thus likely to rotate through the game. This can sometimes lead to confusion, inaccuracy, and, ahem, guesswork.

scrambled seam similar to a cross seam (qv) delivery, but usually from a spinner. Often wrong'uns (qv) and cutters (qv) are scrambled seam by nature. Some bowlers prefer to scramble the seam because the ball can bounce (qv) or shoot (qv) unpredictably depending on whether it lands on the seam or not. Others prefer to do it because it makes them harder to read (qv). Swing bowlers might use it as a variation, as a ball bowled with a scrambled seam will not swing.

screws a shot that 'comes out of the screws' is one that is really, properly, powerfully, comprehensively timed (qv) and middled (qv). Chris Gayle's six into the road outside the Oval during the 2009 World T20 could reasonably be said to have come out of the screws. A puzzling expression, as there are never any screws involved in cricket bat construction. Derivation unknown.

seam (1) the 80 or so stitches in a raised ridge around the equator of a cricket ball.

---

seam (2) of a fast bowler, to bowl with the seam upright, so that when it hits the pitch it is likely to deviate one way or another. This is known as 'jagging' or 'seaming'. Adjective: 'he's a decent seam bowler'; verb: 'he's really getting the ball to seam'.

---

seamer a fast bowler who relies more on seam (qv, 2) movement than swing (qv).

---

seam position the position of the seam as the ball moves through the air during delivery. Seam bowlers will bowl with the seam upright, in the direction of travel, to give it more of a chance of landing the seam (see 'seam 2'). Spinners will often bowl with the seam rotating perpendicular to the direction of travel, again so the ball will land on the seam and grip the surface. See 'scrambled seam' and 'cross seam'.

---

set see 'in' (2)

---

set the field to place the fielders where you want them is to set the field. Usually done by either the bowler or the captain, often together. See 'attack (2)' and 'defensive (2)' and 'fielding positions'.

---

shape 'good shape' might be said encouragingly by team-mates of a delivery, usually from a swing bowler, where the ball is moving in promising ways through the air, he is 'shaping the ball' in or out, but perhaps was not quite on target enough to warrant a full throated 'great ball!' A minor adjustment away from perfection. Also applied to a batsman playing his shots and looking good, (see 'follow through') though it's not yet showing on the score sheet – he's 'making good shapes'. Or, when he's out of position or off balance, he has 'lost his shape'.

---

shine to buff one side of a cricket ball to help it swing (qv). See also 'ball tampering'.

---

shirtfront a dead, flat (qv) pitch.

'shit gets wickets' you may be an excellent bowler having a great day, bowling beautifully, like an artist, and having no success at all. Then you bowl a horrible long hop (qv), the batsman's eyes light up, he flashes at it across the line (qv), and top edges a dolly (qv). Or you may be a bowler of limited ability, brought on, say, after a tight spell full of jaffas (qv) and maidens (qv), and the batsmen lay into you out of sheer frustration and offer up simple catches. Either way, as is evidenced most times cricket is played, at any level, bowling doesn't have to be good to be successful. (At DCC, the 'shit gets wickets' phenomenon is know as 'Burrough's Law', after a particularly successful proponent of the principle, rarely claiming wickets with decent balls, but often with horrible ones.) See also 'pie chucker'.

shooter a ball that, instead of bouncing as expected, keeps very low to the ground and shoots forward. Likely to get you out LBW or bowled. Also known as a grubber.

short (1) a ball that pitches nearer the middle of the wicket than the batsman is said to be short. Can also be 'short of a length' or back-of-a-length (qv), which is only marginally short. See 'cut' and 'pull'. See also 'bouncer'.

short (2) another word for a close fielder; short midwicket is a midwicket closer to the bat. See also 'silly' and 'close'.

short run when running between the wickets, if a batsman doesn't ground his bat (or any part of his body, but the bat is easiest) behind the popping crease (qv) at the completion of a run before turning back to start the next run, the run doesn't count, and is said to be "one short". The umpire signals (see 'umpire signals') 'short runs' to indicate to the scorers that one run should be deducted from the score for that ball.

'shot' contraction of 'good shot', an acknowledgement, directed to the batsman by his batting partner, his team mates in the pavilion, spectators, even his opponents.

shoulder arms to 'leave' (qv) the ball. To 'shoulder' or 'put up' arms in one respect means to disarm or demonstrate non-engagement. Also, usually, in a nice little double meaning, the expression is used to describe the kind of leave played to a rising ball, so the priority is to get both bat and gloves as far out of the way as possible, usually raised high above the head, which can look quite elaborate and formal, not unlike its namesake military parade-ground manoeuvre. The other way to play a leave against the rising ball of course is to lower the bat and drop the hands out of the way; this would not be described as shouldering arms.

shout an appeal (qv). A delivery that hits a batsman in line with the stumps, or looks like it might have got a thin edge that carried, is "worth a shout".

sightscreen large white (or black if playing with a white ball) rectangle positioned 'behind the bowler's arm' ie directly behind the bowler, so the ball shows up clearly and the batsman can see it easily. There's an awful lot of nonsense talked about movement behind the bowler's arm: people fidgeting about, parking cars, having picnics, etc. Hours are wasted fiddling about with sightscreens in the professional game, especially when they have those swanky ones which are effectively giant tellies showing ads when the bowling is from the other end, and invariably break down half way through a game and end up being covered by a sheet or something. More often than not village greens don't have sightscreens, and when they do have them the wheels tend to be rusted solid so they're never in the right place anyway.

silly any fielding position (qv) that is dangerously close to the bat, eg: silly point, silly mid off, etc. Silly because, lets face it, it is not sensible to stand that close to someone who's likely to whack a cricket ball at you any second.

sitter a very easy catch. See 'dolly'.

skiddy bowlers shorter in stature – and thus also kids – are often skiddy bowlers, meaning the ball skids through low and doesn't 'get up' or bounce much. They're not always short though; some just have actions that promote a flatter trajectory, some have a naturally fuller length than 'hit-the-deck' (qv) bowlers.

skier ball played – unintentionally, usually off a top edge (qv) – high in the air, giving an easy catching chance.

skittle to bowl a side out very cheaply.

skip/skipper captain.

sledging to verbally abuse, harangue and otherwise attempt to put off your opponent. Occasionally light hearted banter and quite funny (see 'chirp'), it increasingly seems to be plain nasty gamesmanship, reducing international sportsmen to puerile name-calling and personal insults. Mercifully rare in the amateur game.

slide a fielding technique of running and then timing a slide along the ground on one leg to intercept the ball. If you get it right, you can also use your momentum to get back on your feet again and get into position to return the ball. Like many things in cricket, done well, it looks effortlessly graceful. (Done badly, it looks like a sack of potatoes falling off a lorry and bouncing along the road.)

slider a leg spinner's (chiefly Shane Warne's) variation. A cocktail of a top spinner (qv), an arm ball (qv) and a quicker ball (qv), it was flatter in trajectory, faster, and straight, getting him a lot of LBWs.

sliding an LBW shout that is missing the stumps on the leg side, especially an inswinger that is swinging too much, is said to be 'sliding down leg', and is often abbreviated simply to 'sliding'.

slip fielding position (qv) behind the bat on the offside, set to take catches off edges (qv). The slips run in a roughly diagonal line from the wicket-keeper outwards. First slip is nearest the keeper, second further away, etc. It's unusual to see more than a couple in village cricket, though sometimes you might, if the bowling is fast and/ or swinging away from the bat, and everything is going behind. Dennis Lillee once famously bowled with nine slips, which was doubtless as much of a psychological decision as a tactical one, and tells you everything you need to know about Dennis Lillee. Slips are an attacking position, their primary purpose being to take catches rather than stop runs. In professional cricket, your best and most agile fielders with the sharpest reflexes and safest hands are specialist slip fielders, often batsmen. In village cricket, usually the guy with the injured this, pulled that or dodgy the-other will ask to field at slip, so he doesn't have to run anywhere.

slipper a specialist slip fielder

slog an agricultural (qv) yahoo (qv) of a shot, invariably across the line (qv).

slogger a 'batsman', in the loosest sense (ie a man with a bat) whose only shot is the slog. A classless, talentless thumper of the ball. Maddeningly, can be very effective indeed.

slot a ball that is 'in the slot' is exactly where the batsman wants it, perfect for him to hit, perfect for him to marmalise (qv) through the covers (qv) or wallop through midwicket. See 'half-volley', 'buffet' and 'pick up'.

slow bowling doesn't have to be fast to be good. If you can repeatedly bowl the ball on a good line and length, no matter what speed it's travelling, it'll be hard to hit. However, most serious slow bowlers are spinners. See 'off spin' and 'leg spin'.

slower ball the fast bowler's surprise ball. Expecting a rocket, the batsman may be 'through the shot too early' – ie trying to hit a ball that hasn't arrived yet, often resulting in being bowled or looping up a gentle catch. The best slower balls are very difficult to pick (qv), as the arm comes over at the same speed, with only a slight variation in the grip meaning the ball actually leaves the hand significantly slower.

smear a ball hit low and very very hard. May not be the prettiest of shots perhaps, but shows intent, and a certain contempt for the bowling.

snick a tiny nick (qv) or feather (qv). Onomatopoeic – if you're fielding close or in the slips, the merest of edges sounds just like someone whispering: 'snick'.

snicko tv innovation which registers sound as a visible graphic at the supposed moment of impact, to help determine if a batsman got a little nick (qv). For some reason it currently takes an age to receive this information, so snicko technology is not yet available for reviews (qv).

soft hands to hold the bat loosely so that it gives on impact, more often than not playing the ball down, as opposed to a tight, fierce grip, which is much more likely to chip it up. Also, when catching, loose relaxed hands (not too relaxed, obviously) are much more successful, whereas nervously tense hands are more likely to spill chances. In both instances, infinitely harder to do than to say.

spell the overs a bowler bowls without a break is a spell.

spin To impart lateral rotation on the ball, causing it to deviate from its course after pitching. See 'off spin', 'leg spin', 'left-arm orthodox', and 'bounce'.

spinner a slow bowler who spins the ball. There are three basic types: see 'off spin', 'leg spin' and 'left arm orthodox'. For more in-depth stuff, see 'air', 'flight', 'bounce', 'doosra', 'googly', 'top-spinner', and 'quicker ball'. To get confused, see 'chinaman'.

spirit The Spirit of Cricket is no longer just a vague concept. Since 2000 it has been a 'preamble' part of the Laws (qv), "providing the context in which the game is intended to be played". It talks about conduct, fairness, responsibility and respect.

splice the part of the bat where the handle is joined to the blade. There is no give or power in that part of the bat, so the batsman doesn't want the ball to hit there, and the bowler does.

split the field see 'placement'

square (1) The area in the middle of a cricket pitch from which a wicket (qv, 1) is cut. Wickets are rotated to allow them to recover after games. Confusingly, squares are rarely square, they're usually rectangles. The square is the bit that's roped off when there isn't a game on, to stop people and animals wandering over it.

square (2) The area at right angles to the wicket on the leg side at the striker's end; the batsman has his back to it as he's facing

square leg right angles to the wicket on the leg side at the striker's end, about 22 yards away. Where the second of the two umpires stands.

squarer when fielding, you may often be asked to move 'squarer' or 'finer' or 'straighter'. This is tricky to explain from first principles, but here's a stab. Imagine the batsman is north, and the bowler is south. To move 'squarer' is to move more towards either east or west (in this context it's used for both off and on side). If you move so you're more in line with the north/south axis you are 'finer' if you're behind the bat; 'straighter' if you are in front of it.

stance the way a batsman stands at the crease ready to face the bowling. (Archaically called 'Standing in Attitude'.) Traditionally it is sideways on, knees slightly bent, back foot behind the crease, bat behind the back foot, head towards the bowler, eyes over the bat. But there are a million variations.

stand a partnership (qv). As in 'opening stand' or 'last wicket stand'.

standing back/up for fast bowlers, the wicket-keeper will be anything up to 25 yards behind the stumps. To spinners and sometimes to medium pacers, he will be right up close to the stumps, forcing the batsman to remain in his crease at all times, or risk being stumped (qv) if he misses the ball.

standing umpire the umpire at the bowler's end.

start see 'in' (2)

stay hit a rather foolish expression, when you think about it, but one of those you find yourself using despite yourself. "When he hits it it stays hit," simply means "He really does hit the ball very hard indeed."

steepling of excessive, lively bounce, especially from tall fast bowlers. To 'get big' (qv) quickly, and cramp a batsman for room, often causing a chance off an edge or a glove as he has to unexpectedly defend himself.

steal to steal a single is to run very hard, setting off immediately, to make a single that wasn't really there. To steal the strike is to take a single off the last ball of an over. See 'nick' (2).

stealing a run batsmen attempting to run during the bowler's run up. Pretty underhand behaviour – and punishable with 5 penalty runs (qv) – but also pretty unlikely, unless the bowler has an immensely long run up not seen since the days of Michael Holding pushing himself off the advertising hoardings.

sticky wicket also known as a sticky dog. After overnight rain, a wicket that dries quickly in fierce sunshine so the ball 'sticks' in the pitch (ie slows up very quickly), takes prodigious turn and bounces unpredictably. A nightmare to bat on, an absolute joy to bowl spin on. See chapter 5.

stock ball the ball a bowler bowls most often. Just outside off stump for a seamer, an outswinger for an outswinger, a leg break for a leggie, an off break for an offy.

stonewall to defend, to protect one's wicket. See 'bat time' and 'gritty'.

straight to play straight is to play the ball straight back in the direction it came from. Requires good timing (qv). See 'straight bat' and 'v'.

straight bat playing with a straight bat has transcended the game and entered the language – see chapter 5. It means to play back down the line of the ball with the bat absolutely vertical, minimising the opportunity to miss or edge it. Solid, not risky or flashy. Displays sound technique. Likely the score you runs in the 'v' (qv).

straight through a delivery that seems unable to have missed the stumps, but has, and appears to have passed directly through the batsman as if he was insubstantial, is said to have gone straight through him, or to have 'cut him in half'.

straight up and down dismissive, of a bowler who is getting no movement in the air or off the pitch and is not particularly quick.

straighter see 'squarer'.

streaky to score runs off edges (qv) and chinese cuts (qv) and hit the ball in the air (qv) into gaps (qv). To be lucky, basically. To still be out there batting by the skin of your teeth.

strike to be facing the bowling is to have the strike.

strike rate both batsmen and bowlers have strike rates. A batsman's is an average of the amount of runs he scores for every hundred balls he faces. As with most stats it varies enormously depending on the format of the game – T20 strike rates for better batsmen are over 100, meaning better than a run a ball. A bowler's strike rate is an average of how many deliveries it takes him to get a wicket.

striker's end The end the bowler bowls to, where the 'on strike' or 'facing' batsman awaits.

strip a wicket (qv, 1)

strong of a batsman, to really punish balls in certain areas. To be 'strong off his pads', a batsman will score heavily from poor balls down the leg side. The opposite, of course, also applies. See 'weak'.

stump (1) one of three 28 inch upright poles at each end of the wicket (qv, 1)

stump (2) when a wicketkeeper, standing up (qv), takes a batsman's wicket (qv, 3) by breaking his wicket (qv, 2) with the ball in his gloves, with the batsman out of his ground (qv 2), the batsman is out, stumped. The difference between being stumped and run out (qv) is that the batsman is in the process of attempting a shot rather than attempting a run. Most stumpings occur when a batsman dances down the wicket (qv) and misses the ball.

stumped (2) see stump (2)

stumps (1) The three 28 inch upright poles at each end of the wicket (qv, 1) topped by two bails (qv) to form a wicket (qv, 2).

stumps (2) Contraction of 'draw stumps'. To pull the stumps from the ground and put them away. The end of a game, or the end of a day's play.

sweep (1) cross bat (qv) shot usually played to spinners, hitting the ball as it bounces with a horizontal bat almost touching the floor, smothering the spin. Generally played so the ball goes square or behind on the legside. With the paddle sweep, the ball is guided gently towards fine leg, with the slog sweep, it is walloped.

sweep (2) to clean up the grass, bits of flaky bat tape, scribbled batting orders and empty water bottles from a changing room after a game.

sweeper a fielder right out on the boundary, whose job is to sweep up after the infield (qv) – ie to field anything that gets through the inner ring. Usually set either at cover or midwicket (see 'fielding positions), a sweeper might cover almost a quarter of the ground's perimeter, and will be a fast runner with an excellent arm (qv).

swing for reasons no-one is quite sure about, cricket balls swing in the air. We're sure why they sometimes do. A ball that's, say, 20 overs old can be shined on one side, and left rough on the other. As this ball travels through the air at speed with its seam upright, the shiny side meets less resistance than the scuffy side. The rough side drags and travels more slowly, so simple physics tells us that a ball so treated will swing away from the shiny side. But new balls, equally shiny both sides, swing too. And then sometimes they don't. And sometimes only certain bowlers can get a ball to swing, and others – who usually can swing it – can't. Some makes of ball are more likely to swing than others. White, orange, pink and red balls swing differently. Weather affects it too: if it's cloudy, it's more likely to swing than when it's sunny. And climate: the ball often swings in England, rarely in the Caribbean. It will be more likely to swing at some grounds than others. Sometimes new stands built at a ground will affect the amount of swing bowlers get. To add to the confusion, when bowled very fast, old balls sometimes swing the other way: towards the shiny side. No-one really knows why this is either, though there are lots of convincingly complex aerodynamic theories to do with airflow, turbulence, 'boundary layers' and keeping the ball very dry; it doesn't seem to happen when it's damp. We are sure what it's called though, it's called reverse swing. The ball will only reverse above a certain speed too: usually around 80mph, sometimes as fast as 90mph, depending on conditions. Whereas conventional swing will happen at pretty much any speed – in village cricket you'll find some highly skilful swing bowlers who can hoop it round corners at a gentle 55mph. A ball that starts wide of off stump and swings in towards the batsman is known as an in-swinger. A ball that starts on the stumps and swings away towards the slips is an away-swinger, or out-swinger. Seam position at the point of delivery as well as a bowler's action will help determine the direction and amount of swing. Some have actions that only allow in-swing, others can only swing it away. Bowlers who can do both, at will, and control the amount of movement and even how late it swings, are rare talents. However and why-ever it works, it definitely does. Old ball, new ball, conventional, reverse, in, away: in the hands of a skilful practitioner, the swinging ball is a highly potent weapon, and only the very best batsmen can resist it for long.

swipe a hopeful, cross batted (qv) limp wristed, across the line (qv) effort that the batsman is instantly disgusted at himself for, whether it works or not.

switch hit extraordinary shot pioneered by Kevin Pietersen in which the batsman jumps 180 degrees at the point of delivery so that what was his off side is now his on side, and he is now batting left handed instead of right handed, or vice versa. Not recommended to anyone other than supremely talented ambidextrous exhibitionists.

swivel pull an even more elegant and flowing version of the pull (qv), where the batsman swivels on the pivot of his back foot and rotates 90-180 degrees as he plays the shot, which usually places the ball backward of square. Ricky Ponting does it particularly gracefully, spinning on his heel almost like an ice skater, looking for all the world like he *must* have started playing the shot before the bowler released the ball.

T20 Twenty20 has been played for years in the evenings, after work, as the only real alternative to nothing at all. The 'new' part is that the pros and internationals are starting to take it seriously, largely because of the vast amounts of money pumped into the IPL (qv). Fast, loud, brash, quick-fix cricket, fun to watch and play, but with none of the complexities or subtleties of the longer forms. It is one of cricket's greatest strengths that it is so flexible and malleable, and the two-and-a-half hour version can be as popular and riveting as the five day version, even if its core audience are quite different people.

T20x2R The author's own invention. A format for casual matches, to make sure everyone gets a game. Two innings of 20 overs per side, like a miniature Test match. In the second innings, the batting order is reversed. Max 3 overs per bowler in the first innings, 4 in the second. Batsmen retire at 50, return if everyone's out. The format rewards the unusual tactic of loading the middle of your order, both batting and bowling, with your 'least casual' players. The ICC is on the cusp of organising an international T20x2R tournament. No, it's not, but it should be. I'd go, wouldn't you?

tail the back end of a batting line up, in professional sides composed of specialist bowlers. Many village sides 'bat all the way down' (qv), so that little or no variation in ability is discernable from 1 to 11.

Regardless, if lower order batsmen score runs, the tail, rather quaintly, is said to have 'wagged' (qv, 2).

take on the arm to take on a fielder's arm is to attempt a further run when he has the ball in his hand: to gamble that you can make it to the danger end (qv) before he can throw the ball in. Happens rarely – but does happen – in top flight cricket as the general standard of fielding is now excellent, but happens frequently in village cricket, where it's, y'know, not. Really top class fielders have ridiculously powerful and accurate arms, and will hit the stumps more often than not from fifty yards.

take the pace off of medium and fast bowlers, to bowl deliberately slower than normal on slow wickets, forcing the batsmen, especially the top order, to swing at the ball, rather than be able to time it, which is likely to be their natural game. See 'pace off'.

target (1) one more than what the team batting first have scored: what the team batting second need to score to win a game.

target (2) to target or 'go after' a bowler, is for a batsman individually, or a batting side collectively, to decide to try and score heavily from his bowling, in order to psychologically dominate him, and leave his captain with little choice but to stop bowling him. Also known as 'hitting him out of the attack'. Can easily backfire.

tea the finest of traditions in the most civilized of games. Sandwiches. Cakes. Enormous pots of tea. A meal built into a game. Brilliant.

technology see 'third umpire', snicko (qv), Hawk Eye (qv), and hot spot (qv).

Test Match The ultimate test of a cricketer; the name is no coincidence. An international game played over two innings and five days. The best Tests ebb and flow, with the initiative changing hands frequently. There is time for batsmen to build an innings, time for bowlers to work batsmen out, time for captains to tinker with fields, time for every technical and mental weakness to be exploited.

Only the world's very best cricketers are Test material. The ultimate player and spectator experience.

Test Playing Nations The 10 countries qualified to play international cricket at its highest level, namely: Australia, Bangladesh, England, India, New Zealand, Pakistan, South Africa, Sri Lanka, West Indies, and Zimbabwe.

textbook refers to the mythical 'MCC Cricket Coaching Book' in which all correct and orthodox shots are detailed. The MCC manual may be slightly dated now, nevertheless much of it is still relevant, and a textbook shot remains one perfectly executed. See 'correct', 'top hand', 'straight bat', 'elbow', and 'elegant'.

third man fielding position (qv) on the boundary behind the slips (qv) where an awful lot of streaky (qv) runs are scored against good fast bowling in both amateur and professional cricket.

third umpire in the professional game, a third official (in addition to the two on-field umpires) who sits in a room with a telly in it using slow motion replays and things like Hawk Eye (qv), and hot spot (qv) to help him decide if people are out or not. An abomination ruining the standing and respect for umpires in a gentleman's game, or the inevitable march of progress? Who knows. See chapter 7.

through the gate to be bowled through the gate is for the ball to find the gap between your bat and your pad. More common than you'd believe possible.

throw the bat to hit the ball very very hard indeed. (Does not mean to let go of it.)

throwing illegal delivery, see 'chuck'; fielding, see 'arm' and 'take on the arm'.

tie a cricket match which ends with both teams on exactly the same score. Completely different from a draw (qv).

tied up in knots of batsmen, to have trouble, or at worst no clue at all, facing bowling of superior skill.

timing the essence of batting. A good batsman doesn't hit the ball, he strokes it. The bat meets the ball at the perfect place in its arc, and the ball willingly races off the middle (qv, 1) of the bat without any fuss. Similar to golf; if you time it well the ball rockets off, but it feels like it wasn't even there. (The major difference being that golf balls are still when you try and hit them, rather than coming towards you at motorway speeds.) Also similar to golf, timing is the reason why the biggest and strongest players are not necessarily the biggest and strongest hitters.

toe crusher a yorker (qv).

ton a century (qv).

top edge a cross bat (qv) shot played a little too low – or to a ball that bounces more than the batsman expects – will take the uppermost edge of the bat and go high in the air, offering a relatively easy catch. See also 'skier'.

top hand the hand highest on the bat handle; the left hand for a right hander, right hand for a lefty. The top hand should supply the guidance for a shot, the bottom hand (qv) only the power, not the direction. Top hand shots tend to be graceful, controlled and unhurried looking. See 'correct', 'textbook', 'straight bat', 'elbow' 'elegant'.

top of off pace bowlers often aim to hit the top of off stump, especially to better batsmen, who will pick balls off middle and leg comfortably. There are few more satisfying sights for a fast bowler – or his team mates – than an uprooted off stump cartwheeling back past the wicketkeeper.

top order the batsmen. The first four-six guys coming out to bat. See 'batting order', 'balance' (2), 'tail', and 'pinch hitter', just to confuse the issue.

top-spinner or over-spinner, a delivery from a spin bowler that spins forwards, so that it goes straight on but gets erratic bounce (qv).

toss the toss of a coin before play commences to decide which side will bat or bowl first. Depending on the weather, the toss can be crucial. Some tosses, when the weather and pitch are uncertain quantities, are said to be 'a good toss to lose', as a captain can hardly be blamed for losing the toss, but can certainly be blamed for choosing to bat first on a minefield when you're all out for 30, or putting the opposition in when they rattle up 300 for 1 before drinks. WG Grace had very definite ideas: "If you win the toss, bat. If you are in doubt, think about it, then bat. If you have very big doubts, consult a colleague, then bat." He was, needless to say, a batsman.

toss it up see 'air', 'batsman's eye-line' and 'flight'.

TMS Test Match Special. Ball-by-ball commentary on BBC Radio 4 Long Wave and these days on the digital station 5 Live Sports Extra. The constant companion of many a cricket fan during summer days and winter nights when England are touring abroad, especially now there is shamefully no live cricket at all ever on free-to-air telly. Peerless entertainment from a gaggle of lovable characters, from old Etonions like Blowers to rough barro' boys like Tuffers, whose 'job' it is to follow summer around the world and yarn about it to a niche audience thousands of miles away at often ridiculous times of the night, it justifies the BBC licence fee on its own.

track another term for a wicket (qv, 1).

trigger an umpire prone to giving people out when the decision is marginal, especially LBW.

turn to get a ball to spin is to get turn. Some pitches and conditions favour it, others don't. It's often very difficult to predict. "Is it turning?" is what spinners ask each other eagerly when one gets to bowl before the other. "He's turning it miles" is what batsmen mutter to each other darkly while waiting to go in to bat.

turn and bounce a combination guaranteed to get spinners all excited. See 'flight and guile'.

turner a wicket that takes spin. The exact requirements for a turner are often contradictory, and the pitch inspection guru has something of the air of an alchemist about him as a result. Drying wickets turn, but really wet ones don't. Green grassy wickets won't turn, but straw coloured dry grassed wickets might. Grassless tracks are unlikely to, unless they're really dry – 'dustbowl' wickets turn the most. Simple, see?

twelfth man there are eleven players in a cricket side. The 12th man is the one who just missed out on selection. For a pro, that means he's carrying the drinks. For a villager, it probably means he's going shopping in a really foul mood.

two see 'guard'.

two paced a wicket (qv, 1) that is either deteriorating towards the end of a match, or just plain bad. Produces balls that sometimes leap off a length, and sometimes shoot along the floor, seemingly from identical spots on the ground.

umpire The men in white coats. Adjudicators. There are two required for each game of cricket, one at the bowler's end, and one at square leg. Their roles reverse with each over. The professional game of course has neutral, professional umpires. On village greens it'll often be two of the batting side who have yet to bat or are already out. Or they'll be secretaries, chairmen or older club members who no longer play but who are happy to umpire to remain involved and part of the set-up. Other-than-right though they may frequently be, they are never wrong and their word is final. Go gracefully.

umpire signals sign language from the middle, from the umpire to the scorers. The scorers should acknowledge receipt of the signals. Some umpires will doggedly continue to make the signal until they receive such acknowledgement, which can be quite amusing if both parties are equally stubborn. Some signals are very familiar and everyone knows them, a few are hardly ever used. Some only apply to professional cricket, and still more apply only to televised cricket. The meanings of all the standard signals are defined elsewhere in this glossary (qv) **Out** raises one hand to chest height or above, the index finger raised and the other digits down. **Four** waves one arm back and forth in front of him, horizontally at chest height. **Six** raises both arms straight up. **Bye(s)** raises one arm straight up. **No ball** raises one arm horizontally to his side. **Wide** raises both arms horizontally to his sides. **Leg bye(s)** raises one leg, and taps it with one hand. **Dead ball** leans forwards, with both arms hanging straight down in front of him, and waves them backwards and forwards across his knees. **Short run(s)** raises one hand and taps his fingers to the same shoulder. **New ball** (indicating that the new ball has been taken by the bowling side) raises the new ball above his head, showing it to the scorers. That's all the normal ones. Here are a few of the more arcane: **5 penalty runs to the batting team** taps left shoulder with right hand. **5 penalty runs to the fielding team** taps right shoulder with left hand. (See 'penalty runs'.) **5 runs** (not penalties) raises right hand with all five fingers spread. **Free hit** raises one hand above his head and describes a horizontal circle. **Power play** raises one hand, palm outwards, and describes a vertical circle in front of his face. **Television replay review** describes an oblong in front of him with both hands, like the 'TV show' sign in charades: starting in front of his face, both hands go out to their respective sides, then down, then across to meet again in the middle in front of his waist. **Last hour** raises both hands above his head and points to his watch on his left wrist with his right hand. **Revoke the previous signal** raises both hands crossed across his chest to simultaneously touch their opposite shoulders. **Someone else get out here you bastards** hopping on one leg holding privates, indicating the need to pee; raising an imaginary glass in indignation, indicating the need for a pint; kneeling in prayer or simply slumping melodramatically to the floor, indicating the need for a sit down. (Of player/umpires, indicating to their team mates in the pavilion that they consider themselves to have done more than their fair share of umping.)

---

unplayable a jaffa (qv). A delivery so good that even the best batsman would struggle against it. Usually used to indicate that a batsman was dismissed by excellent bowling, rather than by his own mistake.

up see 'field up'.

uppish any shot that is played into the air (rather than along the ground) offering the possibility of a catch.

vacant of a fielding position (qv), to be unoccupied. Almost invariably used when the ball goes there: "That flew through the slips area and down through a vacant third man for four."

variation the options a bowler has up his sleeve. For spinners, this might be a doosra (qv), googly (qv), top-spinner (qv), or quicker ball (qv), for the quicks it might be a slower ball (qv), yorker (qv) or a cutter (qv). For many a casual bowler, it might be the legendary straight one. The whole point of all this wondrous variety, of course, is to deceive the batsman with something he's not expecting.

'v', the the area of the ground in a narrow 'v' shape behind the bowler, from long on to long off. The most pleasing place to score runs, it means you're hitting the ball hard and straight (qv) with the full face of the bat (qv). Scoring runs in the v is a sure sign of good technique and generally lovely to watch. Unless you're bowling.

village cricket countless thousands of games of cricket are played throughout England every weekend. Rural England still thrums to the sound of leather on willow. It lives and breathes on our village greens, where bent old grandfathers, farmers and stockbrokers continue to dream, and the next generation of internationals learn how to play, how to behave, and what a wrong'un is.

village all-rounder A casual cricketer who bats and bowls okay, but excels at neither. The author places himself firmly in this category. Most village sides will have at least two, sometimes as many as nine. Under no circumstances to be confused with a genuine all-rounder (qv).

waft a pointlessly noncommittal wave of the bat in the vague direction of the ball, as if too tired or inebriated to make a serious attempt to hit it. See 'hang the bat out'.

wag (1) if the 'tail' (qv) of a batting line up scores more runs than it's expected to, it is said, rather endearingly, to wag.

WAG (2) Wives-and-girlfriends: the female entourage of any male team. In professional cricket teams, they are likely to be found following them around the world looking after kids, going shopping, etc. In amateur teams, they are similarly likely to be found looking after kids, going shopping, etc, only with a lot less international travel and significantly more complaining involved.

wagon wheel Hawk-Eye's (qv) graphic representation of where a batsman or team have scored their runs in an innings. Drawn as a circular bird's eye view of the ground, it shows the shots as lines going out from the middle, looking like the spokes of a wheel. The more evenly distributed the spokes, the more impressive, as clearly the batsman is not one-sided (qv, 1), and is scoring his runs all around the ground.

walk to know that you are out and walk off the field without waiting for the umpire's decision. There are some instances, a feather-light nick (qv) behind, for example, when only the batsman himself can really be sure. Even TV replays and snicko (qv) will never be conclusive. To walk is the gentlemanly thing. Used to be simply the done thing, but sadly, due to ever increasing pressure to win by any means (ie cheat), and since the retirement of Adam Gilchrist (as famous for being a walker in an age of standers as he was for being the most destructive wicketkeeper/batsmen and most prolific Test 6-hitter the game has ever known) it is now unusual in the professional game. Still more common than not on village greens. Long may it remain so.

walking in of a fielding side, to move in towards the batsman as the ball is bowled. One of the most cohesive and least energetic experiences in sport.

walking wicket A poor batsman. A rabbit (qv). One who is easy to get out. In first class cricket he'll definitely be a bowler. In casual cricket, he could be anyone.

weak of a batsman, to not be so good in certain areas. A batsman 'weak off his pads' will not score heavily from poor balls down the leg side that other batsmen might punish. The opposite, of course, also applies. See 'strong'.

wheels speed. "Good wheels", as encouragement from a fielding side to a bowler means "That's impressively quick".

wicket (1) the area of a cricket field, 22 yards by 8 feet, on which the ball is bowled to the batsman for the game in question.

wicket (2) the set of three stumps (qv, 1) and two bails (qv) that a batsman defends and a bowler and fielding side attacks.

wicket (3) a batsman's innings – when a batsman is out, his wicket is said to have fallen, or been taken. A score of 50-4 means a team have scored 50 runs and have lost four wickets (four batsmen are out). If it's bowling figures, it'll typically be the other way around: 4-50 means that bowler has had 50 runs scored from his bowling, and removed four batsmen. If you're an Aussie you do it backwards, just because you come from the land down under and you like to rankle the poms.

wicket maiden an over from which no runs are scored and a wicket is taken. One the bowler can be proud of.

wicket-keeper the guy crouching behind the stumps, whose job it is to catch or at least stop anything that goes behind. Many edges (qv) are caught by the keeper. He'll usually be a specialist batsman (obviously not a bowler) and often, though not always, a smallish, agile chap. He is the only fielder allowed to wear pads and gloves. His pads will be slightly smaller than batting pads, covering only up to his knees so they're not in the way when he crouches. Unlike batting gloves, his will be padded on the palms rather than the back of the hands, and also feature hard protection in the fingertips and leather webbing between the first finger and thumb. Due to the nature of the game when a side is fielding, wicket-keepers are often play makers, in the middle of the action, loud, mouthy and highly opinionated. (See 'chirp'.) As a consequence, they can also often be quite an odd breed.

wickets in hand to be in a situation where you haven't lost too many wickets yet, and can therefore afford to be aggressive and risky in pursuit of runs.

wicket taking ball a delivery likely to take a wicket. See 'magic ball'.

wicket to wicket to bowl very straight, with an action that starts very close to the stumps, offering no width (qv).

wide a ball that is theoretically too far away from the batsman for him to hit. Practically, the longer the form of the game, the more lenient the umpires are with wides. In T20 village cricket, as well as professional T20 and ODI games, anything passing the batsman on his legside is a wide. The penalty is one run to the batting side (see 'extras') and an extra ball.

width as subtly distinct from a wide, width really is any delivery that's not going to hit the stumps, and allows the batsman room to 'free his arms' (qv).

Wisden Cricketers' Almanac Since 1864 an annual publication containing comment on the state of the game from the cream of the world's cricket writers, awards for the 'Five cricketers of the year', and records from the international and English First Class (qv) season. The eagerly anticipated yearly cricket 'bible'. See 'Cricinfo'.

World Series Cricket see 'Packer Revolution'.

wrist spin see 'legspin' and 'chinaman'.

wristy batting technique whereby a batsman uses his wrists rather than the bigger muscles in his arms and upper body to flick the ball late (qv). Subcontinental players are typically wristy, as they learn to play on turning pitches. See 'turner'.

---

wrong'un a leg spinner's googly (qv) or an off spinner's doosra (qv). A ball that turns the other way from a spinner's stock ball. The opposite of what the batsman expects.

---

yahoo a wild swipe played with maximum energy and minimum control, sometimes even with eyes closed, with the sole intention of losing the ball in an adjacent field. See also 'agricultural' and 'slog'.

---

yorker a full delivery pitched right up on the batsman's toes. Difficult to defend, let alone score off. Also difficult to get right: too full and it's a full toss (qv), not full enough it's a half-volley (qv). Bowled (or attempted) a lot at the death (qv).

---

zip a pitch with zip in it is a fast, dry, bouncy 'track'. Enjoyed by both fast bowlers and top-order batsmen.

---

zone legendary state of competence. Once a batsman is 'in' (qv) and scoring freely and concentrating easily, it would be fair to say he is in the zone. For bowlers it happens more rarely, but when a good bowler finds his rhythm, suddenly it's an easy game, and few batsmen can live with him.

---

zzzzz favourite crowd activity at mid-table, mid-summer, mid-week County draws.

If my little attempt at elucidation here has confused you even further, I can heartily recommend these other sources.

First and foremost are the Laws of Cricket, available free online or in a nice little booklet for a few quid from www.lords. org/laws-and-spirit. Also helpful is Tom Smith's Cricket Umpiring and Scoring guide to interpretation and application of the Laws, published by MCC.

Then there are three other excellent little books which, while more subjective and less definitive than the Laws themselves, may be easier to read and require significantly less reverence. Rob Eastaway's *What is a Googly?* is more concerned with playing than watching, though he also touches on both. Lawrence Booth's *Arm Ball to Zooter* 'A sideways look at the language of cricket', and Simon Hughes' *Jargonbusting: The Analyst's Guide to Test Cricket* both focus on the professional game, but throw plenty of light on our antics on the village green in the process.

acknowledgements

Many people have helped me shape my thoughts simply by sitting around in the pub garden and talking about cricket with me, which is one of my all time favourite things to do. To that end I would like to thank all the players and people of Damerham Cricket Club, regulars and infrequents, Saturdays, Sundays and Wednesdays, and everyone else I ever play cricket with or against, for making it such a rich experience and so much fun, both to play and to dissect afterwards. Thank you to everyone who read the manuscript and gave me their thoughts, and especially to Dad for the final proof. Thank you to Smithers for his time and his skill in making it look this good. Thank you to Lawrence Booth and Andrew Miller for saying nice things about it and letting me quote them, and to Test Match Sofa for letting me come on and talk about it. You're all ace.

Printed in Great Britain
by Amazon